THE FEMININE CHARACTER

THE FEMININE CHARACTER

History of an Ideology

VIOLA KLEIN

*With an Introductory Essay
for the American Edition
by Janet Zollinger Giele*

UNIVERSITY OF ILLINOIS PRESS
Urbana   Chicago   London

To the Memory of My Mother

Published by agreement with Routledge & Kegan Paul Ltd.
First published 1946; second edition 1971

Introductory Essay for the American edition © 1972
by The Board of Trustees of the University of Illinois

Manufactured in the United States of America

Library of Congress Catalog Card No. 72-83482

Cloth: ISBN 0-252-00294-6
Paper: ISBN 0-252-00298-9

CONTENTS

FOREWORD

Recent changes in the social position of women, their increasing participation in public life and their manifestation of hitherto unexpected psychological qualities, have challenged our views concerning the so-called eternal traits of the feminine character. Discussions on this subject which is now arousing more and more interest have been carried on by a long line of thinkers who have expressed in theoretical terms the change in attitudes which has been developing since the Industrial Revolution. This aspect of the present study will, I suppose, be obvious and interesting to everyone, as hardly anything is more stimulating than the realization that our social life is full of phantasies. For centuries these have been taken for granted and considered as facts until a sudden change has revealed their irrational or ideological nature.

From the point of view of the sociologist I should like to draw attention to another aspect of this investigation. It is an experiment in working out a new pattern of research which I first tried to develop with research students in 1930 at Frankfort University and have since continued, and which I should call Integrating Research.[1] Its task is to combine different aspects of the same problem which previously have been dealt with only in water-tight compartments. If we raise, for instance, the question of the feminine character, we generally approach it by the methods of biology, philosophy, psycho-analysis, experimental psychology, psychometrics, history, literary history, anthropology or sociology. But no one troubles to pool the knowledge of this subject gained in various fields, or to co-ordinate these findings in their bearing upon its various aspects. This lack of integration is due to the shortsighted over-specialization of the past epoch. Accurate results were thought to have been achieved by isolating fragments from various fields and investigating them most conscientiously, forgetting that a fundamental inaccuracy was bound to occur if one lost sight of the whole pattern in which each item has its place and meaning.

This is not an argument against division of labour or specialization in the scientific world, but against blind specialization which

---

[1] For more information on the foundations of integrating research cf. my *Man and Society in an Age of Reconstruction*, London, New York, 1940, p. 164 ff.

sets to work without first surveying the whole field, and continues without fitting the findings of specialized research into a universal framework.

Should anyone in the industrial field try to do the same thing, for instance, to produce accurate parts of a motor car without ever fitting them together, he would be laughed at ; but this is exactly what still happens to a large extent in the social sciences. Each scientist concentrates on a limited field of research without a clear knowledge of approaches, problems and facts which obtain in other branches and have a bearing upon the subject. As regards the social sciences we are working without an assembly plant and lack experts who know how to organize, supervise and co-ordinate our findings. This is precisely the task of the sociologist. Apart from his own province, the study of the basic facts and concepts relating to society (" Elements of Sociology "), his aim from the very beginning is to develop a frame of reference for integrating research.

There are still many who bar the way to integrative methods, among them those who are their incompetent supporters, and those who are sceptical without having studied the experiments made in that direction. The incompetent supporters of the integrative approach are the most dangerous. Paying lip-service to this form of sociological work without themselves undertaking it, they talk generalities or, if they attempt it, do so in a dilettante fashion. They have not been trained in the " Elements of Sociology " which, as I pointed out, is a specialized subject with a well-developed body of problems and facts. These friends of integration embark upon the gigantic enterprise of solving problems of the evolution of mankind as a whole and spread the mistaken idea that synthesis in the social sciences means one man's synthesis.

To this it must be replied that the synthesis of all knowledge by one man is an impossibility, but this is not what is meant by those who plead for the integration of knowledge. To them synthesis means a new method of thinking ; it does not attempt to deal with all subjects at once, but when it considers a social fact such as the family, for instance, it examines many aspects and does not exclude those investigations which may go beyond the boundaries of a scientific department established by tradition. It is a new method because it regards the unity of the subject as more important than abstract approaches to it which, after all, are imposed by an arbitrary division of labour. The family, for instance, is a unity, and biological, psychological, economic, legal or educational analysis of it is artificial if it proceeds in water-tight compartments. We only adhere to the strict separation of these approaches because our research workers have been trained along these lines, and so far we have failed to produce scholars who can move from one field to another without becoming unscientific.

Clearly the synthetic approach does not abandon the division of labour. No single scholar will cover the whole subject but there will be, as it were, specialists in integration. Their partic-ular gift and training will enable them to co-ordinate the results of two or more traditional branches of knowledge concerning one particular subject, such as the " family ", the problem of " nationalism " or whatever it may be.

The old division of labour in the social sciences according to which various abstract aspects (e.g. the economic, legal, educa-tional) of a concrete subject (e.g. the family) were dealt with separately will be supplemented by the work of specialists in integration who, in turn, will also have to subdivide their field. This new division, however, will never lose sight of the unity of the concrete subject (the family, in our example) because it will share out the various units of research in such a way that the dynamic interrelation of functions in one subject will at no stage of the research be disregarded.

A full training of the new type of specialist would consist in making him thoroughly acquainted with his abstract speciality and in enabling him also to transcend the boundaries of his own field whenever it became necessary to absorb facts and methods belonging to a neighbouring branch of learning and to acquire a general orientation in the whole field of the social sciences. This suggestion is, after all, not so formidable, since everyone will admit that a doctor who specializes in heart or eye trouble should also have a knowledge of all the other parts of the human organism. Seen in this light, there is nothing impossible in the synthetic approach. This new division of labour will require a large staff of collaborators, but this should not be an obstacle since the number of persons who study social phenomena will gradually increase.

Of recent years interesting experiments have been made, particularly in America, in an attempt to do justice to the synthetic approach in the social sciences. Once the idea of a one-man synthesis was dropped, attempts were made to encourage co-operation between various specialists by forming a team and giving them a concrete topic to explore. This approach has been greatly helped by the fact that the great Foundations have the funds to support the work of such teams. Important as these experiments in co-operation are, there is the danger that when various individuals with different training meet, they may very often be tempted to divide the work once more according to their traditional training.

It will be easier to assign the psychological aspect to the psychologist, the economic to the economist, etc., than to make the concrete unity of—for instance—the family the common concern of the whole team of workers and to ask them to contribute their own special knowledge to the discussion only when the inherent dynamics of the problem demands it. There is all the difference between a problem which emerges organically in the course of thinking, and random questions and pooled answers without a real connection. The latter method leads to what has been called the book-binder's synthesis, the book-binder being the only person who is concerned with the unity of the various pieces of research in putting them into one volume. In contrast with this, the former method promises to be integrative as it follows the lines dictated by the inner development of a well-defined problem.

This type of synthesis is difficult because when scholars co-operate they can produce anything rather than this inner and consistent development of questions from a central starting-point, since this task, being logical and organic at the same time, will always have to be achieved by the individual mind. If thought is to be consistent the team of scholars should have a leader who represents both the dynamic principle inherent in the problem and integrates the conclusions reached by others. Therefore the future of integration will depend on the extension of such experiments in which the technique of contributing to creative discussion, and guidance of that discussion, may be learned.

Although we admit that this creativeness depends on individual gifts, we wish to emphasize that it has also to be trained. Universities and other learned institutions will have to train for this just as they do for reliable specialized research.

The art of observing details and fitting them into a pattern has to be learned and practised simultaneously by the adult as much as by the child. Scientific thinking, after all, is not very different from that of everyday life when we observe facts and try to form judgments. It may be more exact, more methodical, but fundamentally it is the same kind of intelligence as the one on which we rely in dealing with ordinary experiences.

There is another wide-spread mistake which has to be corrected. Many people agree to the need for integrative research but wish to wait until all the relevant facts have been collected. They believe that the time is not yet ripe for integration, but that in collecting facts piecemeal and laboriously, the synthesis will automatically emerge. They misjudge the nature of the human mind which does not arrive at its more comprehensive knowledge by summing up atoms of information but proceeds by attempting to organize into a pattern whatever knowledge is available.

Thus one way of reaching synthetic sociological knowledge consists in beginning with already established facts, removing, if necessary, the frequently false and obsolete frame of reference, and re-organizing the facts in accordance with sociological problems and principles. For convenience I will choose as examples books which have been published in this Series. This re-organization of existing material around sociological problems characterizes the short study : The *Sociology of Literary Taste*, written by the well-known authority on Shakespeare, Levin L. Schücking, and also the essay *Sociology of the Renaissance*, written by the historian Alfred von Martin. Neither of these studies stresses the accumulation of new facts (although the books contain a great many of them), but the authors have combined and organized new and established facts in such a way that they are able to give at least tentative answers to sociological questions which have never before been formulated so consistently and which are essential to the understanding, not only of the past, but of our own situation.[1]

Thus synthesis usually proceeds from an existing set of facts, stimulates new specialized research, and later leads to a broader integration of more critically analyzed facts.

[1] Professor Bonamy Dobree rightly says in an article on our Universities : " What is important now is not to discover new facts but rather to study the relation of old facts to each other and their significance in the light of contemporary experience . . ." —" The mistake has been and still is that research in the Art subjects can be modelled on the line of ' scientific ' research, since the ' facts ' dealt with are of an entirely different order " (" Art Faculties in Modern Universities ", *Political Quarterly*, 1944. October–December issue, p. 349).

Sociology has two components, one, which is accessible to the methods of the natural sciences, and another which is adequately grasped only through understanding and interpretation, cf. on this crucial topic H. A. Hodges, *Wilhelm Dilthey, An Introduction.* In the Intern. Library of Sociology and Social Reconstruction, London 1945.

This process is in keeping with the natural broadening of our mental horizon and can never be abandoned as a background of social research, unless we wish the latter to become a store-house of disconnected information, each item being accurate in itself but irrelevant to the whole.

Everyone who is acquainted with the present state of the social sciences will realize that this is mostly the case. Research becomes as disconnected as it is specialized, and it does not answer questions which we would like to see explored. If this was the case even before the methods of measurement were introduced into the field of the social sciences, the situation has become even worse, since in certain quarters there is a tendency to suppress nearly everything in the social sciences which cannot be stated in quantitative terms. The tension between the two camps can be best seen in two statements, each of which has characteristically been adopted as the motto of a well-known sociological Handbook. The desire for universal quantitative expression is emphasized in the following passage : " All of the Social Sciences have a common aim—the understanding of human behaviour ; a common method—the quantitative analysis of behaviour records ; and a common aspiration—to devise ways of experimenting upon behaviour." [1] The opposite view is adequately expressed as follows : " It is much easier to measure non-significant factors than to be content with developing a first approximation to the significant." [2]

There is no doubt that a very great advance in the study of human affairs is to be expected from the refinement of measuring techniques and their skilful application. Much has been done in this field, and each new effort should be supported even if at the beginning it does not supply us with the knowledge which is most important to us. But it is one thing to be in favour of developing a technique and another to transform our interests so as to fit them to these techniques. Unfortunately this is what happens : each technician in the scientific field is not only proud of his scientific methods or of his measurement techniques, but tends to arrange his interests and problems so as to enable him to use his skills. But this is not all. Every technician and possessor of a certain skill attempts to develop

[1] Wesley C. Mitchell, " Quantitative Analysis in Economic Theory ", *American Economic Review*, 1925, Vol. 15 (quoted by Murphy, G. & Murphy, L. B. & Newcomb, Th. M., *Experimental Social Psychology*, New York, London, 1937, front page).
[2] Elton Mayo (quoted by Kimball Young ; *Personality and Social Adjustment*, New York, 1944).

a logical system and a methodology according to which only his type of knowledge is true knowledge. All else is mere opinion or fancy.

Thus there are two unprofitable tendencies arising from over-estimating the significance of measurement : (a) we tend to forget the real motives and interests which originally determined the choice of our problem and its formulation, and (b) we neglect all avenues of approach to reality which do not lend themselves to measurement and we call only those aspects of an object real which corresponds to the limited idea of matter-of-factness. Concerning the latter A. N. Whitehead rightly said : " Matter of fact is an abstraction, arrived at by confining thought to purely formal relations which then masquerade as the final reality. This is why Science, in its perfection, relapses into the study of differential equations. The concrete world has slipped through the meshes of the scientific net."

This measurement mania, especially as it developed in the U.S.A., had the following result : data were collected on a host of things in which no one was interested and this multitude of data caused confusion because it diverted attention from the really relevant problem. I uttered a warning against this as early as 1932 in a Symposium arranged by the *American Journal of Sociology* on the occasion of the publication of Stuart A. Rice's " Methods in the Social Science " (cf. Vol. XXXVIII, No. 2, Sept. 1932, pp. 273–82, of the periodical mentioned above). Since then things have changed for the better in the U.S.A. leading to impressive developments. Some aspects of the new point of view are ably stated in Robert S. Lynd's recent article " The Implications of Economic Planning for Sociology " in the *American Sociological Review.*[1]

In the social sciences we are not concerned only with quantities, and it would be fatal at the present time to refuse to make use of technical skill wherever it is useful in the field of measurement ; nevertheless we should not allow our minds to be confused by adopting a *measurement philosophy.*

European scholars who have a long tradition of historical research and methods based on the understanding of man should not fail to realize that a mind which has been trained to allow for its own social and individual prejudices can derive genuine knowledge from carefully observed but unmeasured facts. Even

---

[1] Vol. IX, No. 1, Feb. 1944, pp. 14–20. Cf. also his *Knowledge for What ? The Place of Social Science in American Culture* (Princetown, 1939).

without mathematical spectacles the critical mind is a suitable instrument for perceiving reality. And its power is more seriously endangered if it loses the habit of asking significant questions than if it indulges in a passion for measurement where the nature of the question does not strictly demand it.

Dr. Viola Klein's study undoubtedly starts from a set of significant problems and, apart from collecting new facts, tries to co-ordinate results drawn from various fields of knowledge in order to raise new problems and stimulate further research. In this sense her study is entirely tentative, and exploratory, and she would be the last to claim more. She would be judged by false criteria if one were to expect from a single person at the beginning of a venture the exactness and final answers which would be feasible only if a great team of explorers were to study the various fields. As a matter of fact, in an exploratory study it is an advantage to leave loose ends. This creates scope for scientific imagination to throw new light upon known facts and to explore so far unobserved interrelations between them.

In my view there are two tasks equally important in the present age : to refine our existing techniques which will lead us to ever greater exactness in the study of details, and also to show the spirit of adventure which is willing to experiment, and take risks in suggesting new patterns of research, even if others will have to contribute to their final elaboration.

KARL MANNHEIM.

THE LONDON SCHOOL OF ECONOMICS,
UNIVERSITY OF LONDON.
Cambridge, May, 1945.

PREFACE TO THE SECOND EDITION

This book has been out of print for a number of years. Yet, despite recurrent demands for a new edition, both the author and publishers were doubtful about the wisdom of reprinting it in its original form.

Their dilemma derived in a large measure from the nature of the book itself, that is, from the two purposes it simultaneously tried to serve.

The author did her best to put her cards on the table and to make her dual aim clear from the outset. It seems, however, that the reading public, by and large, was not prepared to take her word for it that the book was concerned with an analysis of existing theories about feminine psychology rather than being itself a psychological study of women. The misunderstanding of the author's intentions went so far that some critics—Rose Macaulay among them—accused her of using " secondary sources " instead of doing " original research ", when in fact the investigation of those sources was the very object of the exercise. I hoped, nevertheless, to be able to learn something new, and to be able to make a constructive contribution to the solution of the " enigma " femininity by comparing and co-ordinating what other authorities who have studied the matter had to say.

Books have their own destiny, and this one had a considerable influence on the author's subsequent fate. That, in turn, added further to our hesitations.

Put briefly, the dilemma hinges on the question whether or not this book is primarily a book about the psychology of women.

Originally, the work was conceived of as the application of the principles of Sociology of Knowledge to the study of a specific, clearly delimited and topical issue. In other words, its main purpose was to demonstrate that scholars—no matter how honestly they endeavour to pursue the truth and nothing but the truth, pure and objective— are intellectually dependant on the social, cultural and historical climate of their time. The book's subtitle, " History of an Ideology ", was meant to convey this idea. (My interest in the ideological elements of knowledge had been aroused, among others, by C. H. Waddington's book *The Scientific Attitude*, widely discussed at the time.)

It was, I think, mainly because of *this* aspect of my study that the late Karl Mannheim took a genuine interest in it from its beginning, offered critical and constructive comment, chapter by chapter, as it advanced, and eventually published it as one of the first volumes in his then newly founded International Library of Sociology and Social Reconstruction.

The tentative experiment in the " integrative method ", whose merits Karl Mannheim set forth in his Foreword to the first edition of this book, was incidental to the above prime purpose.

A number of other issues might equally have served to illustrate the point that human thought, even at its most detached level, is rooted in the cultural soil which has nourished it. If I chose to analyse theories about the alleged personality characteristics of women, it was because this topic seemed particularly suited to my ends for two reasons. Firstly, the subject as such produces such a universal and intense (even if mostly unconscious) ego-involvement that emotional detachment is difficult to achieve. Secondly, the social status of women has been undergoing obvious and far-reaching changes during the last century; it should therefore be possible to detect corresponding changes in the attitudes and observations of those who have made it their profession to theorize about feminine traits.

Looked at from this angle, that is, as a kind of mental X-ray plates of some representative theories about psychological sex characteristics, the value of the book, such as it was, has barely changed. Margaret Mead may have somewhat modified her views under psycho-analytical influence;[1] L. M. Terman with other collaborators may have refined their techniques and added further publications in the same vein as the one described here in chapter VII. Psychometric methods have become much more elaborate since this book was written, and the literature on differential achievements between the sexes in a vast variety of measurable abilities—huge as it was even then—has since multiplied apace.[2]

The arguments presented in this book, which can and should be seen in an historical perspective, have hardly been affected by these variations on a familiar theme, nor by the additions to our stock of knowledge. The number of examples might have been increased, the illustrations could have been taken from a greater range of experience and set in a wider theoretical framework if the book had been written more recently; but the basic structure of the discourse has remained untouched by the passage of time.

The situation is different if the reader is in search of information on the current state of knowledge concerning psychological sex differences and theories about their causation. In this respect the present book—written as it was at the end of World War II—is regrettably but inevitably out of date. In the meantime, all experimental sciences have made tremendous progress, biology and psychology being of special relevance in our context. In sociology, too, theories have been

[1] Cf. *Male and Female* (1949). For this and the following references see the bibliography at the end of this book.
[2] *The Development of Sex Differences*, edited by Eleanor E. Maccoby (1966), includes an extensive annotated bibliography, summarizing the main data and research findings of the relevant recent literature.

developed which cast a new light on the processes of personality development, and by inference on the problem which here for the sake of brevity has been called " the feminine character " but which is now, perhaps more precisely but less euphonically, referred to as " psychosexual orientation ".

Among the empirical sciences, genetics in particular has brought new revelations about the nature of heredity and the psychological as well as physiological effects of chromosomes and sex hormones. There seemed to be good prospects that the tangled question of heredity versus environmental factors in the formation of personality characteristics might be getting a substantial step nearer to being unravelled.

Ethology, too, developed to a point and in a direction which shed new light on human behaviour. There are, however, limitations and even dangers in extrapolating from animal to human behaviour. For one thing, human beings have characteristics not shared with any other species—symbolic communication being the most obvious and important among them—which make man an animal *sui generis*. For another, the variety of animal species is so boundless and their behaviour patterns so diverse that it is possible to find one or another species which will exhibit almost any characteristic social behaviour one wishes to illustrate. It can, e.g., hardly be a chance that at a time of near-equality between the sexes (among humans)—a time, moreover, when the importance of paternal care for the mental and moral welfare of children is increasingly being stressed by psychologists—some bird species whose males have the function of hatching the eggs should have received attention.

On the borderline between sociology and social psychology Rôle Theory has been developed which explains human behaviour essentially in terms of conforming to social norms. Every individual, being member of a stratified society, occupies several social positions, or " statuses ", in each of which certain types of behaviour, i.e. " rôles ", are expected of him. The rôle of a mother differs from that of a teacher or an insurance salesman; that of a schoolgirl from that of an old lady. Each culture defines these rôles differently; learning the behaviour patterns appropriate to one's " assigned " and " achieved " statuses is part of the process of growing up. Male and female rôles are taught the new members of the social group in innumerable and subtle ways almost from birth. They are reinforced by experience, example, innuendos and the various other means by which social control is usually exercised.

Many investigations in a number of disciplines have been carried out in recent years which at least partially support this environmental point of view. Interesting developmental studies were, for instance, carried out by the psychiatrists J. L. and Joan G. Hampson[1] of a number

---

[1] " Determinants of Psychosexual Orientation " in F. A. Beach (ed.), *Sex and Behaviour* (1965).

of persons whose assigned sex did not—for various reasons—coincide with their physical sex characteristics. With very few exceptions most of these pseudo-hermaphrodites had fully accepted their incongruously assigned sex rôle. (The term " gender rôle " has been coined in this context to underline the fact that an individual's psychosexual orientation, due to early socialization, does not necessarily correspond to his, or her, actual sex.) In these authors' view the sex of assignment and rearing are the prevailing factors in establishing masculine or feminine rôles.

The fact that it has now become common usage to speak of " sex rôles " rather than male or female " temperaments " or " character traits " has the obvious implication that human beings are acknowledged as being not only organisms, but organisms in social situations.

It has now been almost universally accepted, among biologically orientated scholars no less than among psychologists and social scientists, that psychosexual orientation is the outcome of complex interactions between genetic, endocrinological and environmental factors.

Reverting to my starting point, namely the question why after all these years and regardless of the intervening scientific advances this book is being re-issued almost unchanged, the explanation is this.

When I first undertook this study, I asked myself the questions: (a) Is there such a thing as " Femininity "? (which I then called " feminine character ") and (b), if so, what does it—in the view of the authorities on the subject— consist in? At the end of my investigation the answer to both my questions was a resounding " Don't know ".

Today, " Femininity " would be defined in terms of a polymorphous " female rôle ". About its intrinsic nature we are today no wiser than before. Our ignorance may have reached a higher level of sophistication, but it is still there in full strength.

Incorporating even only the most important new publications on the subject of psychological sex differences into the body of my old book would have meant rewriting the whole. This was neither possible nor did it seem warranted in the circumstances, especially as some excellent anthologies on the subject are available.

We have decided therefore to publish the book as it was, with only minor modifications, correcting a few printing errors and omitting the appendix, and to expand the bibliography so as to provide the interested reader with references to the more recent relevant literature.

INTRODUCTORY ESSAY
FOR THE AMERICAN EDITION

New Developments in Research on Women*

JANET ZOLLINGER GIELE

Although Viola Klein finished writing *The Feminine Character* in 1945, the book is still enormously useful to the person who today seeks to evaluate the burgeoning literature on feminism and the changing roles of women. Viola Klein not only was the first to show the usefulness of the sociology of knowledge for analyzing such an emotion-laden topic as women's psychology and roles, she also provided us with a kind of handbook to the work of important scholars who wrote on this topic in the pre–World War II era: Havelock Ellis, biologist; Otto Weininger, philosopher; Helen B. Thompson, L. M. Terman, and C. C. Miles, psychologists; Sigmund Freud, psychoanalyst; Mathias and Mathilde Vaerting, historians; Margaret Mead, anthropologist; and W. I. Thomas, sociologist.

Her work begins with a review of the historical situation surrounding women's roles. Showing how the nineteenth century produced an altogether new set of possibilities for women because of industrialization and the opportunity for limiting family size, Viola Klein concluded that the situation of the 1940s was primarily one of role conflict, a conflict between the achievement women might expect of themselves as a result of certain newly won rights and their traditional role as mothers and homemakers. Having set out the historical context, Klein then proceeded to illuminiate the different perspectives on the situation of men and women, or on the "feminine character," that were taken by representative scholars from each major academic discipline. Klein makes it evident that not only the peculiar nature of a discipline shaped the scholar's view, but also his or her

* In preparing summaries of research on women in a variety of fields, I have been fortunate in the advice of a number of people expert in each: *Biology,* Dorothea Widmayer; *Philosophy,* Ann Congleton; *Psychology,* Mary Parlee, Paul Rosenkrantz, Phoebe Williams; *History,* Gail Parker, Martha François; *Anthropology,* Barbara Ayres, Lila Leibowitz, Joan Mark; *Economics,* Anne Carter, Hilda Kahne, Rodney Morrison; *Literature,* Patricia Spacks. In addition Rose Coser, Hilda Kahne, Talcott Parsons, Alice Rossi, and Viola Klein made helpful general comments on an earlier version of the entire essay.

own life history, and the particular social and historical milieu in which the work was done.

A generation after Klein wrote this pioneering work, the student of women's roles (or as we are now more inclined to say, the student of sex roles) may profitably review *The Feminine Character*. It is an illuminating example of the sociology of knowledge that sharpens critical awareness and rational discourse on an emotionally charged subject. It is also a baseline for scholarly discussion of the feminine role against which current understanding can be measured.

The present edition of *The Feminine Character* comes out at a time of new scholarly interest in the topic of women and the changing relation between the sexes. There is also in the United States a very clear revival of feminism. In the face of these developments it is useful to draw some connection between Klein's work and the present. The following essay will accordingly consider each of the aspects for comparison listed below:

I. Historical Developments: Change in Women's Roles, 1945-72
II. Recent Scholarly Research on Women
III. The Rise of Interdisciplinary Work
IV. Continuity and Change in the Conclusions Reached
V. *The Feminine Character* in Contemporary Perspective

I. Historical Developments:
Change in Women's Roles, 1945-72

One truth that seems to be rediscovered every decade is that the Industrial Revolution not only freed women from laborious tasks of farm and home, it also imposed on the privileged some degree of idleness, dependency, and the need to elaborate motherhood and housekeeping to fill the time available. Veblen described the phenomenon in *The Theory of the Leisure Class* in 1899, showing that women's leisure was conspicuous consumption for upwardly mobile males. Viola Klein, when she reviewed the history of women in the nineteenth century, noted the combination of freedom and constriction also.

Have historical developments of the last several decades at all changed the picture? The answer depends on whether one looks at the 1950s or at the 1960s and '70s. Right after World War II women married in larger numbers than ever before and, though birth control was available, bore on the average more than three children each. They devoted themselves to the housewife's role with zeal. But by 1970, this pattern was open to question. A qualitative change appeared to be under way in which the roles of men and women were becoming more similar, rather than diverging. Talk of zero population growth, day-care centers, and anti-discrimination suits against telephone companies and universities emphasized the degree to which women rejected different expectations from those held for men. In America Kate Millett's *Sexual Politics* (1970) followed *The Feminine Mystique* (1963). In England *The Female Eunuch* (1971) and *Woman's Estate* (1971) gave indication of an articulate feminism building there also.[1]

Viola Klein ended her 1945 review of the historical background surrounding questions of feminine character by pointing to the cultural lag and role conflict in which women were caught. Women's tasks had been lightened, their time freed for other activities; but the ideology of the traditional feminine role hung on, making them feel they had to continue in the pattern of earlier generations. While technological advance permitted more freedom, the ancient division of labor did not enable them to use it. Most women still could not see how to pursue *both* family goals and achievement in a job.

Today, the issue for women is not so much that of *role conflict* and cultural lag, though both these problems continue to exist, but rather that of *role-sharing* between men and women.[2] This change in the central issue confronting the sexes derives in America from institutional change since the 1930s. It coincides with the rise of radical perspectives in the social sciences. It has roots in the current feminist movement and an impact on the kind of social scientific research that is now current. Finally, it bears on the shape of the future society in which both men and women will live. Each of these aspects of the shift from the role-conflict ideology to the role-sharing ideology is considered below.

Institutional Change and Role-Sharing. The ideology of role-sharing emerged with the revival of feminism sometime during the 1960s. It assumed that men and women *could* do similar kinds of work—both in child care and cooking, and in factory, office, and the public arena. It is an ideology not yet fully accepted, but it ap-

---

[1] Kate Millett, *Sexual Politics* (New York: Doubleday, 1970); Betty Friedan, *The Feminine Mystique* (New York: W. W. Norton, 1963); Germaine Greer, *The Female Eunuch* (New York: McGraw-Hill, 1971); Juliet Mitchell, *Woman's Estate* (New York: Pantheon, 1971).

[2] Jessie Bernard, *Women and the Public Interest* (Chicago: Aldine, 1971), ch. 8.

pears strongest among the young and those under approximately ages 35-40.

Why did such beliefs about sex roles gain ascendency and displace the older role-conflict beliefs? The answer is to be found in the experience of the generations born and reared in the Great Depression and the years following. These generations experienced change in societal institutions that carried the implicit lesson of possible role-sharing between men and women.[3]

Ever-increasing task differentiation broke up a job to be performed into many component operations, divesting the original of its sex-linked mystique and basis in craft knowledge. Thus men could as easily cook prepackaged food as women; women could as easily perform many machine-aided operations of production and defense as men. The possibilities became apparent not only in the United States but also in Israel, Sweden, Russia, and China. The overall effect was to make possible a cross-over in the duties and responsibilities of each sex (though the possibility was not realized to the same degree in every country or in every area of life). The crossover permitted a sharing of consciousness across sex roles such that the expectations held for each sex were more nearly similar than they had been before. The increasing similarity was apparent in moral and psychological expectations, in familial responsibilities, and in economic roles.

Morally, the same standards began to apply to the two sexes. Young women were permitted greater sexual freedom, approaching that of men. Young men were active in political reform, the peace cause, and humanitarian movements that had until World War I (at least in the United States) been largely the interest of women.[4]

Psychologically, there was also a convergence between the motives of achievement felt to be natural to men and the motives of nurturance and service thought to be characteristic of women. Family-centered instincts were recognized in the men who puttered around their suburban homes. Needs for some sort of societally recognized achievement were evident in women who answered "just a house-

[3] The argument presented below is given fuller treatment and documentation in my article "Changes in the Modern Family: Their Impact on Sex Roles," *American Journal of Orthopsychiatry* 41 (1971): 757-766.

[4] Evidence for women's humanitarian interests in other countries may be found in R. Patai, *Women in the Modern World* (New York: Free Press, 1967); and in Raden Adjeng Kartini, *Letters of a Javanese Princess* (New York: Knopf, 1920).

wife" to survey questionnaires and expressed dissatisfaction at the endless "stuffing and stamping" routine of volunteer work.[5]

In the realm of the family, parental roles of each sex began to take on more nearly equal weight in the public eye. In the United States evidence for this trend is found in welfare measures of the 1930s and 1960s. The program for Aid for Dependent Children instituted during the Depression emphasized the value of the maternal role to young children and in effect provided an income to the mother for performance of this function. By the 1960s, however, there was increased appreciation of the *paternal* role—the value of father as role model for his sons. Proposals for family support centered on keeping the father in the family and preventing his desertion. The growing frequency of the househusband in Sweden and the similarity between parents' roles in the kibbutz provide additional evidence of rapprochement between parental functions of the sexes in other societies.

Men's and women's roles in the economy are also increasingly similar. Men, particularly as they grow older and approach retirement, are likely to enter into consumer decisions with a fervor that approaches their wives'. Women, as they pass child-bearing age, are more likely to enter the labor force. With longer life expectancy and the family-oriented life of the retired, men's and women's power in the family is more nearly equalized—women's rising and men's falling, creating over the life span, if not in any single moment in time, conditions for a universalization of consciousness across the boundaries of male and female roles.[6]

These changes in moral and psychological consciousness, then, coupled with institutional and demographic changes in contemporary society, help to account for current attitudes toward sex roles that emphasize role-sharing. But it is now necessary to show how this ideology of role-sharing has any relevance for the social scientific work on women that we wish to review. To make this connection it is necessary to give initial brief consideration to the relation between ideology and science.

[5] Martin Gruberg, *Women in American Politics* (Oshkosh, Wis.: Academia, 1968); Jessie Bernard, "The Paradox of the Happy Marriage," in V. Gornick and B. K. Moran, eds., *Woman in Sexist Society* (New York: Basic Books, 1971).
[6] Bernice Neugarten *et al.*, *Personality in Middle and Late Life* (New York: Prentice-Hall, 1964); Ethel Shanas, *Old People in Three Industrial Societies* (New York: Atherton, 1968).

Social Science and Value-Involvement. In reviewing the historical background of change in the feminine role, Klein noted the importance of science, its part in eroding traditional beliefs, and its contribution to the study of social and psychological phenomena. But a central theme of *The Feminine Character* is that objective and scientific though each scholar tried to be, his or her views were shaped by personal experience and the thought of the era in which the research took place.

In the 1970s, after a decade of student protest against American universities' involvement with the military-industrial establishment, Klein's skeptical attitude toward the "objectivity" of scholars seems altogether in keeping with contemporary mood. In fact her work provides visible support for the emerging contemporary view that it is impossible to be altogether objective. The current trend in the social sciences appears to be in the direction of "value-involved" research, i.e., research which asks questions from a confessed ideological position and then follows the scientific canons of assessing evidence from that perspective.[7] Klein's book could be interpreted as giving support to the view that any other course is self-deception.

What would value-involved research on women look like if the researcher were dedicated to the cause of maximum possible health, happiness, and self-fulfillment for women? This question is implicit in some of the new critical work being done in feminine psychology. Recent research shows that professional psychologists hold a negative and stereotyped image of women that characterizes the normal adult female as considerably below the standard for a normal adult male. Psychoanalytic views of women are under similar attack for casting women in a passive role. Sociological analysis which characterizes the male role as instrumental and the female role as expressive has been

---

[7] Max Heirich uses the term "value-engaged" research as distinguished from "value-free" research done on student activism; see "The Student Revolt: Afterthoughts and Prospects," *Contemporary Sociology* 1 (1972): 13-18. For general criticism of the value-free functionalist tradition in sociology, see Alvin Gouldner, *The Coming Crisis in Western Sociology* (New York: Basic Books, 1970). Everett Mendelsohn recently pointed out that medicine is such a "value-involved" science, i.e., concerned with health and the use of science to some good purpose (Radcliffe Conference on Women, April 1972). This value-involvement does not mean the distortion of data, but rather the direction of inquiry toward certain kinds of questions and not others. I would suggest that Keynesian economics provided this possibility for economics also—perhaps a reason that economists are much more visible in public policy-making and government than are sociologists.

criticized for its implicit prejudice against working wives and mothers.[8]

What each of these criticisms seems to imply is that earlier research and theorizing in the social sciences was anything but objective. In other words, it merely takes a researcher with an alternate view of women to point out the biases, the prejudices, and the stereotyping that influence which research questions are chosen, which data are collected, and what interpretation is given. The avowedly feminist researcher need not knowingly distort or falsify the findings any more than earlier social scientists. The scholar sympathetic to women would simply pose problems in a different way, be sensitive to a different section of the possible evidence, test different kinds of hypotheses, and ultimately emerge with different conclusions as a result of starting from a different value position. Indications of what these conclusions might be are sketched below both in connection with present feminist perspectives and with possible future ones.

Role-Sharing and Current Scientific Research. When the prevailing ideology of women's roles is that of role-sharing, one expects to find a search for similarities in traits of males and females and for dysfunctions of existing role arrangements that make sharp distinctions between the sexes. Research of this kind has only recently been produced and is just beginning to be well known. Eleanor Maccoby's book *The Development of Sex Differences* is particularly respected, not only because of the quality of the research reported therein, but also, I suspect, because many of the articles in it show the conditions under which male and female performances approach similarity. Alice Rossi's essay on "Equality between the Sexes" has been widely anthologized. One of its central points is the dysfunctionality not only for women, but also for children of the full-time mother who may over-control and over-nuture her child. One line from that essay is frequently quoted: ". . . for the first time in the history of any known society, motherhood has become a full-time occupation

[8] Friedan, *The Feminine Mystique;* Inge K. Broverman, Donald M. Broverman, *et al.,* "Sex-Role Stereotypes and Clinical Judgments of Mental Health," *Journal of Consulting and Clinical Psychology* 34 (1970): 1-7; Alice Rossi, "Transition to Parenthood," *Journal of Marriage and the Family* 30 (1968): 26-39; Phyllis Chesler, "Patient and Patriarch: Women in the Psychotherapeutic Relationship," in Gornick and Moran, eds., *Woman in Sexist Society;* Pauline B. Bart, "Sexism and Social Science: From the Gilded Cage to the Iron Cage, or, the Perils of Pauline," *Journal of Marriage and the Family* 33 (1971): 734-745.

for adult women." Naomi Weisstein's articles are also popular with proponents of current feminist ideology. Her point: that the social conditions under which performance occurs have more effect than the individual differences between people being tested. The implication is that, provided with similar social conditions and identical expectations of what they could do, women and men would not differ that much in their performance.[9]

However, one may ask how lasting this research will be. Presumably, if ideology changes so will the nature of the social scientific research that is in vogue. To foresee what that ideology will be requires either a crystal ball, a theory of social change that enables prediction of future trends, or the willingness to make an educated guess on the basis of possibilities currently visible. On the basis of the fact that "men's liberation" is occasionally mentioned as a reform long overdue, I shall venture here an educated guess that the next important ideological phase of the woman question will be an active effort to change men's roles. The ideological underpinnings of that position and its likely effects on research are sketched in the following paragraphs.

Feminine Values, the Future Society, and Future Research. If feminist ideology goes through another transformation, one possible result is greater attention to feminine values. The current emphasis on role-sharing is linked with women's liberation, i.e., with the demand that women be able to share equally in the man's world. But the theme of men being able to share in the woman's world, i.e., men's liberation, is an alternate possible emphasis.

What is distinctive about the ideology of men's liberation as compared with women's liberation is its attitude toward the larger society in which sex roles are found. Feminism of the last century has by and large accepted the values and structure of the larger society in which it is found. It has sought to get women into the system. Significantly, perhaps, Viola Klein did not include a Marxist or other entirely radical scholar who placed the woman question in the context of criticizing the structure of society as a whole (as did Engels or Bebel). This is not an omission that a sociology of knowledge

---

[9] Eleanor Maccoby, ed., *The Development of Sex Differences* (Stanford, Calif.: Stanford University Press, 1966); Alice Rossi, "Equality between the Sexes: An Immodest Proposal," in R. Lifton, ed., *The Woman in America* (Boston: Beacon, 1964, 1965); Naomi Weisstein, "Woman as Nigger," *Psychology Today* 3 (October 1969): 20ff.; and "Psychology Constructs the Female," in Gornick and Moran, eds., *Woman in Sexist Society.*

would make today. For one thing, "radical" economists, "radical" sociologists, and "radical" historians are part of the scholarly landscape today, even in America.[10] (In Europe such criticism of the system itself has for a long time been standard in that branch of its intellectual tradition that is Marxist.) In the last ten years in America, a radical perspective has sprung from native sources, perhaps as a result of an awful military technology that continues to grow even in peacetime, perhaps as a result of continuing poverty in some sectors of the population, or the rapid depletion of the earth's natural resources. What seem to have been largely "masculine" goals—of invidious competition and economic success, of military competition and capacity for aggression and destruction, of exploitive use of human beings and the environment—are now called into question. Whether "feminine" goals—of cooperation, of preservation of life, of encouragement of individual growth and self-realization, of peace and harmony with the natural order—can be restored to some better balance with "masculine" goals is likely to be the question of the day.[11] Women's liberation has by and large sought the opportunity to share in the man's world. Men's liberation by contrast would mean the opportunity for men to break out of purely masculine notions of achievement and share in the nurture and life-preserving orientation that is stereotypically associated with women.

The outlines of such an ideology are still so fuzzy that one can only speculate on the effects that it might have on scholarly perception of sex roles and on the social order itself. There would undoubtedly be a "division of labor" in ideology and scholarship between the piecemeal reformers and intellectuals who accept existing social arrangements and merely seek a better place for women in a masculine system and the more radical visionaries who question the basic values of the system itself. (I say "division of labor" because I

[10] "The Radicals Gain Professional Chic," *Business Week* (Economics), March 18, 1972, pp. 72-74; "Historians' Conference: The Radical Need for Jobs," *New York Times Magazine,* March 12, 1972, p. 38ff.

[11] While I believe that men and women each are capable of qualities thought typical of the other sex, I have recently argued the value of certain stereotypically "feminine" qualities which both men and women should strive to emphasize a great deal more than is done now, e.g., awareness of context (or "field dependence"), cooperativeness, responsiveness rather than aggressiveness, etc. Janet Zollinger Giele, "Women's Strength: An Affirmation," paper delivered at Radcliffe Conference on Women, April 1972. See also R. Lifton, "Woman as Knower: Some Psychohistorical Perspectives," in Lifton, ed., *The Woman in America;* David McClelland, "Wanted: A New Self-Image for Women," in *ibid.*

believe both views have validity and neither alone is adequate.) Representatives of such ideological positions are even now apparent among social scientists and historians. But by and large such an ideological division of labor has not yet had its effects for scholarly research on sex roles. If and when it does, there may be a correspondence between the alternative values that radical observers think society should try to attain and the qualities which women are found to possess. There then would likely be studies that once again seek to pinpoint some differences between men and women and point out that the qualities which women have to offer are valuable and have been excluded from rewards by existing society to its detriment as well as to the women's. There might even be an effort to prove that men are just as capable of exhibiting these qualities (awareness of context, cooperativeness, responsiveness, concern for life, etc.). Then the argument could be developed that men have been discriminated against in the socialization process and in the social expectations held for them so that they have not been able to develop to their fullest potential their "feminine" as well as "masculine" qualities.

A radical critique of our current social system and an ideology of equality between masculine and feminine *values* would likely uncover a much greater overlap in men's and women's abilities and accomplishments than is today thought possible with the ideology of equality and role-sharing, or than formerly was thought possible with the ideology of equality and role conflict. At present, however, a review of recent research shows that past investigation concentrated primarily on phenomena growing out of role conflict—an analysis that Viola Klein foresaw and described. The impact of the role-sharing ideology is still very recent. That of more radical social criticism is yet to be seen.

II. RECENT SCHOLARLY RESEARCH ON WOMEN

Although it is obviously not possible in a short essay to describe the present research situation as regards women with a degree of thoroughness parallel to Viola Klein's collection of views on the feminine character, it is possible to sketch some of the major developments within each of the disciplines that she considered and some new areas as well. Factors in the personal backgrounds of each of the authors are not by and large accessible to us (other than gross facts such as whether the person is a man or a woman), but there is internal evidence in the works themselves to indicate whether an author largely accepts the system as given and deals with sex differences within that framework or, on the other hand, takes a critical view of existing arrangements and is not averse to their alteration. Generally speaking, in the United States, social scientific work on the sexes in the 1950s was used to explain the functionality of existing arrangements and the existence of role conflict. The research of the 1960s, however, became much more critical in nature, and gave support to those impatient with continuing inequities who wished to document the degree of discrimination that existed. The development of a third trend toward scholarly research on alternative ways of organizing the social system, rather than on the mere justification or critique of current sex roles, is only just begun. Examples of these trends are sketched below, following the order of Viola Klein's chapter outline, in the fields of biology, philosophy, psychoanalysis, psychology, history, anthropology, sociology, and several other fields in which interest in sex roles has recently emerged.

Although there are possible distortions in following an oversimplified description of developments in each field, it is convenient to characterize the general trend of research as being conservative in the 1950s, i.e., maintaining continuity with pre–World War II research, critical with a sharp change of direction in the 1960s, and holding out the possibility of a radical outlook in the 1970s and beyond.

Such a characterization of the intellectual orientation of each decade corresponds not only to trends in sex-role ideology but also to the general stance of the scientific establishment vis-à-vis the society at large. Not only were the 1950s the heyday of the role-conflict ideology, they were a time when science and the intellectual community in general were reestablishing continuity with pre-war standards of normalcy. The shift from the role-conflict ideology to role-sharing corresponds with a shift from status quo orientation to a critical stance that occurred among intellectuals in a number of societies around 1960. In the United States the launching of Sputnik by the Russians and the growth of an active civil rights movement for blacks caused soul-searching and uneasiness about the established order. In Russia, Khrushchev's campaign for deStalinization precipitated redirection. A few years later, China's Cultural Revolution and France's withdrawal from the Algerian war caused enormous upheaval in each of those societies. By 1968, student uprisings with their radical overtones were a worldwide phenomenon occurring in France, Mexico, Japan, Great Britian, and the United States.

The consequence of all these events was a pervasive mood of skepticism toward the status quo. It had its parallel in the social sciences in the United States, though the connections are not direct or obvious. In anthropology an interest in evolutionism which for seventy-five years had been out of fashion was revived. In psychology, long dominated by experimental method and an atomistic S-R logic, humanistic concerns for individual self-actualization found wider following. In sociology, functionalism came under attack and was challenged by sociologists who had a stake in social criticism. How such developments bear on research into women's psychology and roles is examined below in each of the fields examined by Klein, ranging from biology through sociology, and finally in the humanities and law, fields not considered by Klein at the time her book was first issued.

Biology. A wide variety of data on sex differences is available from biological research. The important question is which of these findings will be selected for special attention and application to the issue of sex equality. Havelock Ellis chose the evidence that argued for the female's superior adaptability. Today several different points of view compete in the interpretation of the available evidence.

Biological differences between the sexes have been examined under at least three major headings:

1. Male/female traits—chromosomal definition, morphological types and anomalies, hormonal levels and reproductive behavior and response. Advanced techniques for studying human chromosomes date from 1956. Not until after that time was it absolutely clear that certain sexual abnormalities were the result of chromosomal deviations such as the xo or xxy pattern. Then studies of fetal development showed the development of masculine or feminine features to result from hormone levels which were in turn regulated by the sex chromosomes. In addition, hormonal levels, such as that of testosterone, were found correlated with the frequency of particular responses, such as aggression.[12] Research by Money and the Hampsons, however, pointed out that male or female identification is based on a number of variables—genetic, morphological, hormonal, and gender of early psychological identification—all of which may not

---

[12] David Hamburg and Donald T. Lunde, "Sex Hormones in the Development of Sex Differences in Human Behavior," in Maccoby, ed., *The Development of Sex Differences.*

perfectly coincide. After observing persons with anomalous sexual characteristics, they suggested that the sex assigned a person during early childhood was the strongest single influence on the gender of identification.[13]

2. Sex-linked instincts or behaviors. This line of inquiry draws impetus from the ethological tradition exemplified in the work of Konrad Lorenz. Like Desmond Morris's book *The Naked Ape,* much of this work relies on considering men as primates, who like all animals find certain social behavior natural, perhaps even instinctive. Lionel Tiger, in his book *Men in Groups,* argues that men have something like an instinct for male-bonding: they find it easier to group together for defense or other mutual interest than do females. Harlow's studies of monkeys show strong mother-infant bonding and disorientation of the baby monkey and its inability to mate if such bonding is prevented.[14]

3. The evolution and natural selection of sex differences. Here the concern is with what patterns in male and female mating, nurture of the young, aggression, or food-producing may have been particularly adaptive for the species and therefore been selected to continue as characteristic of each of the sexes. An example is the relative frequency of agonistic behavior and the establishment of a dominance hierarchy among large male mammals. Such behavior is relatively rare among females. A possible interpretation is that there is advantage (in terms of natural selection) to the dominant male who can inseminate more females, whereas such dominance has much less reward for the female since she can bear only one offspring at a time. Her aggression may be more adaptive in protecting the interests of her infant, fending off if need be the approaches of other infants or threatening adults, but would not be of selective advantage in the mating process. Another evolutionary question has to do with the evolution of the human family (mother, father, infant): why did it emerge among humans alone when other higher primates are typically organized in troupes or bands?[15]

It is still too soon to draw clearly the implications of biological

[13] John L. Hampson, "Determinants of Psychosexual Orientation," in Frank Beach, ed., *Sex and Behavior* (New York: Wiley, 1965).

[14] Desmond Morris, *The Naked Ape* (New York: Dell, 1967, 1969); Lionel Tiger, *Men in Groups* (New York: Random House, 1969); Harry F. Harlow, "Sexual Behavior in the Rhesus Monkey," in Beach, ed., *Sex and Behavior.*

[15] Course given by Irven B. DeVore and Robert Trivers, "The Biological Basis of Human Sexuality," Harvard University, Faculty of Arts and Sciences; Lila Leibowitz, "Dilemma for Social Evolution: The Impact of Darwin," *Journal of Theoretical Biology* 25 (1969): 255-275.

x

evidence for the current debate over sex roles. One fairly obvious possibility is that such findings will be rejected as being largely irrelevant to the social questions at issue today. Such response stems from historical experience such as that of feminists who in the 1870s heard Dr. Edward Clarke of the Harvard Medical School warn against higher education for women. He based his argument on the delicate nature of the female organism and the hazards of the menstrual cycle. To those who find little evidence that the last century of higher education has harmed women, contemporary evidence of physical sex differences is likely to seem no more relevant than was Dr. Clarke's.

There is, however, the opposite argument, supported by such works as that of Katharina Dalton, *The Menstrual Cycle*.[16] It gives evidence for women's higher accident rates during particular days of the cycle and evidence of other variations in performance as a result of hormonal fluctuation. Persons reading this book might find justification for preventing women from flying airplanes. Of course, one might ask whether there is cyclical variation in men's hormone levels. Work on this problem is only rudimentary. In all, the effect of such research, like that of the pathetic baby monkeys reared by the Harlows, is taken by some as a warning against too rapid or unthinking change of traditional sex roles.

There is, however, a third alternative which seeks to specify somewhat further the nature of the interactions between organism and environment. Such refined information shows the limits within which the organism can modify its responses under different social and psychological conditions. Several recent studies point up the possible relationships. McClintock shows a correlation between timing of ovulation in college girls and that of their roommates, indicating a social factor in a biological process. Douvan, on the other hand, interprets the divergence between boys' and girls' scores on various tests at time of puberty as possibly resulting from biological changes in the girls that make them more dependent on external than internal cues.[17] Although such findings have not yet been integrated

<hr>

[16] Katharina Dalton, *The Menstrual Cycle* (Pantheon, 1969, 1971).

[17] Martha McClintock, "Menstrual Synchrony and Acceleration: A Possible Parallel with Phenomena in Mice," B.A. honors thesis, Wellesley College, 1969; Elizabeth Douvan, "New Sources of Conflict in Females at Adolescence and Early Adulthood," in Judith Bardwick *et al.*, *Feminine Personality and Conflict* (Belmont, Calif.: Brooks/Cole, 1970). The most comprehensive recent treatment of the interplay between biological forces and psychological processes in women may be found in Judith Bardwick, *Psychology of Women* (New York: Harper and Row, 1971).

into a coherent whole, they do suggest the ways in which biological data on sex differences may be brought to bear on the issue of women's changing roles. The challenge is to describe more precisely the nature of the interaction between organism and environment so that the limits of the organism's adaptation to changed conditions can be foreseen and taken into account.

Philosophy. From questions about limits on human freedom that are posed by biology, we turn to philosophy for consideration of ethical and normative standards that men and women should strive to achieve in their relationships to each other. Probably the single most important contribution to this question in recent years has been that of Simone de Beauvoir. In her book *The Second Sex*,[18] she reviews the biological and historical condition of women and characterizes their state as one pervaded by "immanence," whereas that of men holds greater possibility for "transcendence." Men make tools and are free for that experience that carries them beyond the bounds of nature. Women, however, are tied to their biology in a way that limits their freedom. De Beauvoir's message, of course, is that women should seek liberation from the boundedness of their role so that they may also experience transcendence.

This call for liberation has echoed in feminist ideology of recent years. However, it should be noted that the goal thus set up is for the female to approach the male's state of "transcendence." The opposite possibility, that males seek liberation to pursue female patterns, has yet to be stated clearly. However, Philip Slater, in *The Pursuit of Loneliness,* does pass a normative judgment on western culture that indicts its repression of emotion and its single-minded pursuit of success, and traces the pattern to the relation between men and women that prevails not only in the family but in society at large. His analysis suggests the need for men's liberation as de Beauvoir's suggests women's liberation.[19]

Psychoanalysis. Psychoanalysis provides one sort of synthesis between biological limits and philosophical purpose. It not only analyzes the individual's situation, it also offers therapy.

Freud's work and that of Helene Deutsch and Karen Horney had been published when Klein wrote *The Feminine Character*. Since

---

[18] Simone de Beauvoir, *The Second Sex,* trans. and ed. H. M. Parshley (New York: Modern Library, 1952).

[19] Philip Slater, *The Pursuit of Loneliness* (Boston: Beacon, 1970). Slater traces the anxiety about masculinity to Greek culture in *The Glory of Hera* (Boston: Beacon, 1968).

then there have been two major developments in psychoanalysis—one the work of Erik Erikson, the other a critique of psychoanalytic assumptions and method by contemporary feminists.

In *Childhood and Society,* published in 1950, Erikson shows that the inclusive, extrusive, and intrusive modes of infantile sexuality are laid down in both boys and girls, creating for each the precedent of relating to the world in a receptive or initiating way. From the oedipal stage on, however, it is primarily the intrusive mode that is emphasized for the boy and the introceptive for the girl. Yet each sex has in the process of normal development learned the full complement of possible modes of relating to the environment. Abnormalities result when the child gets "stuck" at one phase or another. Though one of Erikson's later articles argues that there are differences in boys' and girls' block play, the importance of the earlier work for understanding basic similarities has perhaps been overshadowed and is due fresh attention in an era that emphasizes role-sharing.[20]

Current critics of psychoanalysis focus not only on the Freudian concepts that are prejudicial toward women, such as "penis envy," but also point out that psychotherapy has held up a model of the "normal" woman who is receptive, submissive, not career-oriented. The conditions of therapy frequently place a woman patient in a dependent position vis-à-vis a powerful male authority figure—the doctor. Feminists beginning with Betty Friedan and continuing through Phyllis Chesler have asked whether such patterns lead women to health or instead foster illness.[21] While theirs is representative of the radical perspective that has questioned the underlying tenets of the field, other more sympathetic observers have argued that "the feminine mystique" was a popular misapplication of psychoanalytic insights regarding the maternal role. They point

[20] Erik Erikson, "The Theory of Infantile Sexuality," in *Childhood and Society* (New York: W. W. Norton, 1950). Differences in block play are described in Erikson, "Inner and Outer Space: Reflections on Womanhood," in Lifton, ed., *The Woman in America.*

[21] Phyllis Chesler, "Patient and Patriarch" and "Women as Psychiatric and Psychotherapeutic Patients," *Journal of Marriage and the Family* 33 (1971): 746-759. Bart points out that the Freudian myth of the vaginal orgasm made many women think something was wrong with them. But the recent work of Masters and Johnson, *Human Sexual Response* (Boston: Little, Brown, 1966) and the earlier work of Kinsey, *Sexual Behavior of the Human Female* (Philadelphia: Saunders, 1953), destroyed that myth. Bart, "Sexism and Social Science," p. 739.

out that an unusually high proportion of psychoanalysts are professionally successful women who have also maintained continuity with feminine interests. One of the most famous examples is Anna Freud.[22]

Psychology. In psychology, too, as in psychoanalysis, there has been a general shift in recent years toward much more critical outlook on the basic assumptions and methods of the field—particularly as regards research on women. Advances have been made not only in identifying the psychologists' own prejudices about male and female personality, but also in refining relatively global concepts and creating more complex designs for the collection and ordering of information.

Research of the 1950s continued the tradition of describing similarities and differences between the sexes, a tradition to which Terman and Miles had made notable contribution in 1936 with their book *Sex and Personality.* However, as the decade progressed, many of the findings were put to a prescriptive use, to judge whether the person was normal or deviant in terms of past M-F test results. Not surprisingly, consciousness of role conflict emerged along with this prescriptive research.

Criticism of these prescriptive assumptions has come only very recently. Broverman and others show that psychologists' expectations for a normal adult female are considerably below those for a normal adult male. However, other studies show that such invidious stereotypes toward women also exist in the culture at large. For instance, Goldberg showed that an article purportedly written by "John T. McKay" was given higher ratings by students than an identical one by "Joan T. McKay." Matina Horner has clarified the relationships between such stereotypes and women's achievement. Because most girls believe that achievement is inconsistent with femininity, they have a fear of success and actually welcome failure because it resolves internal conflict.[23]

Such research not only attacks the implicit stereotypes of masculinity and femininity and forces a refinement of these global concepts

[22] Helen Tartakoff, "Psychoanalytic Perspectives on Women: Past, Present, and Future," Radcliffe Conference on Women, April 1972.

[23] Inge Broverman, Susan Vogel, *et al.,* "Sex-Role Stereotypes: A Current Appraisal," *Journal of Social Issues* (in press); Philip Goldberg, "Are Women Prejudiced against Women?," *Trans-Action* 5 (1968): 28-30; Matina S. Horner, "Femininity and Successful Achievement: A Basic Inconsistency," in Bardwick *et al.,* eds., *Feminine Personality and Conflict.*

into variables (such as need for achievement) that can be comparably measured in both sexes, it also shifts the focus of investigation from primary concentration on individual *traits* and shows the force of *social expectations*. Thus, as well as a more radical value orientation entering into the research, there is evolution of a more complex model for explanation of male and female differences. This model makes necessary the consideration of environmental influence as well as biological determinants. In addition it fosters definition of more universal traits than masculinity or femininity or emotionality, and substitutes instead variables such an aggression, dependency, autonomic lability, or hostility.[24]

Having moved through a stage of research on "psychological sex differences coincident with the ideology of role conflict," psychologists are now interested in research on "sex-typing and socialization."[25] This latter not only illustrates a more complex conceptual apparatus, it also is more relevant for the ideology of role-sharing because it underlines the dissimilarity of the socialization process for males and females and the disadvantages in it for women. If a future ideological phase will emphasize men's liberation, it is not unlikely that coming research will show the adverse effects of sex-typing for boys.

History. Historical works on women were out of fashion until relatively recently. Then, in 1959, Eleanor Flexner's *Century of Struggle,* a sympathetic, scholarly description of the woman's movement in America, attracted fresh attention. More recently William O'Neill's critique of the suffrage movement, *Everyone Was Brave,* has brought analysis of nineteenth-century feminism into conjunction with the American revival of feminism.[26]

Until Flexner's book, much of the history and biography of early feminists was devotional in character, lacking the perspective of distance and the techniques of modern historical scholarship. Flexner

[24] Mary Parlee, "Psychological Studies of Sex Differences: An Historical Survey" (unpublished manuscript).

[25] Parlee points out the categories used in Oetzel's bibliography on sex differences and the titles of chapters in the 1954 and recent revised editions of the *Handbook of Child Psychology* as evidence of this change in perspective. See the Oetzel bibliography and Walter Mischel, "A Social-Learning View of Sex Differences," in Maccoby, ed., *The Development of Sex Differences.*

[26] Eleanor Flexner, *Century of Struggle* (Cambridge, Mass.: Harvard University Press, 1959); William O'Neill, *Everyone Was Brave* (Chicago: Quadrangle, 1969). For the English case, see Margaret Hewitt, *Wives and Mothers in Victorian Industry* (London: Rockliff, 1958); Constance Rover, *Women's Suffrage and Party Politics in Britain, 1866-1914* (London: Routledge, 1967); and Rover, *Love, Morals and the Feminists* (London: Routledge, 1970).

brought to the subject not only a meticulous sense of detail and accuracy, she also saw the feminist movement as engaging a broad spectrum of women—not only suffragists, but those in women's clubs, missionary societies, and labor unions; those seeking not only political goals but also educational and economic reform.

Published nearly ten years later, O'Neill's work introduced yet other perspectives on the earlier movement. He included reference to the psychological and sociological research of the 1950s that dealt with role conflict. He touched on changes in the family that isolated women in the suburbs. But finally, he ventured into a critique of early feminism that departed radically from Flexner's matter-of-fact description. O'Neill argued that the earlier feminists had narrowed their focus to the vote at the expense of a larger and more radical effort to change social institutions such as the family.

O'Neill's work roughly corresponded with the radical reorientation of many American scholars in the 1960s. Rather than merely accept events and describe them faithfully as Flexner had done, he ventured into social criticism. We may ask what new approach can be expected to develop next. One very likely possibility is greater attention to demographic history and the changing structure of the family and economy that are crucial variables underlying women's status. The question for such research is: what were women's lives— that of all social classes, not merely the privileged ones—really like? In her study of *The Southern Lady* Anne Firor Scott made some progress in this direction by examining myriad documents of the region and giving attention not only to the leaders of the woman's movement but also to letters of anonymous women.[27] But other detailed demographic analysis still waits to be done. For instance, examination of parish registers for indications of fertility rates, age at marriage, etc. would reveal more precisely the structure of the family and economy that shaped the roles of ordinary women. Examination of membership lists in labor unions and other organizations could reveal characteristics of members not yet otherwise known.[28]

Another likely possibility is more intense analysis of women's biog-

[27] Ann Firor Scott, *The Southern Lady: From Pedestal to Politics, 1830-1930* (Chicago: University of Chicago Press, 1970).

[28] An example of such historical demography is found in John Demos, *A Little Commonwealth* (London: Oxford University Press, 1970), ch. 5, "Husbands and Wives." Analysis of membership lists of two women's organizations is given in Janet Zollinger Giele, "Social Change in the Feminine Role: A Comparison of Woman's Suffrage and Woman's Temperance, 1870-1920," unpublished doctoral dissertation, Harvard University, 1961.

raphy to reveal sources of frustration and sources of energy, thereby approaching the question of what women's lives were really like from an individual perspective. Gail Parker views the life of Elizabeth Cady Stanton from this angle, seeking to answer how she "got it all together"—having babies, managing a household, dealing with a somewhat lackluster marriage, and all the while producing remarkably original and vital arguments for women's rights. Other such biographical attempts should be made. Until a study equivalent to Erikson's for Martin Luther or Gandhi is done for some outstanding woman, the possibilities for appreciating feminine sources of creativity fall far short of realization and prevent understanding of similarities and differences between the sexes in this regard.[29]

Anthropology. Some of the major recent developments in physical anthropology have been treated above in the section on biology. The main trend to be described here is in the growth of cross-cultural research. Following the lead of Margaret Mead, Ruth Benedict, and others, much of the cross-cultural comparison of the 1950s was relativist in perspective. That is, anthropologists examined the role of women within the bounds of individual cultures, describing it with ethnographic detail, rather than searching for principles that accounted for cross-cultural similarities and differences.

Several studies provide rich ethnographic description of women's roles. For a modern society, there is the account by Seeley *et al.* in *Crestwood Heights* of men's and women's lives in a Canadian suburb. Audrey I. Richards gives a meticulous description of a girls' initiation ceremony among the Bemba of northern Rhodesia in *Chisungu*. Phyllis Kaberry had in 1939 published a study of Australian aboriginal women. In 1952 her *Women of the Grassfields* gave a detailed account of the economic and family roles that characterized several groups of Bamenda women of West Africa. Catherine Berndt examined the effects of western contact on Australian women's roles in her study, *Women's Changing Ceremonies in Northern Australia.*[30]

[29] Gail Parker, essay in Elizabeth Cady Stanton, *Eighty Years and More: Reminiscences, 1815-1897* (New York: Schocken, 1971).

[30] John R. Seeley *et al., Crestwood Heights: A Study of the Culture of Suburban Life* (New York: Wiley, 1956); Audrey I. Richards, *Chisungu: A Girl's Initiation Ceremony among the Bemba of Northern Rhodesia* (Glasgow: University of Glasgow Press, 1956); Phyllis Kaberry, *Aboriginal Woman Sacred and Profane* (London: Routledge, 1939); and *Women of the Grassfields,* Colonial Research Publication 14 (London: Her Majesty's Stationery Office, 1952); Catherine Berndt, *Women's Changing Ceremonies in Northern Australia* (Paris: Librairie Scientifique, 1950).

Studies such as that of Richards and Kaberry gave excellent raw material for cross-cultural comparison. Each considered the underlying economic and political variables that affected family structure and in turn the position of women.[31] It was several more years, however, until the implications of such detailed reports were gathered together in a landmark comparative work, *Matrilineal Kinship,* edited by David Schneider and Kathleen Gough. That book reviews earlier theories regarding matrilineal kinship and suggests a revised hypothesis that matriliny is most likely in rich horticultural societies where continuity of generations in the same geographical area is rewarding. Only when mobility is necessary and a division of the patrimony among brothers is necessary, as in a herding society or one with plow agriculture, does the economic contribution of the women lessen and dispersion of brothers become advantageous.[32]

Other important cross-cultural studies have followed the method of George Murdock and made use of the Human Relations Area Files at Yale University. Two such studies seemed to reinforce traditional stereotypes regarding sex roles. Zelditch found that "instrumental" roles in the nuclear family were nearly universally performed by men and "expressive" roles by women.[33] Also, William N. Stephens, comparing the roles of husband and wife in a number of cultures, concluded with what are apparently three "near-universals of husband and wife roles": (1) a standard division of labor by sex; (2) the "essential femininity" of some tasks, such as child care, and the "essential masculinity" of other tasks, such as fishing;

[31] Kaberry made this method explicit: "In other words, one's starting point is not the women but an analysis of a particular aspect of culture. On that basis one may then proceed to examine in more detail the way in which the structure and the organization of rights, duties and activities within a group of institutions affect the position of women" (*Women of the Grassfields,* p. viii). Kaberry examined several different variations in women's roles and underlying structural features among the Bamenda. Audrey I. Richards likewise made comparative studies among the Bantu: "Some Types of Family Structure amongst the Central Bantu," in A. R. Radcliffe Brown and D. Forde, eds., *African Systems of Kinship and Marriage* (London: Oxford University Press, 1950). A more recent collection of essays with comparative possibilities is Denise Paulme, ed., *Women of Tropical Africa,* trans. H. M. Wright (Berkeley: University of California Press, 1963).

[32] David Schneider and Kathleen Gough, eds., *Matrilineal Kinship* (Berkeley: University of California Press, 1961). See particularly the introductory chapter by Schneider and the chapter by Aberle.

[33] Morris Zelditch, "Role Differentiation in the Nuclear Family: A Comparative Study," in Talcott Parsons and R. F. Bales, *Family, Socialization, and Interaction Process* (Glencoe, Ill.: Free Press, 1955).

(3) power and privilege: the husband's status is either equal to or higher than the wife's; matriarchies are rare.[34]

More recently, however, precise research among hunter-gatherers, reported in *Man the Hunter,* has established that women gather 60 to 80 percent of the total food consumed, although men provide the scarce and highly valued meat that is gained through hunting.[35] In addition, precise psychological measurement of such characteristics as field dependency in boys and girls by use of the rod-and-frame test in a number of cultures reveals that similar experience can make boys' and girls' test results more similar. There is also indication that as societies become more modern, test results in general become "more masculine."[36]

Taken together, these developments speak for a shift from a cultural relativist stance to a search for universal principles that explain not only differences in men's and women's roles in various cultures but also similarities. Even Margaret Mead as early as 1949 in *Male and Female* suggested such a shift from relativism toward a search for explanations that handle similarities in men's and women's roles in different cultures.[37] Current cross-cultural research bears out the trend even more clearly.

Sociology. If there has been a shift of comparable importance in sociology, it has been from functionalist thinking that dominated the

[34] William N. Stephens, *The Family in Cross-Cultural Perspective* (New York: Holt, 1963), p. 324. Other important comparative studies are George P. Murdock, *Social Structure* (New York: Macmillan, 1949); Beatrice B. Whiting, ed., *Six Cultures: Studies of Child-Rearing* (New York: Wiley, 1963); Leigh Minturn and William W. Lambert, *Mothers of Six Cultures: Antecedents of Child-Rearing* (New York: Wiley, 1964); Frank W. Young, *Initiation Ceremonies* (Indianapolis: Bobbs-Merrill, 1965).

[35] Richard B. Lee and Irven B. DeVore, eds., *Man the Hunter* (Chicago: Aldine, 1968); Judith K. Brown, "A Note on the Division of Labor by Sex," *American Anthropologist* 72 (1970): 1074-78.

[36] Unpublished research of John and Beatrice Whiting, Harvard University. For other studies reporting psychological test results and sex differences in a cross-cultural setting, see H. Barry, M. K. Bacon, and I. L. Child, "A Cross-Cultural Survey of Some Sex Differences in Socialization," *Journal of Abnormal and Social Psychology* 55 (1957): 327-332; Carol Ember, "Effects of Feminine Task-Assignment on the Social Behavior of Boys," unpublished doctoral dissertation, Harvard University, 1971; Sara B. Nerlove, Ruth Monroe, and Robert Monroe, "Effect of Environmental Experience on Spatial Ability: A Replication," *Journal of Social Psychology* 84 (1971): 3-10.

[37] Margaret Mead, *Male and Female* (New York: William Morrow, 1949). Mead understood the similarities in the role of a given sex across cultures to be rooted in biological universals that created for all cultures similar problems in the socialization of the sexes and set limits on the number of possible solutions.

1950s to change-oriented thinking that gained prominence during the 1960s.[38] Corresponding with this general change in emphasis, the most prominent sociological theory and research on women during the decade following World War II tried to show that the differences between men's and women's roles were functional for the family and other social systems. Since then, there has been a steady swing toward emphasizing the dysfunctionality (or maladaptedness) of existing sex roles and the need to change them.

The best-known functionalist theories of sex roles are those of Parsons and Bales. In the 1940s Parsons had shown the fit between the conjugal family system and industrial society, with the woman primarily devoted to the home and the man to the productive system. In 1955 he and Bales together elaborated this theme, arguing that the instrumental and expressive functions found in small groups had their parallel in the family in the roles of husband and wife.[39]

A number of role-conflict studies took such traditional role allocation as a point of departure for examining the effects of the working wife on the children and on allocation of power within the family. Blood and Wolfe showed that a wife's relative power rose when she worked. In their study of *The Employed Mother in America,* Nye and Hoffman examined whether a mother's working had harmful effects on her children and found no conclusive evidence that it did.[40]

Betty Friedan made one of the earliest and clearest attacks on functionalism as a way of freezing women into traditional roles that no longer fitted reality or their interests. Her plaint was soon joined by other criticism of contemporary sex roles that came from women

[38] Gouldner, *The Coming Crisis in Western Sociology.*

[39] Talcott Parsons, "The Kinship System of the Contemporary United States," *American Anthropologist* 45 (1943): 22-38; "Age and Sex in the Social Structure of the United States," *American Sociological Review* 7 (1942): 604-616; Parsons and Bales, *Family, Socialization, and Interaction Process.*

[40] Robert Blood and Donald M. Wolfe, *Husbands and Wives: The Dynamics of Married Living* (New York: Free Press, 1960); F. Ivan Nye and Lois Wladis Hoffman, *The Employed Mother in America* (Chicago: Rand McNally, 1963). A quite positive view toward the role-conflict question appears in Alva Myrdal and Viola Klein, *Women's Two Roles: Home and Work* (London: Routledge, 1956, 1968). Other books that marked the transition toward greater acceptance of working women were *Womanpower,* published by the National Manpower Council in 1957 (New York: Columbia University Press), and *American Women,* the report of the President's Commission on the Status of Women, published in 1965, Margaret Mead and Frances Bagley Kaplan, eds. (New York: Charles Scribner's Sons).

sociologists themselves. In 1964 Jessie Bernard found evidence for
discrimination against women in the academic community. In the
same year Alice Rossi underscored the discrepancy between American ideals of equality and the demands made on American women
to be full-time wives and mothers that in effect deny them equal
opportunity.[41]

From these beginnings, the documentation of discrimination on
the job and the dissatisfaction of housewives at home has continued
to grow. In *Woman's Place* Cynthia Epstein shows that the proportion of women in an occupation declines as its status rises. Women
sociologists are blatantly underrepresented in positions at the top
universities, though women who have completed the Ph.D. at these
universities appear to be even more highly selected than their male
colleagues.[42] Turning to the family, analyses by both Jessie Bernard
and Pauline Bart suggest that the housewife role carries restrictions
on freedom and demands to make such emotional investment in husband and children that many women's personalities are stunted and
inordinate depression or other symptoms ensue.[43]

Little wonder then that the newest trend in the sociology of sex
roles points toward role-sharing. Only by such sharing does it seem
possible to mitigate the isolation and restrictions of the housewife
role and free women for greater commitment to a job or other outside interests. Alva Myrdal and Viola Klein early perceived the bene-
ficial aspects of this trend in their book *Women's Two Roles:
Home and Work*. Dahlstrom's subsequent description of role-sharing
in Sweden shows that it can be done by means of training boys as
well as girls for household tasks and by creating a tolerant public
attitude. In addition the study of *Dual-Career Families* by the Rap-
oports in England and of similar families by Holmstrom, Garland,
and Poloma in America provides detailed information on precisely

[41] Jessie Bernard, *Academic Women* (University Park, Pa.: Pennsylvania
State University Press, 1964); Rossi, "Equality between the Sexes."

[42] Cynthia Epstein, "Encountering the Male Establishment: Sex-Status Limits on Women's Careers in the Professions," *American Journal of Sociology* 75
(1970): 965-982; Alice Rossi, "Status of Women in Graduate Departments of
Sociology," *American Sociologist* 5 (1970): 1-11; Michelle Patterson, "Alice in
Wonderland: A Study of Women Faculty in Graduate Departments of Sociology," *American Sociologist* 6 (1971): 226-234.

[43] Pauline Bart, "Mother Portnoy's Complaints," *Transaction* 8 (1970):
69-74; Bernard, "The Paradox of the Happy Marriage"; Erik Gronseth, "The
Husband-Provider Role: A Critical Appraisal," in Andrée Michel, ed., *Family
Issues of Women in Europe and America* (Leiden: E. J. Brill, 1971).

how institutional arrangements and *ad hoc* family decisions can be bent to accommodate two careers.[44] Such research is as yet largely oriented to the middle class, but work by Rainwater, Komarovsky, and others on women's roles and family structure in other classes provides raw material for a more comprehensive treatment of the role-sharing issue.[45]

Thus in a generation the sociology of sex roles has changed its stance from accepting and explaining inevitable role conflict to one that labels needless suffering that can be avoided by changed institutional arrangements and redefinitions of male and female roles.

Economics, Law, Humanities, Theology. In a miscellany of several additional fields, scholarly attention to the status of women has so newly emerged that it is not yet possible to delineate competing theories or traditions of research. None of these fields were covered by Klein in the first edition of *The Feminine Character.* A brief notation of them is made here for the student who may wish to examine some of the leading contributions and be abreast of further developments as they unfold.

In economics the position of women is considered largely as a problem of supply and demand in the labor market. Both Robert Smuts, an economic historian, and Valerie Oppenheimer, a demographer, give interpretation to the historical trend toward women's greater participation in the labor force. Oppenheimer, differing with

[44] Edmund Dahlstrom, *The Changing Roles of Men and Women* (London: Duckworth, 1962, 1967); Lotte Bailyn, "Notes on the Role of Choice in the Psychology of Professional Women," in Lifton, ed., *The Woman in America;* Rhona and Robert Rapoport, *Dual-Career Families* (Baltimore: Penguin Books, 1971); Lynda Lytle Holmstrom, *The Two Career Family* (Cambridge, Mass.: Schenkman, 1972); Margaret M. Poloma and T. Neal Garland, "Jobs or Careers? The Case of the Professionally Employed Married Woman," in Michel, ed., *Family Issues of Women;* and *Dual Careers: A Longitudinal Study of Labor Market Experience of Women,* Manpower Research Monograph 21, vol. 1 (U.S. Department of Labor, 1970).

[45] Lee Rainwater *et al., Workingman's Wife: Her Personality, World, and Life Style* (New York: Oceana, 1959); Mirra Komarovsky, *Blue Collar Marriage* (New York: Random House, 1962, 1964); Herbert Gans, *The Urban Villagers* (New York: Free Press, 1962); Hyman Rodman, *Lower Class Families: The Culture of Poverty in Negro Trinidad* (New York: Oxford University Press, 1971). One other kind of comparative material should also be mentioned. This is analysis of role change, such as that in the kibbutz, where sex roles became *less* equalitarian over time. See Yonina Talmon, "Sex-role Differentiation in an Equalitarian Society," in Thomas Lasswell, ed., *Life in Society* (Glenview, Ill.: Scott, Foresman, 1965). Like the anthropologists Kaberry and Richards, Talmon points to the underlying structural conditions that promote or frustrate equality.

Smuts, argues that the rapid post–World War II increase was due
to a sharp rise in demand in such traditionally female occupations
as teaching and clerical work.[46] Cain and Mincer give close attention
to the variables that determine a particular woman's decision to
work: her own education weighs positively; her husband's income
and the youth of her children weigh negatively.[47] Eli Ginsberg
examines the personal and social backgrounds of highly educated
women and points to life-style factors that either reinforce or frustrate their continued work history.[48]

Another possible line of inquiry has to do with the nature of the
economic system that creates demand for women's labor. Oppenheimer dealt with this question in the United States by comparing
periods of high and low demand. Norton Dodge examined the question by his study of *Women in the Soviet Economy*. He found the
high labor-force participation rate of Soviet women to be in large
part explained by heavy war casualties of men in certain age groups.
Such work provides a basis for national comparisons to which Barbara Ward made an early contribution in her writing on Asian
women and questions of economic development.[49]

If there is any radical economic thought which has implications
for women comparable to that in other fields, its roots perhaps lie
in the attitude of radical economists that continued economic growth
is not necessarily good and that some contributions to the economy
which are not now assigned a dollar value (such as the cost to the
environment of absorbing waste) should be reckoned in our ac-
counting system. Among such currently "free" goods and services
that perhaps should be paid for are certain child-care functions and
home maintenance that women have traditionally provided.[50]

[46] Robert Smuts, *Women and Work in America* (New York: Columbia University Press, 1959); Valerie Oppenheimer, *The Female Labor Force in the
United States: Demographic and Economic Factors Governing Its Growth and
Changing Composition,* Population Monograph 5 (Berkeley: University of California, 1970).

[47] Glen G. Cain, *Married Women in the Labor Force* (Chicago: University
of Chicago Press, 1966).

[48] Eli Ginsberg, *Life Styles of Educated Women* (New York: Columbia University Press, 1966).

[49] Norton Dodge, *Women in the Soviet Economy* (Baltimore: Johns Hopkins
Press, 1966); Barbara Ward, *Women in the New Asia: The Changing Roles of
Men and Women in South and South-east Asia* (Paris: UNESCO, 1963).

[50] Juanita Kreps, *Sex in the Marketplace: American Women at Work* (Baltimore: Johns Hopkins Press, 1971), p. 75.

In law, many issues such as women's jury duty or right to equal pay that had lain quiescent since the right to vote was granted in the United States over fifty years ago were revived by President Kennedy's appointment of a Commission on the Status of Women and the publication of their report in 1963. Since then Leo Kanowitz's book *Women and the Law* has been the best general reference to women's legal position throughout the country. More recently several law journals have carried special issues on women. To the sociologist, historian, or anthropologist, the question of women's comparative legal status in various countries is a potentially valuable basis for analysis. Kanowitz is currently engaged in comparative work on women's legal status in Europe. Other valuable sources of information, though uneven in detail, are Koyama's description of change in Japanese women's status after the war, and other UNESCO publications. Patai's compilation of reports on women's status in a number of different countries is also a useful starting point for comparative work.[51]

Developments in the humanities are most visible in literature, where Kate Millett and Germaine Greer have recently achieved fame for their critical assessments of the imagery surrounding women. Such beginning assaults on male chauvinist attitudes seem likely to be followed by more painstaking reassessment of the strengths of famous women authors such as Jane Austen or the Brontës and by serious attention to the recent autobiographical and confessional writing of women like Doris Lessing, Mary McCarthy, and Anaïs Nin.[52] Other studies like that of Fiedler's *Love and Death in the American Novel* and Katherine Rogers's history of misogyny in literature are likely to spark further inquiry into the imagery surrounding women in different times and places. Further question may center on whether indeed our own reading of many of these images

[51] Mead and Kaplan, eds., *American Women;* Leo Kanowitz, *Women and the Law: The Unfinished Revolution* (Albuquerque: University of New Mexico Press, 1969); "Symposium: Women's Rights," *Hastings Law Journal* 23, no. 1 (1971); "Symposium—Women and the Law," *Valparaiso University Law Review* 5, no. 2 (1971); Takashi Koyama, *The Changing Social Position of Women in Japan* (Paris: UNESCO, 1961); *Report of the Royal Commission on the Status of Women in Canada* (Ottawa: Information Canada, 1970); A. Afertinan, *The Emancipation of the Turkish Woman* (Paris: UNESCO, 1962); R. Patai, *Women in the Modern World.*

[52] Patricia Meyer Spacks, "Free Women," *Hudson Review* 24 (Winter 1971-72): 559-573; "A Chronicle of Women," *Hudson Review* 25 (Spring 1972): 157-170.

need be as necessarily misogynous as we currently believe.[53] An image is after all to some degree ambiguous until spelled out in connection with other elements of culture. This very ambiguity could be expected to engender alternative interpretations of classic images. Work on such unraveling is largely yet to be done.

Closely tied to the question of images are theological questions about the position of women. The best-known recent venture into such issues in America is that of a Catholic theologian, Mary Daly, in her book *The Church and the Second Sex*. Krister Stendahl earlier examined the question of women's status in an argument for admitting women to the clergy in Sweden. Daly's statement largely pinpoints negative stereotypes of women derived from traditional religious belief. Stendahl points out the positive elements in the Judaeo-Christian tradition that argue for equality.[54]

Recent developments in such a wide spectrum of disciplines clearly indicate that the woman question is a richly varied issue with many ramifications that can be examined from many sides. We turn next to a consideration of the means by which knowledge of women in different specialties can be integrated.

III. THE RISE OF INTERDISCIPLINARY WORK

Although the foregoing review of recent developments in research on women in a number of disciplines gives the impression that such work is neatly confined within the boundaries of each specialty, this is anything but the case. More frequently it is becoming the pattern for scholars in any given discipline to take into account work in neighboring fields. Yet intellectually the problem presents itself of how research on sexuality and sex roles in a discipline such as ge-

[53] Leslie Fiedler, *Love and Death in the American Novel* (New York: Dell, 1960, 1966); Katherine Rogers, *The Troublesome Helpmate: A History of Misogyny in Literature* (Seattle: University of Washington Press, 1966); Wendy Martin, "Seduced and Abandoned in the New World: The Image of Woman in American Fiction," in Gornick and Moran, eds., *Woman in Sexist Society*. Alternatives to the solely misogynous interpretation of images are presented in Janet Zollinger Giele, "Centuries of Womanhood: An Evolutionary Perspective on the Feminine Role," *Women's Studies: An Interdisciplinary Journal* 1 (in press).

[54] Mary Daly, *The Church and the Second Sex* (New York: Harper and Row, 1968); Krister Stendahl, *The Bible and the Role of Women: A Case Study in Hermeneutics*, trans. Emilie T. Sander, Facet Books Biblical Series 15 (Philadelphia: Fortress Press, 1966).

netics has any relation to that done in social psychology. One possible solution is the "integrative method" that Karl Mannheim mentioned in his Foreword to the first edition of *The Feminine Character*. He pointed to Viola Klein's collection of representative work from a number of disciplines as an example of the method. Today it is appropriate to consider what changes have occurred in the "integrative method" and whether other more streamlined approaches to interdisciplinary work on the "feminine character" have yet arisen.

Klein made, so far as I know, the first conscious attempt to integrate work that had been done on women in a wide variety of disciplines. It is evident that the disciplines she chose, with the possible exception of philosophy, are still most prominent in the research being done on women.

The one important change since her initial effort is that the researchers have become more interdisciplinary in their work. The integration of findings on women gathered in several disciplines no longer has to await the efforts of the intellectual historian or the sociologist of knowledge. The very nature of the research questions posed takes for granted the interaction of a number of variables and seeks to describe the complex process of causation more precisely. I shall cite some examples and then suggest why this growth in interdisciplinary research took place when it did.

Examples of Interdisciplinary Orientation in Recent Research. It somehow appears fairly obvious to the modern human mind that the person can affect his surroundings, that innate characteristics of the organism give rise to character traits, social behavior, and cultural products. What is more surprising is the demonstration that environmental forces "act back" on the organism, that culture affects personality structure, that personality affects the physiological processes of the body, etc. The tendency is the same in the realm of male-female differences. No one is particularly surprised if one finds that the male and female, with their different physical characteristics, turn out to have different psychological makeup, capacities for different social roles, and a preference for certain cultural configurations. But if it can be shown that male and female modes of behavior are as much the *result* of psychological, social, and cultural conditioning as their *cause,* then a new kind of thinking has been introduced. This form of thought that sees causation leading not only directly from the physical to the mental but also turning back and affecting the physical self is particularly conducive to interdisciplinary efforts at understanding.

Among the scholars working on female roles and psychology, there was certainly awareness, as in Freud, W. I. Thomas, or Margaret Mead, of the feedback principle, though that term had not yet been invented. But their perception of the complexities of causation needed to be more clearly specified. In her conclusions, Klein pointed to this need and saw in it a special role for the sociologist:

The contribution the sociologist has to offer to the discussion of this problem consists in an attempt to define more closely the concept of mental traits of sex by marking out its limits. . . . By eliminating those feminine traits which are due to other factors than sex he narrows down the definition of psychological sex character, making it at the same time more definite. His aim is not to prove that the organic constitution does not exert some influence, but rather to elucidate the nature of this influence by excluding those traits which can be shown to be due to such factors as a cultural pattern, including social functions, historic tradition, prevailing ideologies, etc. [p. 171].

Klein was absolutely right about the need for such delimitation of the effects of biological sex. Rather than making such delimitation alone, however, sociologists have been joined by workers in other disciplines who in their own investigations seek to refine somewhat more the complex chain of causation. Each in his experiments or logic of explanation has had to weigh the relative effects of innate organic traits as compared with the effects of myriad possible variations in the social environment. As a result, the orientation of many workers has become truly interdisciplinary because they have had to "control for," or take into account, the variables that are central to a neighboring discipline. Two recent examples of research that bear on sex roles will demonstrate this new tendency.

The first example is the work of Ariès in *Centuries of Childhood* on the evolution of the nuclear family. His work has implications for the woman's role because it suggests that the nuclear family is a fairly recent invention, emerging in the middle classes no earlier than the Renaissance, and that it was when the family became such a small private unit making great emotional investment in the child that the woman's role became peculiarly distinct within it. What caused this change was a new importance accorded to the child's personality combined with a sharp subsequent decline in infant mortality that resulted from better hygiene. Up to that time families knew children had only a precarious chance of surviving; children were treated from a very young age as small adults. Activity of women and children mixed with that of men and of other families in courtyard and field. The particularly emotional closeness of the post-Renaissance family had not yet been created, nor were the lives of women so narrowly restricted within it.[55]

Whether Ariès's thesis is ultimately upheld or not, his argument demonstrates a long chain of causal reasoning linking physical conditions (mortality), psychological factors (unwillingness to make emotional investment), social structure (nuclear family), culture (the child-oriented preoccupation of the middle classes), and finally, changes in the feminine role. It is apparent that demographic, social, and cultural factors have in this instance had an immense impact on the feminine role, "acting back" on it rather than being an emanation from it. The kinds of variables considered further demonstrate the need for an interdisciplinary theory that permits the historian (in this case) to approach a full and satisfying explanation. He must deal not only with demographic fact but also with psychological and sociological principles and their interaction.

A second example comes from a contemporary anthropological study by Carol Ember of boys and girls in Kenya.[56] Using natural conditions, she followed the logic of experiment to conclude that boys who were given girls' tasks, such as tending the fire or watching younger children, turned out to have cognitive patterns more similar to those of girls than did other boys. Conversely, girls who were given boys' tasks, such as carrying water from some distance or performing other duties that required mobility, developed psychological test results more likely to be characteristic of boys.

In this example, as in that of Ariès, there is an effort at explanation that links together several levels of experience. Ember shows the relation between particular facts of *culture* (Kenyan boys' and girls' typical task assignments), *social structure* (peculiarities of a particular family—a boy not being available and a girl having to perform the task, etc.), *psychological characteristics* (e.g. cognitive

---

[55] Philippe Ariès, *Centuries of Childhood,* trans. Robert Baldick (New York: Random House, 1962), pt. I, ch. 2; pt. III, ch. 1.

[56] Ember, "Effects of Feminine Task-Assignment on the Social Behavior of Boys." See also Nerlove, Monroe, and Monroe, "Effect of Environmental Experience on Spatial Ability."

style, performance on a test of field dependence, test performance typical of boys or girls), and characteristics of the *organism* (male or female). Here, too, the thesis is striking because it shows culture and social structure "acting back" on the organism to produce certain psychological traits, rather than these traits emanating simply from the male or female nature of the organism.

It is significant, perhaps, that in both the Ariès and Ember contributions the starting point of explanation is an example where there has been a reversal of some sort in what is expected of the female. Ariès shows a historical reversal; Ember a psychological reversal. The circumstance of reversal provides a particularly convincing demonstration that certain characteristics of males and females may not arise so much from innate differences in potential as from feedback mechanisms in social experience that are differently selected by the fact of being male or female. Of the authors Klein considered in *The Feminine Character,* Margaret Mead came the closest to selecting the kind of examples that produced such insight. By choosing cultures where there was a reversal in expectations held for males and females from what we normally expect, she made clear the powerful effect of culture and socialization. But her method was ahistorical; she took differences in culture as her starting point. Both Ariès and Ember lead us somewhat closer to understanding the *dynamics* behind different cultural expectations for men and women.

To describe more precisely the advance in interdisciplinary work, I shall present a diagram of the causal model that was implicit in much of the scholarly research done prior to the first edition of *The Feminine Character* and the causal model that appears to be implicit in research done now.

Causal Models and Interdisciplinary Work. When Viola Klein wrote her summary chapter for *The Feminine Character,* one of her central points was that thinking about male-female differences had gone beyond a logic that assumed biological traits to be the primary causal factors in behavior. The thought which replaced the logic of innatism was one that saw the importance of social and cultural influence on the psychology of women. This was an exceedingly important insight that is still central to the topic today. The changes that have occurred since then are greater precision in measurement and a more explicit awareness of the model that integrates the findings.

Little need be said about increasing precision in measurement. The elaboration of various kinds of tests in psychology, of survey techniques in sociology, or measurement of hormones and genetic characteristics in biology are familiar phenomena. But the underlying model for interdisciplinary work is little discussed.

This model is that of a system with many different subsystems, each one of which has effects on the others, and all of which together respond to and affect a larger environment. In other words, no one system can be considered closed. It is open both to the environment and to its own internal parts. Thus the challenge of explaining sex differences at any one level of organism, personality, or social role is that all other levels have to be taken into account. The prior model of explanation was unidirectional as follows:

Body ————————▶ Mind ————————▶ Action
(sex   (sex   (sex
diff.)   diff.)   diff.)

The current model of explanation incorporates a number of feedback loops as follows:

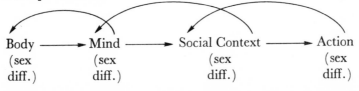

Body ————▶ Mind ————▶ Social Context ————▶ Action
(sex   (sex   (sex   (sex
diff.)   diff.)   diff.)   diff.)

Such a model facilitates exchange of information between disciplines and leads to more adequate understanding because each research specialty is concerned with a different segment of reality and no one of these segments can be isolated from the others except by artificial means. The organism, personality, social organization, and cultural beliefs are all entities interlaced with each other. The student of any of these systems must picture it as both receiving influence and having impact on each of the surrounding systems. Scholarly fields are caught up in a division of labor where each specializes in examining particular segments of the reality but in turn takes the others into account. This can be done through the logic of experimentation and statistical assessment or qualitative judgment of the relative weight of various factors in a given outcome. A diagram representing the division of labor between the disciplines is represented by Figure I.

FIGURE I. Academic Disciplines and Aspects of Research on Women

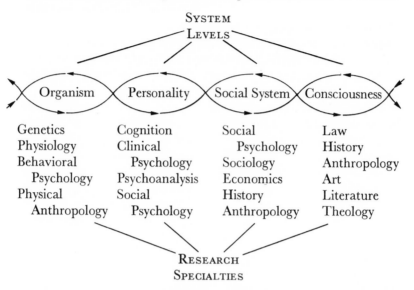

SYSTEM
LEVELS

Organism	Personality	Social System	Consciousness
Genetics	Cognition	Social	Law
Physiology	Clinical	Psychology	History
Behavioral	Psychology	Sociology	Anthropology
Psychology	Psychoanalysis	Economics	Art
Physical	Social	History	Literature
Anthropology	Psychology	Anthropology	Theology

RESEARCH
SPECIALTIES

Ember's research exemplifies the advances in conceptualization and measurement that are associated with this more complex model. Her work, like that of much of the recent work in all the disciplines, exhibits a knowledge not simply of a narrow specialty but of the interrelated interests of several specialties that are discovered when trying to evolve satisfying explanations in the field of women's psychology and sex roles.

IV. CONTINUITY AND CHANGE IN THE CONCLUSIONS REACHED

In her summary and conclusions Viola Klein particularly mentioned several sociological approaches that could give additional perspective and provide new evidence in the debate on women's character. She mentioned the change in the concept of femininity and showed several stages in the recent thought about the feminine character. She also showed how creativity and innovation, long thought lacking in women, were as much the result of training and the social situation as of any inherent deficiency in women.

After reviewing change in the social roles of women over the last generation and change in the kinds of research done on women, do we find that Klein's conclusions are in any way substantially changed? I think not. But I think her conclusions can be elaborated and specified somewhat further on the basis of what we now know. We can elaborate (1) on the nature of the interplay between social change in the feminine role and the categories we use to describe the feminine character, and (2) on the conditions in history when women's essential traits and their marginality are an asset and when their opportunities to be creative are enlarged.

Changes in the Feminine Role and the Concept of Femininity. Klein outlined three stages in the nineteenth-century development of the concept of femininity: an initial stage where women were discovered to have souls like men; a second stage in which women were thought to have characteristics the reverse of men's; and a third stage where individualism held sway and it was recognized that "personality traits are the 'by-products of immediate interests and incentives' and develop in accordance with the individual's social role in a given culture" (p. 170).

I believe we could now characterize these stages as a process of cognitive differentiation. Initial stereotypes yield to more complex perceptions. When this happens, it is evident that certain traits are neither masculine nor feminine, but rather found in both men and women. The process of cognitive differentiation parallels the process of social differentiation of roles and tasks that goes along with industrialization. In treating historical changes since 1945 I sketched several further stages of thought about women that appear to have gained acceptance in recent years—that of role conflict, role-sharing, and perhaps eventually that of value-sharing. Each of these stages is a further example of the principle of cognitive differentiation and weakening of stereotype. Each is also correlated with major societal changes that increased task differentiation and societal complexity. With each new stage of thought there was more opportunity for crossover in the roles performed by men and women. The relationship appears circular. People living in a changing social structure may well have cause for criticizing ancient beliefs because they no longer describe reality. But new ways of thinking can also in turn be used to affect social institutions and change the course of scientific inquiry.

Thus after a review of recent historical changes in sex roles and of the research that has been done on men and women, Klein's original insight is upheld. The intimate relationship between categories of thought about women and social experience continues to account for changes not only in ideology but also in scientific point of view.

Women's Marginality, Creativity, and Cycles of Social Change. Klein made an important connection between marginality and women's roles. And she sensed the importance of proving women's capacity for creativity and achievement if they were given an encouraging environment. But she did not clearly link the two insights together. This I think we can now do as a result of experience since she first wrote. We can make the connection because we have lived through a time in which there has been a striking changeover from the fifty-year period between the climax of the suffrage movement and the rise of women's liberation. During the period just finished women's marginality to the industrial system was a handicap and was legitimated by reference to their expressive functions. In the present period, however, the sense of feminine value is revived and is on the point of being turned into a benefit for the larger society.

What is apparent from this brief span of 150 years of rapid change in women's roles is that there are ups and downs in feminine contribution to the society. Women made striking innovative contributions at the turn of the century, when the criticism of new industrial conditions gave women an opportunity to contribute in the new and marginal field of social reform. Later their percentage in the professions declined—at least in the United States—and their sense of self-worth went into the doldrums. Women will probably again make striking contributions as criticism of the industrial society mounts. Their marginality will again be an asset, for, standing somewhat at the periphery of the established system, they are in a better position to make creative suggestions for change, much as a Jane Addams or a Beatrice Webb did at the turn of the century.[57]

Not only is it women's historical experience of the last several decades that enables us to see the connection between cycles of social

[57] Of course, as the universalization of traits, roles, and consciousness continues to occur, blurring sex lines, it may in the future be less obvious that it is *women* who are drawn into heightened activity during periods of rapid social change; it may instead become clear that it is a class of *men and women*, somewhat marginal to the system, who are drawn in at such periods, and another class of *men and women* who hold power during periods of relative stability. For documentation of the point that their very marginality was in women's favor at the end of the nineteenth century, see Janet James, "Introduction," in Edward T. James, Janet Wilson James, and Paul S. Boyer, eds., *Notable American Women 1607-1950* (Cambridge: Harvard University Press, 1971).

change and the benefits of marginality, it is also the identification of a central issue in the social sciences—the problem of explaining social change and personality change—that helps us to make this connection. If there is one debate that has attracted more interest in sociology than any other, it is the theoretical problem of explaining social change. The functionalists have been criticized for their slighting of the problem. The conflict theorists and other critics of functionalism have pointed to the importance of explaining change as well as order and stability. With the feminist example, there is suggestion of how these two important areas of inquiry can be integrated—in a cyclical model that comprises alternating phases of change and stabilization. For many periods of history, there is evidence that women's status flourishes during periods of radical reorientation in the social structure. Women were visible in the French Revolution as well as in the nineteenth-century reform movements in England and America.

V. Conclusion: *The Feminine Character* in Contemporary Perspective

It is Viola Klein's distinction to have been the first to see, more than twenty-five years ago, the fruitfulness of bringing the sociology of knowledge to bear on such an emotion-laden question as that of woman's nature and capacities. In so doing, she brought together the issue of cognition, on the one hand, and the issue of how social norms evolve, on the other. Although she did not develop an explicit argument of how the two are related—scientific knowledge and social change—she did, both in the body of the book and particularly in the selection and ordering of her conclusions, suggest a back-and-forth relationship between the knowledge scientists look for, the understanding people carry around in their heads, and the ideal social arrangements that they try to evolve. Even today, this understanding of the relationship between ideology, scientific knowledge, and programs for changing or preserving present social conditions is not well understood. Countless people seem to think of knowledge as some pure distilled essence, available in the same form to anyone who looks for it, no matter what their orientation, unsullied by human bias and partial understanding. Klein dispelled that illusion by placing side by side the differing conclusions of some of the most respected authors of the day who wrote on women.

Since Klein's original excursion into this field, new theories in the history of science, such as that of Thomas Kuhn's *Structure of Scientific Revolutions,* raise the possibility that the variety of scholarly views may not be merely random, but may itself be ordered into stages of thought that are compatible with some central paradigm that dominates an era. Kuhn, dealing with the stages of thought in such physical sciences as astronomy and physics, shows the impact of culturally derived "paradigms" on the gathering and ordering of scientific knowledge, causing some perfectly valid findings to be at first rejected because they do not fit the paradigm. If culture has an effect on knowledge in the physical sciences, how much more obvious its effect in the social sciences and on the handling of such a topic as the psychology of women! Klein of course demonstrated the impact of culture and the personality of the observer on the findings beyond reasonable doubt. The issue for students in the future is to unravel the paradigms that prevail in one era as compared with another. Klein began this task by suggesting three stages in the understanding of the feminine character in her conclusions. A challenge to the contemporary student is to spell out these stages somewhat further and grapple with the question of what precipitates movement from one stage to the next.

If knowledge and self-awareness have given men and women advantage in the evolutionary scheme, it is because they enhance their adaptability to changing conditions and their capacity for self-modification. In such a rapidly changing world as our own, it is altogether fitting that great scholarly effort go into the collection of knowledge about our own human limitations and potential. If this knowledge no longer proves adaptive or in tune with people's actual experience, then it is right that it be questioned critically and replaced by new, more adequate understanding that better helps human beings to cope with their environment. *The Feminine Character* leads us into these realms of inquiry and charts a course that has stood the test of time and will continue to provide direction for the future.

THE FEMININE CHARACTER

CHAPTER I

INTRODUCTION: AIMS AND METHOD

This book tries to contribute to the clarification of the idea of " femininity ". Its object is to discover whether there are traits which can be called typically feminine, what these traits are, and whether they have always been regarded as characteristic of women.

It approaches this question by studying a number of authorities who have developed their different theories during the second half of the nineteenth century and later. This co-ordination of various and often contrasting views will, it is hoped, lead to a better understanding of the complex problem of femininity. At the same time it will reveal the extent to which these theories reflect the idiosyncrasies of their time and have changed with a changing age.

As people generally tend to live up to what is expected of them, it seems important to expose the particular set of views held in our culture with regard to woman's social rôle, characteristic traits and psychological abilities. These views, transmitted by custom, social attitudes, public opinion, and in many other ways, are the framework within which personalities develop and to which, in one way or another, they have to adjust themselves. This cultural pattern however is anything but static. In our own civilization it has been subjected to radical changes, particularly during the last century. It is the observation of these changes and of their effect on the development of personality traits which enables us to make assumptions as to the influence on character formation of such social factors as cultural traditions, prevailing ideologies, the approval or disapproval of certain kinds of behaviour, the rewards allotted by an established community for a given conduct, the membership of a group with a defined social status, professional preoccupations, etc.

What are the transformations undergone by the feminine ideal? Which new traits have been developed in accordance with it? What have been the effects of their inferior social status upon the personality of women? What characteristics have they in common with other suppressed or minority groups? Before these questions have been answered satisfactorily no fair judgment can be made with regard to woman's innate characteristics and potentialities.

One aim of this book therefore is to show the changes in society's expectations of women and the corresponding changes in the feminine character. In order to sketch the background of opinion against which the " feminine character " develops, a number of theories on the subject have been studied. It is in the nature of the task that the selection of examples should not be comprehensive. It represents but a summary of some expert views and is meant to be a basis and stimulus for further investigations.

Another aim of this study is to observe how far scientific knowledge is affected by the general trend of intellectual and emotional development, i.e. by what has been called " the mental climate " of an age. Although the idea that knowledge, particularly in matters of man and society, could stand apart from the general social and cultural development of its time is to-day shared by a diminishing number of people, we still frequently find the " scientific attitude " represented as a completely detached and autonomous mental act, as if it were, in fact, an immediate and objective approach to facts.

In contrast to this view it is proposed here to demonstrate in a limited field that scientific knowledge, especially in the social sciences, does not exist in splendid isolation, but is an organic part of a coherent cultural system. It shares in the development of that culture both in a passive and in an active sense : it expresses its total state at a given time, and it actively fosters certain trends in the general development.[1] The choice of a particular problem as a subject for study and the specific approach to it both betray the spirit of their time. They reveal the influences of the contemporary state of social, spiritual, and technical development as well as personal bias. What becomes the subject of scientific interest, and the way it is presented, are dependent partly on social and historical factors, partly on the general level of scientific development, and are also coloured by the very individual factor of the investigator's personality —his style, his personal experiences, his character and temperament. " It could be shown in all cases that not only do fundamental orientations, evaluations, and the content of ideas differ, but that the manner of stating a problem, the sort of

---

[1] K. Mannheim has set forth the method of this " Sociology of Knowledge " in his *Ideology and Utopia* and other writings.

approach made, and even the categories in which experiences are subsumed, collected and ordered, vary according to the social position of the observer." [1] These influences may be, and probably are in most cases, unconscious. Nevertheless, no scholar —or for that matter any creative writer or artist—fails to reflect the ideologies of his time as well as his personal attitude, however much he may consciously strive for detached impartiality.

It is important to stress—as K. Mannheim has done—that the study of the effects of such irrational influences upon knowledge does not imply a relativist philosophy ; nor does it lead to the conclusion that objectivity can only be achieved in the exact sciences. What follows from the Sociology of Knowledge is the observation that " objectivity " in the social sciences is established in a different way and its achievement requires specific methods. The search for truth in sociological matters calls not only for a thorough examination of facts, but for a dynamic process of self-criticism, in which the diagnosis of our own " perspective " (i.e. our place in the historical and social process) and a continuous analysis of the unconscious motivations guiding our observations are of prime importance. " Perhaps it is precisely when the hitherto concealed dependence of thought on group existence and its rootedness in action becomes visible that it really becomes possible for the first time, through becoming aware of them, to attain a new mode of control over previously uncontrolled factors in thought." [2]

" Truth " in social matters presents itself in terms of various " perspectives ". By the method of a Sociology of Knowledge these " perspectives " are exposed to criticism and, as time goes on, an ever richer " integration *sui generis* " of these aspects becomes possible by an ever fuller understanding of their partiality. Relativism is thereby avoided, and a theory of " Relationism " established which takes into account the fact that knowledge of social matters is connected with the social and cultural background.

In support of this thesis a subject has been chosen which by its emotional character seems particularly suited to showing up these unconscious, irrational influences upon scientific theories. The scholars' views on women reflect : (*a*) the status of women in a given society ; (*b*) the prevailing ideologies concerning women in a certain historical period ; and (*c*) the author's

---

[1] K. Mannheim : *Ideology and Utopia* (Kegan Paul, London, 1936), p. 13.
[2] Op. cit., p. 4.

personal attitudes towards women. Sometimes these theories amount, in the last resort, to the use of a scientific apparatus for the rational justification of emotional attitudes. Only after all these influences have been laid bare, and a comparison between the many ways of approach to the problem of femininity has been made, will a really sound and well-founded judgment on the elusive " feminine character " be possible.

The method adopted here, therefore, is, first, to give a short historical survey of women's position in society from the Industrial Revolution to the present day, and then to present characteristic examples of the different scientific ways of approach to the problem of women during that period. These examples are outstanding rather than comprehensive. No claim is being made that all shades of opinion within each discipline are included. One representative has been selected from every field of science, and there is one chapter each on the biological, the philosophical, the psychoanalytical, the experimental-psychological, the psychometric, the historical, and the sociological methods of approach. This juxtaposition of various methods gives, at the same time, an indication of the great number of different ways that have been developed to deal scientifically with the problem of the feminine character.

To examine the different " perspectives " existing with regard to the problem of feminine psychology is one intention of this book; to show their historical and sociological background is another.

What effects the existence of prejudgments about the abilities, interests and limitations of women as a group has on the development of individual personalities is a question to which there is, and can be, no answer.

In a society whose standards are predominantly masculine, women form an " out-group ", distinguished from the dominant strata by physical characteristics, historical tradition, social rôle and a different process of socialization. As in the case of other groups in a similar situation, preconceived opinions are applied more or less summarily to the class as a whole, without sufficient consideration of individual differences. Similar stereotypes exist with regard to foreigners, Jews, Negroes, etc. Members of these " out-groups " are subject to collective judgments instead of being treated on their own merits.

While such stereotypes may encourage some qualities in the members of a group, their general effect tends to be inhibitive.

To be judged, not as an individual but as a member of a stereo-typed group, implies an incalculable amount of restrictions, discouragement, ill-feelings and frustrations—even if the occasional flattering generalization may help to bolster up a weakening ego.

CHAPTER II

THE HISTORICAL BACKGROUND

It may, at the first glance, seem arbitrary to confine a study of various theories about the feminine character to rather less than the last hundred years. It is a subject which through the ages has given rise to much pondering and theorizing on the part of philosophers, poets, theologians and laymen. But as a subject-matter of science woman did not appear on the scene before the second half of the last century. All theories expounded on this theme before that time were in the nature of personal opinion, of prejudice, religious taboo, or superstition. They were, in short, emotional rather than rational, and uncritical of common-sense observations. They lacked that air of impartiality and systematic method which we usually associate with the scientific attitude.

To discover how far scientists succeed in their attempt at unbiased and purely rational investigation, and to what extent they are influenced by contemporary ideologies and personal disposition, is one of the aims of this study. But there can be no doubt that in their method as well as in their aim scientific theories on feminine traits are fundamentally different from those personal reflections expressed in novels, poems and plays, or in philosophical and religious doctrines.

The reasons for the character, abilities and social functions of women becoming a problem of scientific investigation during the nineteenth century are essentially of two kinds. The first was bound up with the profound social changes which arose in connection with the Industrial Revolution and affected the life of the family as well as the position of women. Economic development made necessary a re-definition of their sphere of work and, consequently, of their status. In this and other ways to be discussed later, public interest and attention were drawn to the phenomenon Woman.

Secondly, science made such progress in the course of the nineteenth century that it not only widened its field of competence enormously, but also began to colour the general outlook and to create a universal willingness to submit to scientific scrutiny all problems that may arise.

The inclusion of woman within the scope of scientific enquiry at a certain period was, therefore, due to the topical interest of the problem on the one hand, and to the general scientific orientation—very recently applied to social problems—on the other.

This interest in social problems was aroused not only by the material conditions of economic change, but by a humanitarian, individualistic philosophy which was the prevalent ideology of the time.

If the restriction of this study to fairly recent theories seems justified on the ground that they all have a common scientific character which distinguishes them from previous deliberations on the subject, a limitation seems even more indicated because of the enormous change which the social position of women has undergone during the same period. This change cannot be measured in terms of legal and political rights and of economic functions alone, but is expressed in the attitudes of society towards women and, accordingly, in the character and attitudes of women themselves.

Our historical memory is so short, and our imagination so limited, that we fail to be sufficiently aware of the striking contrast between our present attitudes and those of, say, a hundred years ago. With amazement we read the following note in *The Times* of July 22, 1797 : [1] " The increasing value of the fair sex is regarded by many writers as the certain index of a growing civilization. Smithfield [2] may for this reason claim to be a contributor to particular progress in finesse, for in the market the price was again raised from one half a guinea to three-and-one half." This trend in the " progress of finesse " (to adopt for a moment the standard of *The Times* of 1797) does not seem to have persisted, as the following story indicates : [3]

In 1814 Henry Cook of Effingham, Surrey, was forced under the bastardy laws to marry a woman of Slinfold, Sussex, and six months after the marriage she and her child were removed to the Effingham workhouse. The governor there, having contracted to maintain all the poor for the specific sum of £210, complained of the new arrivals, whereupon *the parish officer to Effingham prevailed on Cook to sell his wife.* The master of the workhouse, Chippen, was directed to take the woman to Croydon market and there, on June 17, 1815, *she was sold to John*

---

[1] Quoted from *Woman's Coming of Age, A Symposium*, ed. by S. D. Schmalhausen and V. Calverton, Liveright, New York, 1931.
[2] A market particularly reputed for its sales of women.
[3] Recorded by Ivy Pinchbeck in : *Women Workers and the Industrial Revolution* (p. 83), George Routledge & Sons, London, 1930.

Earl for the sum of one shilling which had been given to Earl for the
purchase.   To bind the bargain the following receipt was made out :

> 5/- stamp   June 17, 1815
> Received of John Earl the sum of one shilling, in full,
> for my lawful wife, by me,
>   HENRY COOK.
>
> Daniel Cook ⎱ Witnesses.
> John Chippen ⎰

In their satisfaction of having got rid of the chargeability of the woman
the parish officers of Effingham paid the expenses of the journey to
Croydon, including refreshments there, and also allowed a leg of
mutton for the wedding dinner which took place in Earl's parish of
Dorking . . ."

Miss Pinchbeck rightly remarks : " That the expenses incurred by such transaction could be entered up in the parish
accounts and regularly passed by a parish vestry, is sufficient
evidence, not only of the futility of parish administration under
the old Poor Laws, but also of the straits to which women were
reduced by the weakness of their economic and social position."

These instances do not seem to be isolated cases.   More
examples are recorded in the " Sale of Wives in England in
1823," by H. W. V. Temperley (in *History Teachers' Miscellany*
for May 1925), and as late as 1856 such a benevolent critic of
this country as R. W. Emerson has to report, in his *English
Traits* : " The right of the husband to sell his wife has been
retained down to our times."   All this in England, a country
which was proverbially called a " Wives' Paradise ", and of which
Defoe had said in 1725 that, if there were only a bridge between
the Continent and England, all Continental women would like
to come across the Straits.

Judging this situation from our distant point of observation
we must not, however, adopt an attitude of righteous indignation
and fail to see the facts in their correct perspective.   We must
not overlook the fact that we are dealing with a pre-individualistic
period : and although women's lot no doubt was, in every
respect, harder than men's, woman was no more than one stage
behind man in the social evolution.   We should misrepresent the
situation if we conceived of the " Subjection of Women " as the
submission of the weaker sex to the superior physical and economic
power of free and independent males.   It would seem more
exact to say that women remained serfs after men had already

outgrown the state of serfdom. If we adopt Müller-Lyer's [1] classification of the historic development into three main phases —the Clan Epoch, the Family Epoch, and the Individual Epoch —according to the social unit which ideologically forms the basic element of the social organization, and which is felt to be the ultimate " end in itself " at a given period, we should say that the capitalist period marks the transition from the family phase to the individual phase generally, but that this transition was delayed in the case of women. Keeping in mind the power of persistence of all those attitudes, customs, and traditions which are linked with the family and handed down by the very personal, very emotional contact within the primary group, we cannot be surprised at the retarded social development in the case of women.

Another error into which we easily fall through the shortness of our memories and the influence of an ill-conceived feminist propaganda, is the idea that women were, of old, excluded from the economic life of society, and are only now reluctantly and gradually being admitted into the masculine sphere of work. This is a misrepresentation of facts. Before the agricultural and industrial revolution there was hardly any job which was not also performed by women. No work was too hard, no labour too strenuous, to exclude them. In fields and mines, manufactories and shops, on markets and roads as well as in workshops and in their homes, women were busy, assisting their men or replacing them in their absence or after their death, or contributing by their own labour to the family income. Before technical inventions revolutionized the methods of production the family was, first of all, an economic unit in which all members, men, women and children, played their part. The advice given in *A Present for a Servant Maid* in 1743 : [2] " You cannot expect to marry in such a manner as neither of you shall have occasion to work, and none but a fool will take a wife whose bread must be earned solely by his labour and who will contribute nothing towards it herself ", expresses a general attitude. Society as a whole was not rich enough, and the methods of work not sufficiently productive individually to admit of dispensing with anyone on the score of age or sex. Marriage, at that time, was not looked on, as it was later, as a liability for the man and

[1] E. Müller-Lyer : *The Evolution of Modern Marriage* (Engl. transl., Allen & Unwin, London 1930), from *Phasen der Liebe*, first published in München, 1913.
[2] Quoted in *London Life in the 18th Century*, by Dorothy George (Kegan Paul, London, 1925).

as a sort of favour conferred upon woman, involving for her a life insurance for a minimum premium, but was regarded as a necessity for all, both for their personal fulfilment and their economic benefit.   Only when growing industrialization transferred more and more productive activities from the home to the factory, when machines relieved woman of a great part of her household duties, and schools took over the education of her children, woman's economic value as a contributor to the family income declined, particularly in the middle-classes. Where before women and children had assisted in providing for the needs of the family, this responsibility now devolved upon one man.   Women and children became an economic liability rather than an asset, and marriage was increasingly felt to be a burden for the man.   The emotional satisfaction which it may have offered to both, man and woman, was not enough to make good the loss of self-respect incurred by women by the knowledge of their economic uselessness.   The endeavour to reinstate women in the economic process, on the one hand, and to restrict the size of families, on the other, has continued from then on up to the present day.

At all times, however, the common characteristic of women's work, as contrasted with men's, was, first of all, that it was subsidiary, i.e. that it involved assisting the men of the family—fathers, husbands, brothers—rather than independent ; secondly, and closely connected with this fact, that it was paid at a lower rate, if it received any payment at all and was not included in the family wage ; and, thirdly, that it was mostly unskilled. Although they were accepted as members by some guilds and apprenticed in their crafts, women generally played the part of odd hands, doing useful work of many kinds, but acquiring their skill in a casual way rather than by systematic training.   Here we find one of the reasons for the emphasis on education which was so prominent in the feminist movement ever since Mary Wollstonecraft first raised her voice in support of the emancipation of women.   It seems significant that, prior to her famous *Vindication of the Rights of Women* (1792), she should have published her *Thoughts on the Education of Daughters* (1786).   The lack of sufficient training was felt to be one of the major disabilities in women's struggle for independence.

For her personal happiness, her social status, and her economic prosperity marriage was for woman an indispensable condition. But it was left to a later period, when all the economic and social advantages of marriage seemed to have weighed in her favour alone, that she had to develop the "clinging vine" type as a feminine ideal in order to "appease" men. Only by flattering his vanity could she make up for the loss of the practical contribution she had to offer in the matrimonial relation.

A good woman has no desire to rule [says Mrs. Graves] where she feels it to be her duty, as it is her highest pleasure "to love, honour and obey"; and she submits with cheerful acquiescence to that order in the conjugal relation which God and nature have established. Woman feels she is not made for command, and finds her truest happiness in submitting to those who wield a rightful sceptre in justice, mercy and love.

"Nothing is so likely to conciliate the affection of the other sex," advises Mrs. Sandford,[2] "as the feeling that women look to them for guidance and support." In other words, nothing befits the slave so well as servility.

To win a husband—woman's only aim and preoccupation— must, in fact, have been a formidable job at that time, if we keep in mind what enormous obstacles Victorian morality put in the way of the only end they thought worth achieving. "Acquaintances with the other sex should be formed with excessive caution"[3] was the general opinion held at the time, and everything was done to prevent free association of the sexes. "It would be improper, nay, indecorous, to correspond with the gentleman unknown to your father," an anxious questioner is warned. Young ladies were, however, protected not only from contact with "gentlemen unknown to their father", but from their brothers' friends, and all other men who were not selected as prospective husbands by their parents.

J. should not walk with a gentleman much her superior in life, unless she is well assured that he seeks her society with a view to marriage, and she has her parents' approbation of her conduct. All young girls should study so to conduct themselves that not even the whisper of envy or scandal should be heard in connection with their names . . .

Moreover, apart from seclusion, her job of finding a husband was rendered more difficult by the " maidenly reserve " enjoined

---

[1] *Women in America*, by A. J. Graves (Harper Bros., New York, 1858), quoted from *Woman's Coming of Age*, ed. by S. D. Schmalhausen and V. F. Calverton, New York, 1931.

[2] *Woman*, quoted from *Woman's Coming of Age*, op. cit.

[3] This and the following quotations are taken from " Advice to Young Ladies ", a collection of answers to correspondents published in the *London Journal* between 1855 and 1862, Methuen & Co. London, 1933.

on her which forbade her to seek a man's attention or to show him signs of sympathy.

All the poets and prose-writers who have written upon love are agreed upon one point [is one advice given in the correspondence column of the *London Journal*], and that is that delicate reserve, a rosy diffidence, and sweetly chastened deportment are precisely the qualities in a woman that mostly win upon the attention of men, whether young or old. The moment she begins to seek attention, she sinks in the esteem of any man with an opinion worth having.

A few more quotations from the same source will make it clear with what immense difficulties, imposed by etiquette, the Victorian girl had to struggle in her main pursuit of captivating a husband.

We cannot lend any countenance to such glaring impropriety as trying to " catch the gentleman's attention ! " It is his duty to try to catch yours ; so preserve your dignity and the decorum due to your sex, position and usages of society.

Violet must wait. Is she not aware of the motto IL FAUT ME CHERCHER (I must be sought after) ? The gentleman will propose when he finds Violet is really a timid, bashful girl.

Mary F. is deeply in love with a young gentleman and wishes to know the best way to make him propose ; she thinks he is fond of her, but is rather bashful. The best way is to wait. He will propose quite time enough. If Fanny were to give him a hint, he might run away. Some men are very fastidious on the subject of feminine propriety.

Lavina wants to be married—but cannot obtain even a sweetheart. She is afraid her commanding appearance intimidates the young gentlemen of her acquaintance. Nothing of the kind. It is her anxiety, her feverish stepping out of her maidenly reserve, which has shocked their preconceived notions of feminine propriety—and so frightened them into dumb significance. Lavina must be more retiring, think less of herself, and learn to spell better.

The number of quotations, all in the same vein, could be increased indefinitely. They go to show that almost insuperable obstacles were laid on the Victorian girl's only road to happiness, and it seems as if the peculiar feminine affliction called " decline ", and which consisted in " a form of suicide by acute auto-suggestion ", [1] was by no means only a matter of fashion and a " desire for ethereality ". " It might be said of a large number of Victorian ladies that there was, literally, ' no health in

[1] *The Genteel Female. An Anthology*, ed. by Clifton Joseph Furness (A. Knopf, New York, 1931).

them '. The ideal of a fair young maiden wasting away for no apparent reason or from love unrequited was universally upheld in polite literature," says C. J. Furness in his interesting book. But, considering the inner conflicts and the shattering frustration which must have resulted from the circumstances just described, it is questionable whether the melancholy and " decline " of so many Victorian girls were entirely due to fashion and literary model (the two classic examples quoted by Furness are Dickens's " little Nell " and " little Eva " in *Uncle Tom's Cabin*). It is probable that they were at least partly the outcome of a situation which made marriage for woman the only career and purpose in life, while at the same time depriving her both of the sense of social usefulness and of the means of successfully pursuing her interests or of expressing her emotions. Frailness and disease were, moreover, the only means by which a woman could " catch " attention without offending contemporary morality.

The number of characters in Victorian fiction—sometimes meant to be touching, sometimes not (but always tiresome viewed from the standpoint of to-day)—who could not put a foot on the ground for weakness and yet had no actual disease is amazing. To most Victorian women, this type of invalidism appeared not merely interesting but attractive : it was almost the only way in which they could attract attention to themselves, while remaining models of propriety, in a world indifferent to their potential intellectual or athletic endowments ; and the fancies of young girls who would nowadays see themselves pleading at the bar or playing championship tennis at Wimbledon, dwelt then on pictures of themselves as pathetically helpless creatures in the grip of lingering (but not painful) illness and the objects of the constant concern of their doting families.[1]

A radical change in the life of Western society had been brought about in the second half of the eighteenth and in the beginning of the nineteenth century by new technical inventions which caused an entire reorganization of the productive process. The economic and social effects of the Industrial Revolution are familiar enough to everyone for a brief summary to suffice. Not at once but gradually

the industrial revolution cast out of our rural and urban life the yeoman cultivator and the copyholder, the domestic manufacturer and the independent handicraftsman, all of whom owned the instruments by which they earned their livelihood ; and gradually substituted for

[1] Irene Clephane : *Towards Sex Freedom* (John Lane, London, 1935).

them a relatively small body of capitalist entrepreneurs employing at wages an always multiplying mass of propertyless men, women and children, struggling like rats in a bag, for the right to live.   This bold venture in economic reconstruction had now been proved to have been, so it seemed to me, at one and the same time, a stupendous success and a tragic failure.   The accepted purpose of the pioneers of the new power-driven machine industry was the making of pecuniary profit ; a purpose which had been fulfilled, as Dr. Johnson observed about his friend Thrale's brewery, " beyond the dreams of avarice ". Commodities of all sorts and kinds rolled out from the new factories at an always accelerating speed with an always falling cost of production, thereby promoting what Adam Smith had idealized as " The Wealth of Nations " . . .   On the other hand, that same revolution had deprived the manual workers—that is, four-fifths of the people of England—of their opportunity for spontaneity and freedom of initiative in production.   It had transformed such of them as had been independent producers into hirelings and servants of another social class ; and, as the East End of London in my time only too vividly demonstrated, it had thrust hundreds of thousands of families into the physical horrors and moral debasement of chronic destitution in crowded tenements in the midst of mean streets.[1]

The decline of domestic industries deeply affected the life of women.   While the increasing specialization of labour created a multitude of new jobs in factories and homes with very low wages for the women of the new proletariat, it narrowed the lives of the middle-class women and robbed them of their economic usefulness.   Not only industrial activities, but more and more of the specifically feminine types of work formerly connected with household duties, were carried out on an increasing scale by the factories, e.g. bread-baking, beer-brewing, soap-making, tailoring, etc.   Moreover, the enormous prosperity created by the new industrial organization produced a growing veneration of wealth (now no longer expressed in terms of landed property but of the more flexible commodities of money, shares, factories and interest-bearing securities).   It produced, in the new upper and middle classes, an ambition to compete with each other in the outward signs of prosperity ; in consumption, in finery, in the idleness of women.   A man's prestige required that his wife and daughters did not do any profitable work.   The education of girls was aimed at producing accomplished ladies, not educated women.   Frances Power Cobbe recalls in her memoirs : [2]

Nobody dreamed that any of us could, in later life, be more or less than an ornament to society.   That a pupil in that school should

[1] Beatrice Webb : *My Apprenticeship* (Longmans, London, 1926).
[2] *The Life of Frances Power Cobbe as Told by Herself* (Swan Sonnenschein & Co., London, 1904).

become an artist or authoress would have been regarded as a deplorable dereliction. Not that which was good and useful to the community, or even that which would be delightful to ourselves, but that which would make us admired in society was the *raison d'être* of such requirement. The education of women was probably at its lowest ebb about half a century ago. It was at that period more pretentious than it had ever been before, and infinitely more costly, and it was likewise more shallow and senseless than can easily be believed.

If by ill chance the daughter of a middle-class family had to earn her living, there were only two possible careers open to her : that of the much despised governess, or that of needle-woman. Both involved a loss of caste, and, besides, were not sufficiently remunerative to make her self-supporting.

Under these circumstances it was not surprising that, among the women of the middle classes, more and more voices were clamouring for equal opportunities and higher education.

It is worth recalling that these were aspirations of the upper and middle classes. They were not identical with the interests of the working women. Whereas the women of the upper and middle class claimed political freedom, the right to work, and improved educational facilities, working women wanted protection ; while middle-class women were fighting for equality, working-class women demanded differential treatment. This claim for differential treatment of women in industry has been recognized by everyone except the doctrinaire feminists and the rigid free-trade economists, and, in fact, the first historic examples of State interference in private enterprise are those laws protecting women and children : the Factory Acts applying to the cotton industry, from 1802 onwards ; the Mines Act in 1842 which made illegal the employment underground of women and children under the age of seven ; and the Ten Hours Act (1847), which limited the working hours of women and children in industry. The flogging of women had been prohibited in the eighteen-twenties.

The appalling conditions of the industrial proletariat on one side, the increase of wealth on the other, gave rise to a growing concern about social problems. The poverty of the masses gradually penetrated public consciousness and created among the ruling classes of Victorian England what Beatrice Webb characterizes as a collective " sense of sin ". No longer was poverty accepted as a necessary evil with devout resignation. It was realized more and more that the misery of the poor was not unavoidable and, therefore, that it should be remedied. Charles

Booth's extensive investigation into the *Life and Labour of the People* and Karl Marx's *Kapital* are two outstanding examples of this development.

The decline of Christianity, brought about by the unprecedented progress of physical science during the nineteenth century, no longer admitted of the passive acquiescence in the state of affairs as being ordained by God. No longer was one satisfied that human suffering will be rewarded by heavenly bliss beyond the grave, but one asked for remedy here and now. The poverty of the poor—and, to some extent also the " Subjection of Women "—were no longer considered as irremediable natural states, but as the result of social institutions for which Man and not God was responsible. The following quotation from John Stuart Mill's *Utilitarianism* [1] gives a very good illustration of this new attitude towards human misery and the prevailing optimism with regard to the power of science and education :

No one whose opinion deserves a moment's consideration can doubt that most of the great positive evils of the world are in themselves removable, and will, if human affairs continue to improve, be in the end reduced within narrow limits. Poverty in any sense implying suffering, may be completely extinguished by the wisdom of society, combined with the good sense and providence of individuals. Even that most intractable of enemies, disease, may be infinitely reduced in dimensions by good physical and moral education and proper control of noxious influences ; while the progress of science holds out a promise for the future of still more direct conquests over this detestable foe.

The characteristic state of mind of that period cannot be better summed up than in Beatrice Webb's words :

. . . it seems to me that two outstanding tenets, some would say, two idols of the mind, were united in this mid-Victorian trend of thought and feeling. There was the current belief in the scientific method, in that intellectual synthesis of observation and experiment, hypothesis and verification, by means of which alone all mundane problems were to be solved. And added to this belief in science was the consciousness of a new motive ; the transference of the emotions of self-sacrificing service from God to man.[2]

Philanthropic activities expanded on an increasing scale, and, in keeping with the scientific spirit of the time, systematic investigations were made into the conditions of the poor, investigations which mark the beginning of social science. Underlying, and partly motivating, these activities were the prevailing optimism

[1] Chapter 2.   [2] Beatrice Webb, op. cit.

of the period, created by the success of expanding capitalism, and the almost naïve belief in the power and possibilities of science.

It was a forward looking age, simple and serious, believing in the worthwhileness of things. The reigning theory still regarded the removal of restrictions as the one thing needful ; it trusted human character and intellect to dominate their environment and achieve continued progress. It was an age content with its ideals, if not with its achievements, confident that it was moving on, under the guidance of Providence, to the mastery of the material world and the creation of certain nobler races, now very dimly imagined.[1]

There is a peculiar affinity between the fate of women and the origin of social science, and it is no mere coincidence that the emancipation of women should have started at the same time as the birth of sociology. Both are the result of a break in the established social order and of radical changes in the structure of society : and, in fact, the general interest in social problems to which these changes gave rise did much to assist the cause of women. Both, too, were made possible by the relaxation of the hold which the Christian Churches had for centuries exercised over people's minds. But the relation of woman's emancipation to social science does not only spring from a common origin ; it is more direct : the humanitarian interests which formed the starting-point of social research, and practical social work itself, actually provided the back-door through which women slipped into public life.

Owing, presumably, to the emotional character of philanthropic work and to the absence of pecuniary profit attaching to it, it did not seem " improper " for women of standing to engage in charitable activities, and soon we find ladies of rank and consequence running charity organizations, working for prison reform, collecting rent in the slums of the East End of London, embarking on propaganda for the abolition of slavery, against cruelty to children, against alcoholism and prostitution, and for the emancipation of women. The social history of the nineteenth century is full of women pioneers in all fields of social reform. *Francis Wright*, a disciple of Robert Owen, who worked for the practical solution of the slavery problem; *Harriet Martineau*, the political economist, translator of Auguste Comte, who became one of the most distinguished publicists and political leader-writers of her day and who worked for the Reform Bill ; *Octavia Hill*, one of

[1] R. M. Butler : *A History of England 1815-1918* (Home University Library, London, 1928).

the founders and leading spirits of the Charity Organization Society, who became famous by her work for the improvement of working-class houses ; *Elizabeth Fry*, the Quaker, who worked for prison reform, founded committees of visiting ladies to care for the prisoners, and who made missionary journeys for her cause all over Europe ; *Florence Nightingale*, who during the Crimean War reorganized the military health services after their complete break-down under the military authorities and who created a new career for women as hospital-nurses and probationers ; *Louisa Twining*, one of the most active pioneers in Poor Law Reform and in improving the lot of the inmates of workhouses ; *Frances Power Cobbe* and *Mary Carpenter*, who tried in Ragged Schools and Reformatories to promote the welfare of neglected children ; *Beatrice* and *Katherine Potter*, who were rent collectors in the East End of London and social investigators into the living and working conditions of the poor (Beatrice, later married to Sidney Webb, becoming one of the outstanding social investigators of our time) ; the Baroness *Angela Burdett-Coutts*, who, with money and influence, actively supported most of the charitable organizations ; *Josephine Butler*, reputed for her agitation for the repeal of the Contagious Diseases Acts, but equally active in promoting better education for women—these are only a few selected names, and do not include those who worked more directly as the propagandists of the women's cause : for their parliamentary suffrage, their university education and occupational equality, and against discrimination in moral questions.

All this work helped, first, to demonstrate women's ability to organize, to investigate, to do administrative and all kinds of intellectual work ; and, secondly, it created a new feminine type, distinct from the prevailing Victorian ideal of the submissive and " respectable " wife whose sphere of activities and interests was circumscribed by the triad Church, Child, Kitchen.

Speaking of Miss Cons, another social worker in the East End slums, Beatrice Webb notes in her diary (1885) : " To her people she spoke with that peculiar *combination of sympathy and authority which characterized the modern type of governing women* . . ." and she prophetically adds : " These governing and guiding women may become important factors if they increase as they have done lately." As distinctive characteristics of this new type of women she stresses their " eyes clear of self-consciousness " and their " dignity of habitual authority ".

Not a few of these women were aware of the fact that, while they were fighting poverty, slavery and disease, they were, at the same time, fighting in the cause of women. And many of them had consciously accepted this as a secondary aim. They felt that, by creating new openings for women and by furnishing evidence of their ability to work, they contributed to the future improvement of women's position, and they preferred their method of missionary work to the political and journalistic activities of their feminist sisters. As Harriet Martineau put it in a refutation of feminist polemics : " The best advocates are yet to come—in the persons of women who are obtaining access to real social business—the female physicians and other professors in America, the women of business and the female artists in France ; and the hospital administrators, the nurses, the educators and substantially successful authoresses of our own country ".[1] This prognosis seems to be essentially correct.

The fact that women entered " social business " by way of public relief work, as journalists, and as " substantially successful authoresses of novels ", illustrates an interesting sociological phenomenon : the fact namely, that new crafts, new industries, or new arts, afford the opportunities for hitherto excluded social groups to take part in the life of the community and to rise in the social scale. It is not by admittance to the traditionally established professions that newcomers are accepted. The old taboos excluding specific groups from certain spheres of work live on in the form of prejudices and are an effective barrier to their admission. It is the development of new branches of trade, of art, or industry, which enables outsiders to force their way, or to slip, into the established system. Once they are settled there they may have a chance of making an entry into the formerly reserved occupations if they have succeeded by their skill, their acknowledged character, or the power that they have meanwhile accumulated, to conquer old prejudices. The same process may be observed in the case of women, of Jews, of foreign immigrants. In the case of women it was the spheres of social investigation, of charity organization, of the expanding educational system, and of social health services, which were the places of least resistance through which the bastion of masculine business was penetrated. The expansion of industry further increased the scope of possible work and created new types of occupation.

---

[1] Quoted from *The Adventurous Thirties, a Chapter in the Women's Movement*, by Janet E. Courtney, Oxford University Press, 1933.

In the same way, for instance, shorthand typing has to-day replaced the needlework of times past as a characteristic feminine occupation.

In the arts it was the novel, developing during the nineteenth century as a new literary form, which attracted women and in which some of them won fame as writers of the first rank. One has only to mention the names of Jane Austen, the three Brontë sisters, George Eliot, and Olive Schreiner, to illustrate this point. Among the lower ranks of fiction the number of successful women authors was legion.

Women thus began, by their achievements, to make themselves conspicuous. The fact could no longer be overlooked that there were a number of women—a small minority still, but an impressive *élite* which could be increased—who did not conform to the traditional definition of the type. There was in consequence a feeling among some contemporaries that the definition needed readjustment. In this way women became a problem for philosophers, psychologists and sociologists.

Women themselves became restless. Some of them felt frustrated by the lack of useful work and did not think, with Dr. Gregory, that passing their time with " needlework, knitting and such like " was a sufficiently agreeable way of " filling up their many solitary hours ".[1] Even more of them felt humiliated by the fact that their sex was their only means of getting a livelihood and thought it a degradation of marriage that it should, first of all, have to be considered a business arrangement securing their income and social status. Love and marriage being the main concern of women, it was only natural that their revolt should not have sprung from thirst for knowledge or a desire for freedom or adventures, but that, first of all, it should have been expressed as a protest against the humiliation of having to barter their love for support. As Olive Schreiner said in *The Story of an African Farm* : [2]

It is for love's sake yet more than for any other that we look for that new time . . . when love is no more bought or sold, when it is not a means of making bread, when each woman's life is filled with earnest, independent labour, then love will come to her, a strange

[1] The respective paragraph in Dr. John Gregory's *A Father's Legacy to His Daughters* runs : " The intention of your being taught needlework, knitting and such like is not on account of the intrinsic value of all you can do with your hands, which is trifling, but . . . to enable you to fill up, in a tolerably agreeable way, some of the many solitary hours you must necessarily pass at home." (Quoted from John Langdon-Davies, *A Short History of Women*, Cape, London, 1928.)
[2] First published in London, 1833.

sudden sweetness breaking in upon her earnest work ; not sought for, but found.

Moreover, the chances of marriage were more uncertain than they ever were before, owing, partly, to the increased economic difficulties arising from a social ideal which required the dependence of a whole family on the remunerative work of one member only, partly to the greater liabilities involved in rising social standards, and partly to a growing individualism. The number of people remaining single became large enough to permit their being termed, as a group, " protestants of marriage " and for these to become a social problem. Contrary to the general assumption, however, the surplus of women which would at any rate have deprived a number of them of the chances of getting married, and which as a serious problem was very much on women's minds at the time, was not a new phenomenon. Although the data available are incomplete it appears, according to Karl Bücher,[1] that during the Middle Ages the numerical superiority of women was even greater, varying from 10 per cent. to 25 per cent. (the present rate is on an average 7·5 per cent. in most European countries). But owing to the fact that most industrial activities were carried out in the house the chances of female employment then were bigger. Women were admitted to a number of trades (such as woollen and linen weaving, braiding, tailoring, fur-dressing and tanning, baking, leather-cutting and armorial embroidery, goldsmith's work and gold-spinning. In addition they worked in trades not submitted to regulations, in marketing, huckstering, copying, as musicians in taverns, as nurses, doctors, midwives, as sutler-women accompanying armies and crusades, as porters, gaolers, in the excise, in money-changing, in herding, and in many other professions). Living in homes of relatives they were no useless addition to the household. Moreover, various institutions were provided— apart from nunneries—where single women or widows found board and accommodation. It was industrialization with its separation of home and work, and with its improvement of the social standards of the middle and upper classes, which made the fate of the unmarriageable woman so acute a problem from the nineteenth century onwards.

In this way it happened that

middle class women, by force of circumstances, were being more and more compelled to seek a greater development of their powers in order

[1] Karl Bücher : *Die Frauenfrage im Mittelalter* (Tübingen, 1882).

to become better able to maintain themselves in an honourable independence in case of need . . .   Great numbers of women have, of
course, aimed at higher education who are in no possible need of it
for the purposes of gaining a livelihood thereby ; but the incentive
spoken of has been one of the strongest factors in the situation.   As
large numbers of women became more and more dependent on their
own exertions for self-maintenance they found that school French, and
school music, dancing, flower-painting, needlework, and a diligent use
of the back-board, did not necessarily qualify them to undertake
remunerative employment, and play their part in the struggle for
existence ; while as for the old tradition that anything more than
elementary education might unfit a woman for becoming a wife and
mother, that was set aside by the stern logic of statistics, which proved
that there were many thousands of women who could not hope to enter
the matrimonial state at all or who became widows and self-dependent
after doing so.[1]

The need for making some provision in the event of their
having to depend on their own resources was felt by women to
be imperative.   The following quotation from a report on the
" Emigration of Educated Women " read by Miss Rye at a
meeting of the Social Science Congress in Dublin in 1861 will
shed some light on the urgency of the problem :

. . . my office is besieged every day by applicants for work, and
there is scarcely a county or city in the United Kingdom that has not
sent some anxious enquiries to me.   Unfortunately my experience on
this point is not singular : Miss Faithfull at the Printing Press, Miss
Crowe at the Register Office, Mrs. Craig at the Telegraph Station,
have all a surplus list of applicants.   A short time since 810 women
applied for one situation of £15 per annum ; still later (only ten days
ago) 250 women applied for another vacancy worth only £12 a year
(the daughters of many professional men being among the numbers) ;
and, on the authority of Mrs. Denison, lady superior of the Welbeck
Street Home, London, I may state that at an office similar to those
already alluded to 120 women applied in *one day* to find that there was
literally *not one situation for any one of them.*[2]

The demand not only for a better general education, but
for such special training as would enable women to take up
independent careers, had its root in the practical necessity of
not having to rely on one's feminine charm only in providing for
one's future.

In addition, ideological factors played an important part in
creating a " Women's Cause ".   The contrast between their
position as the dependents of men and the prevalent individualist
philosophy was one of the things which gave women most cause

[1] Edwin A. Pratt : *Pioneer Women in Victoria's Reign* (Newnes, London, 1897).
[2] Ibid.

and most incitement to protest. The spreading democratic ideology taught that all human beings had equal rights by nature ; that man must never be used as a means to anything else but is to be considered an " end in himself " ; and that everyone should have an equal chance of free development as an individual.

Although the ideal of the Rights of Man did not explicitly include the rights of women (and these were certainly not endorsed by all who stood up for the democratic ideal), they may be assumed to be implicit. The demands for women's emancipation, i.e. for their equal citizenship and rights to education, were engendered by the democratic propaganda for equality and liberty and were its logical consequence. Women's struggle for enfranchisement, for equal opportunities, and full legal rights, was incidental to the struggle of the rising bourgeoisie for political power and social ascendancy.

Whether they fought for a reform of the marriage laws on the ground that no one should have property rights over other persons, whether they fought for equal educational facilities, or whether they emphasized the importance of the suffrage as a means and the expression of their equality, the trend of thought behind all shades of feminist opinion was the democratic ideology. (The same is true with regard to the illusion, held by a section of feminists, that the vote was the key to the earthly paradise.)

The opposition to feminist claims was strong and bitter not only among those who had vested interests in the legal, political and personal submission of women. It was at least equally strong among the majority of women themselves. While the claim to equality challenged the masculine feeling of power and superiority, it attacked, in women, those symbols which they had developed as substitute gratifications for their lack of real power, and which were no less close to their hearts than the feeling of superiority was to man's. Queen Victoria's appeal to all women of good will " to join in checking this mad, wicked folly of Women's Rights with all its attendant horrors, on which my poor feeble sex is bent, forgetting every sense of womanly feeling and propriety " [1]—certainly found a readier emotional response among the majority than the unorthodox claim of the feminists. Queen Victoria was not the only eminent woman who, though by her own character and achievement defying the familiar notion of the weak and mentally inferior female, objected

[1] Quoted from *The Adventurous Thirties*, by J. E. Courtney, op. cit.

to the equalitarian claims of Feminism. Hannah More, the moral writer, for instance, held that " that providential economy which has clearly determined that women were born to share with men the duties of private life, has clearly demonstrated that they were not born to divide with them its public administration ",[1] and although " pestered to read the *Rights of Women* ", Mary Wollstonecraft's famous book, she was " invincibly resolved not to do it ".

Caroline Norton, known for her struggle to secure for mothers some rights over their children, wrote in 1838 : " The wild and stupid theories advanced by a few women of ' equal rights ' and ' equal intelligence ' are not the opinion of their sex. I, for one (I, with millions more), believe in the natural superiority of man, as I do in the existence of God. The natural position of woman is inferiority to man." And Beatrice Webb (who, how-ever, later regretted this action) signed a manifesto in 1889, drafted by Mrs. Humphry Ward and some other distinguished ladies, against the enfranchisement of women, and in indignant protest against the suffragettes she allowed herself to be carried away at a public luncheon to make the statement : " I have never met a man, however inferior, whom I do not consider to be my superior." [2]

Nowhere were feminists more than a small, much despised, and even more ridiculed minority. Their unpopularity resulted in part from their militant methods of agitation ; in part from their over-emphasis on enfranchisement, which was a repetition of the struggle for the Reform Bill, with similar methods and bound to have the similar result described, with regard to the workers, by Esmé Wingfield-Stratford in these words : " They had roared for the Bill, the whole Bill and nothing but the Bill, and it took them a little time to discover that what they had got was—nothing but the Bill." [3] But the main shortcoming of Feminism was that, a child of the Victorian era, it presented woman as a sort of sexless creature, as a mere abstraction with-out flesh and blood. The suffragettes' exaltation of woman into a rational super-person " beyond the coarseness of animal instincts ", their hatred of Man as their Enemy Number One, their contempt of his unsatiable sensuality, were the weakest points in their theory. It laid feminists open to ridicule and

[1] Quoted from Irene Clephane, op. cit.
[2] *My Apprenticeship*, op. cit.
[3] Esmé Wingfield-Stratford : *The Victorian Tragedy* (Routledge, London, 1930).

attack, and deprived them of the sympathy of the younger generation of women who, in the dilemma between " Rights " and emotions, would always be prepared to sacrifice abstract principles to emotional satisfaction. In spite of all its revolutionary *élan* the feminist movement had but little appeal to youth, and the report published in the *Vossische Zeitung* in 1932 is probably characteristic not only for Germany but applies to some extent to other countries as well : " Almost all meetings of women's organizations . . . show the same picture. At least three-fourths of the women present are over forty. The generation between twenty and thirty is almost completely lacking, that between thirty and forty is sparsely represented."[1]

It is the more remarkable that in spite of all their failings feminists saw almost all their demands gradually realized—in several instances by frankly anti-feminist statesmen (such as Asquith in this country or President Wilson in the United States, who, himself an anti-suffragist, enfranchised the women of his country in 1917)—simply by force of practical necessity, and because their claims were in accordance with the general trend of social development.

The smaller size of families, made possible by the increased knowledge of birth-control methods ; compulsory school education and the greater attention given to education generally, growing interest in psychological factors, and the more and more general practice of pre-marital employment of women, are among those conditions fostering the development of feminine individuality. After it had been achieved it was only natural that the Rights of Man should be extended to women as well.

During the last decades of the nineteenth and in the beginning of this century women were gradually admitted to secondary school and university education ; property laws were reformed in their favour ; marriage and divorce laws were altered with a view to improving their position (although complete equality of rights has not been achieved yet either in this or most other countries) ; women were enfranchised, first in municipal elections only and later, at the end of the first World War, generally.

The development was, if not simultaneous, more or less the same in almost all European countries and in America—except in the Catholic countries of France, Italy and Spain. (In Spain, however, the Republic enfranchised women in 1931.) The

---

[1] Hiltgunde Graef—Berlin : " Die vergreiste Frauenbewegung " (The Senile Feminist Movement), *Vossische Zeitung*, Nov. 20, 1932.

enormous impetus Ibsen's plays gave to the Women's cause shows that the development was not confined within national frontiers. It went furthest in Soviet Russia, where after the Revolution complete equality of the sexes was introduced. The fact that in spite of legal and nominal equality of the sexes a complete equality could not in practice be achieved has been explained by the Russian professor Nyemilov as " the biological tragedy of woman ".[1] But, as Fannina Halle [2] points out, the tragedy seems to be psychological rather than biological, based, namely, on the fact that the younger communist generation had neither time nor interest for love beyond the merely physical union. All their emotions were absorbed by problems of political and economic reconstruction and they had an ideology according to which " in communist society the satisfaction of the instincts, of the craving for love, is as simple and unimportant as ' the drinking of a glass of water ' ".[3] Lenin found it necessary to intervene and with his personal authority to denounce this " glass of water theory " which " has driven some of our young people crazy, quite crazy. It has been the destruction of many young men and women." It was the women who suffered more than the men from this emotional nihilism. In letters written to Professor Nyemilov and published in a supplement to the fifth edition of his book, the

correspondents complain most that they suffer from the discrepancy between the masculine and feminine attitude towards love, the lack of restraint and the frivolity of men in face of the sexual act . . . But one note rises above all the rest : " it is not from the ' biological tragedy ' that we suffer, but from the men's KHAMSTVO—a term which combines in Russian the pleasing conceptions of coarseness, truculence, bestiality, and brutality, in a word the climax of all that is uncultured. In many cases this statement doubtless penetrates to the core of the problem." [4]

Whether we are here faced with a genuine psychological sex difference, it is, after only one generation of " equality ", too soon to make any definite statement. Moreover, great changes in Soviet policy, abolishing the equality of the sexes in many respects, have taken place during recent years, which cannot be dealt with here.

[1] A. V. Nyemilov : *The Biological Tragedy of Woman* (Allen & Unwin, London, 1932).

[2] Fannina W. Halle : *Woman in Soviet Russia* (Routledge, London, 1933).

[3] Lenin in a conversation with Clara Zetkin in 1920, quoted in F. W. Halle's book, *Woman in Soviet Russia*, op. cit.

[4] Fannina W. Halle : *Woman in Soviet Russia*, op. cit.

The most radical changes in women's status were everywhere brought about by the 1914-18 War and during the years that followed. The participation of women in many important jobs was needed during the war and women were willing to work, and proved themselves capable of the most diverse and responsible activities. The fact that daughters of " good families " went out to work and walked about unchaperoned was suddenly accepted as a matter of course and without a murmur. Technological changes, moreover, brought about new methods of production and organization, and an increasing number of industrial processes no longer required arduous physical work but mechanical skill, diligence, intelligence, patience—abilities with which women were no less endowed than men. It is obvious that a society which depends more and more on activities of an administrative character can very well make use of human qualities which were not considered essentially masculine prerogatives.

Thus, women were gradually admitted, more or less willingly, into an increasing number of professions, and sex ceased to be a general criterion for the division of labour. There are to-day hardly any jobs from which women are excluded on principle. Even to such an exclusively masculine sphere as soldiering women were given access as a result of the exigencies of modern warfare and the shortage of man-power. It must, moreover, be stressed that the continuance of the old tradition according to which women's work is paid at a lower rate than men's, formed in many instances a special incentive to the employment of female labour. It made women, particularly during the years of economic crisis between the two wars, a very unpleasant competitor on the labour market. On the other hand—

although woman continued to enlarge her economic opportunities, she still found that man could earn higher wages and earn them more continuously. To compete for the hand of an able, well-paid man offered [and still does offer] to most women a greater hope of raising their standard of living than did a personal career. It offered emotional satisfaction as well.[1]

As far as the legal position goes, one is probably not far from the truth if one judges women's position to-day as being almost, if not quite, equal to men's. True, Ethel M. Wood,[2] in a report for the Committee on Woman Power, has been able to fill a

[1] Joseph Kirk Folsom : *The Family, its Sociology and Social Psychiatry* (Wiley, New York, and Chapman & Hall, London, 1934).
[2] Ethel M. Wood : *Mainly for Men* (Gollancz, London, 1943).

whole book with examples of discrimination against women existing even at the present day. She has pointed out that—although the " Sex Disqualification (Removal) Act " has been passed in 1919, declaring that " a person shall not be disqualified by sex or marriage from the exercise of any public function, or from being appointed to or holding any civil or judicial office or post, or from entering or assuming or carrying on any civil profession or vocation ", and a resolution in the House of Commons was passed in 1920 without a division : " that it is expedient that women should have equal opportunity of employment with men in all branches of the Civil Service within the United Kingdom and under Local Authorities . . . and should receive equal payment "—women are still excluded from a number of positions (e.g. in the foreign service), are only seldom to be found in the higher ranks, are expelled from employment on grounds of marriage, and are paid at a lower rate. Equal pay, although accepted in principle in 1920, was discussed in the Houses of Parliament and refused in 1924, 1926 and 1929 on the grounds that the country could not afford it. The Baldwin Government in 1936, as well as the Churchill Government in 1944, succeeded in refusing equality of payment against the majority of the House by turning the question into a vote of confidence.

In 1943 a Court of Appeal in this country has decided that a housewife's savings belong to her husband even if she has taken in lodgers to make by her own work these savings possible.

But in spite of these and similar examples, it can be said that with regard to political rights, property rights, and educational facilities—the three items which make up the feminist programme—the progress achieved during the last decades was immense.

These three references, however, do not give the whole picture. For human life is ruled less by laws and regulations than by customs, habits and prejudices, by unwritten codes of conduct, by attitudes and values of other persons with whom one comes into contact—all of which constitute the practical experiences of every-day life.

It is true that women have acquired equal political rights—but the fact that they are allowed to vote once every few years and to attend political meetings does not consciously affect their daily life, nor does it play a vital part in their minds.

It is true they have got property rights, but, first of all, these rights affect only a certain class of women—those who own property—and, secondly, one generally does not resort to the law except in extreme cases of conflict.   As family life is governed by many other considerations and sentiments, women's improved legal position does not in fact lessen their financial dependence nor prevent conflicts with their husbands and fathers.   As we have seen, it is still an easier and more profitable career for most women to marry than to work.

The most comprehensive reform certainly was the improvement of educational facilities for women and their practically equal opportunities in this respect.   But even here the institutional equality does not cover the whole situation.   It is true that women are admitted to the universities ; but it is likewise true that higher education of girls is generally considered a luxury, whereas it is regarded as a necessity for boys of the same social class.   How much the old superiority-inferiority attitude between the sexes is still prevalent can be seen from the complaint of an American professor about " the election by college women of the humanistic subjects in such numbers as to drive the men from those courses on the ground that they are ' feminine stuff ', thus depriving men of the liberal culture they greatly need ".

Moreover, equal education does not imply equal opportunity of employment.   The chances for women to get into leading positions are small, and in spite of equal qualification their payment, except in special cases, is less.   The legal and medical professions seem to be the only ones in which there is no discrimination of reward between men and women.   Even to-day women are considered subsidiary workers in almost all occupations.   It is characteristic, for instance, that an article in the *Observer*, in autumn 1942, dealing with the thousand-and-one jobs performed by women in war-time Britain, should be subtitled :   " Understudies at Work ".

Of the professional women the largest percentage is engaged in teaching, which is increasingly becoming a feminine domain. Of all other occupational fields which demand some education clerical work absorbs the largest number of women, as shorthand-typists, book-keepers, cashiers, secretaries, telephone operators, etc.   In most of these fields women are not replacing men, and therefore are not their " competitors " in the actual sense, but have been introduced into the economic process by new industrial and commercial techniques.   Equally, in the nursing profession, which is another large field of feminine employment, women entered a sphere of work newly created by expanding health services, without thereby supplanting men formerly engaged in it. " The bogey of male displacement by female workers seems to rest on exaggerated fears rather than facts," says Dr. Joseph Tenenbaum,[1] and he gives the following figures in support of this view : In Great Britain

in 1911 the percentage of population, 10 years and over, engaged in gainful employment was 83·7 males and 32·3 per cent. in females.   In 1921, the same proportion for males was 82·8 to 30·8 females.   In the United States, the proportion for males gainfully employed per population group was 78·8 per cent. against 21·1 females, in 1920—a decrease of 1·5 for males against 0·8 for females as compared to 1910.

According to figures available for Great Britain in September 1943 the proportion within the age groups between 14 and 64 inclusive was 93·75 per cent. males and 45·82 per cent. females fully employed either in services, civil defence, or other paid occupations—not including voluntary and part-time workers. The increase in employment thus was, owing to war-time conditions, much higher among women than among men, but it is fairly safe to assume that this stepping-up of feminine employment is only temporary and will diminish when the country no longer has to draw on labour reserves.   Although, of course, a number of women—and mainly those in responsible or remunerative positions—will like to go on working outside their homes, it must not be overlooked that a great number of occupations involve hard, strenuous or monotonous work which is undertaken only under stress and, as war factory reports show, with very little enthusiasm.   Women engaged on such work will probably avail themselves of the first opportunity to go back to home and family life.

But it seems fairly certain that the independence and the social recognition which they enjoyed on account of their work, the self-respect which it inspired in them, and the greater social contacts which it involved, will have had a permanent influence on their attitudes and their character.

The psychological state of women at the present time is characterized by a dilemma, which is another of the many conflicts inherent in our present cultural situation.   It results from the contrast between a materially changed situation and the simultaneous survival of traditional ideologies and attitudes. Woman's position at present is therefore rather ambivalent, which is typical of a state of transition.   Some traits of the

[1] Dr. Joseph Tenenbaum : *The Riddle of Woman* (John Lane, London, 1939, first published in New York, 1936).

cultural pattern have changed more rapidly than others, and there is a cleavage between the material conditions of our lives and persisting traditional attitudes which have not yet been adjusted to the new facts. The rates of change in the different parts of a social system are unequal, owing, as J. Kirk Folsom points out, to the " differential cultural resistances at the time ".[1]

The processes of cultural change he places in the following order :

    1. Material invention or discovery (i.e. scientific ideology),
    2. Change in the economic social structure,
    3. Change in the other parts of the social structure,
    4. Change in cultural attitudes and popular ideology.

If one keeps to this grouping the obvious influences on woman's social position have been as follows. Under the first heading the most obvious technical invention was power-driven machinery. Industrial organization, urbanization, easier transport, a wider radius of communications, and reduction of household duties are its immediate consequences. The introduction of gas and electricity likewise affected women's life enormously. It greatly reduced household labour ; while such apparently simple things as street-lighting no doubt increased their liberty of movement. (Evening walks were no longer hazardous adventures.) Cinema, radio and printing techniques led to a wider and faster spreading of information and a levelling of cultural standards. Progress in medical science and in hygiene reduced infant mortality, improved obstetric methods, developed contraceptives, and increased the general standard of health and the average expectation of life. Psychology developed as a new science and drew attention to the importance of psychological factors on the general mental and physical well-being. Child-psychology in particular, with its emphasis on encouragement rather than prohibition as an educational method, promoted greater tolerance and understanding. Last, but not least, the progress of sciences generally reduced the realm of superstition and taboos, and fostered a more rational outlook and a greater readiness to experiment.

Changes in the economic and social structure, resulting from these scientific discoveries and technical changes, and directly affecting women's life are, as seen before, the separation of work from home, a reduction of muscular effort required in almost all types of work, increasing specialization, and a generally

[1] Joseph Kirk Folsom, op. cit.

improved standard of living involving increased consumption and a more easy-going philosophy of life.

Less immediate and slower were the changes in other parts of the social structure. Those affecting women's life more than anything else are the changes in the function and in the pattern of the family.

The modern family is no longer an economic unit; its educational functions have decreased and " it is losing its rigid social control over the individual, but is elaborating other functions, most important of which is the more complete satisfaction of the love wish, both with regard to marital and parent-child love ".[1] Perpetuation of the race, regulation and control of the sex impulse and provision of opportunity for the most intimate contacts, protection and care of the young, transmission of the social heritage from one generation to another, and education in such attitudes as loyalty, sympathy, altruism, co-operation and goodwill—these are the functions of the modern family mentioned by various sociological authors.[2] The economic function is, if at all, mentioned last.

Also the form of the family is changing. There is no longer one generally accepted paternal family pattern, but co-existing with it are (a) the maternal family, characteristic of the upper bourgeoisie in larger cities; (b) the equalitarian family—both in a conventional and an emancipated type—mainly to be found in the middle and professional classes; and (c) the filiocentric family, which alongside the conventional equalitarian family is chiefly a middle-class family pattern.

This means that the power is no longer exclusively centred in the father, but that a democratization of the family has taken place.

Slowest to come are the changes in cultural attitudes and popular ideologies, and it is here that the causes of the typical conflict of contemporary women are to be found.

True, the competitive economic system fosters individualism and an ideal of full expression of human potentialities, both of which are important ideological influences upon the improvement of women's social position. But it is the sphere of emotions and unconscious attitudes which offers the most stubborn resistance to changed material circumstances. The contrast between

[1] Joseph Kirk Folsom, op. cit.
[2] Quoted from Ernest R. Mowrer : *The Family, its Organization and Disorganization* (Univ. of Chicago Press, 1932).

contradictory social ideals, characteristic for the present situation, originates from the lag of family mores, emotional attitudes, and deep-rooted prejudices behind the rate of social change in general.

Though there is nominal equality of the sexes, there are still two different spheres of work as they existed in former times : the one connected with the home and the family which is exclusively woman's domain, and the other one, the sphere of business and the professions, which to-day is shared by men and women. This means that women have acquired a multitude of new functions but have lost few of their old ones. A woman worker, doctor, or soldier, still keeps her household, brings up her children (at least to some extent), and mends not only her own but her family's stockings. A girl coming home from the office is, as a matter of course, expected to help her mother wash up, while her brother is excused from domestic work.

The differential treatment is not confined to the sphere of work only. There are, in fact, two ideologies living side by side, the one stressing equality of rights and abilities, the other emphasizing the contrasting interests of women. While woman appears as citizen and worker on the front pages of our daily press, its advertisement columns appeal to her specifically " feminine " emotions : her desire to please men by her looks and charm, and her longing for romance. Whereas the bulk of papers and books is addressed to all citizens without regard to their sex, there is a flourishing department exclusively for women, assuming, as of old, that they are interested chiefly or only in clothes, make-up, needlework, cookery, and romantic love. The American film, which openly takes its standards from the taste of the chief cinema-goer, the middle-class woman, caters for her emotional needs in supplying the " glamour " and " romance " in which her daily life is lacking. In short, the changes in the social structure have not been accompanied by a corresponding change of wishes, emotions and aims.

The characteristic feminine conflict of our time is that between the divergent claims put forward by the domestic sphere on the one side, and the business sphere on the other. Woman's business functions require such qualities as efficiency, courage, determination, intelligence, sense of reality, responsibility, independence ; in the professional sphere she is expected to act in a fair and " businesslike " manner, to be straightforward and unsentimental. Apart from this, and in a different setting, there still exists the whole set of attitudes which came down to us practically unchanged from our forefathers. In addition to the characteristics just mentioned—and partly in conflict with them—a woman is expected to be pretty, sensitive, adaptable, unassertive, good-humoured, domesticated, yielding and soft and, if possible, not too intelligent. It is possible therefore that the traits which a woman develops in connection with her business activities—her self-reliance, independence of judgment and executive abilities—may form a real handicap in finding a mate. If this happens she is likely to feel frustrated, and often she will curse "Emancipation" which has deprived her of the simple happiness of husband, child and home. (This is one among other reasons why the call " Back to the Home " had so strong an appeal to the women in Germany.)

Another sense of frustration is connected with the fact that women gradually gained access into a ready-made culture which by its origin and peculiar character is masculine. In the formation of state, law, science, morality, religion and conventions women had no share. Being in the position of outsiders, intruding into a finished system, and restricted by a century-old history of submission, which had bred in them a sense of inferiority, women's chief aim in their struggle was, as a natural result, to prove that in all respects they were " just as good " as men. Their situation is comparable to that of a worker who, rising in the social scale, seeks to prove himself a bourgeois, or, in fact, to the situation of any outsider entering a cultural system from an inferior social position. In all cases the result is an increased feeling of inferiority ; for in addition to the former sphere of competition and the old standards of comparison there now exists a new one. The outsider lives with two different sets of values at the same time. Crudely speaking, to the sense of inferiority which grows in an individual woman by being forced to compete on the marriage market is added the further sense of inferiority at having to compete on the labour market which she entered under the double handicap of a newcomer and of a member of a subordinate class. The modern girl tends to see men as objects of admiration and imitation and, at the same time, as competitors and, in some ways, as the enemies of her sex. Men are the examples which she strives with all her might to copy. On the one hand this struggle to equal man is an enormous impetus to the modern girl and accounts in part for her surprising energy, industry and efficiency. On the other hand, the danger of frustration, implied in an ideal to be " just as good " as somebody else, is obvious. The knowledge that one is able to perform a task as well as another person does not impart self-confidence and does not make a person feel indispensable. At the first crisis, whether individual or national, such persons will feel superfluous and will be prepared to relinquish their work.

This situation of inner conflict and frustration has been made one of the strongest objections to the emancipation of women. It has been pointed out that the increased liberties and responsibilities have not added to women's happiness ; that, on the contrary, women are psychologically worse off than they were before. In a state of submission, it is maintained, they had at least the claim to protection. Their weaker social position was counterbalanced by certain privileges which they forgo only reluctantly. In a certain sense this is undoubtedly correct.

But, in the same way, it could be argued, the state of slavery afforded to the slave certain rights to protection, to food and shelter, and a guaranteed standard of treatment. Equally, serfdom meant not only subjugation of the smallholder and tenant, but involved certain emotional satisfactions, among which the feeling of safety, of a defined status, and the right to protection are the most obvious. In mediaeval society " although a person was not free in the modern sense, neither was he alone and isolated. In having a distinct, unchangeable and unquestionable place in the social world from the moment of birth, man was rooted in a structuralized whole, and thus life had a meaning which left no place, and no need, for doubt . . ." [1] Erich Fromm has shown that humanity has not yet completely recovered from the loss of the sense of security and " belonging " and that the appeal of totalitarianism to so many people to-day is due to their feelings of aloneness and frustration which have been the corollaries of growing individualism. The plight of women's present psychological situation is thus only one aspect of the problems involved in the growth of individual freedom.

Nevertheless nobody in his senses would suggest to-day that slavery or feudalism ought to be revived. Nor can attempts to restore obsolete social systems be successful. " Medieval society did not deprive the individual of his freedom, because the ' individual ' did not yet exist ; man was still related to the world by primary ties." These ties having been severed it is no use trying to go back to an anterior phase—to regress, as it

[1] Erich Fromm : *The Fear of Freedom* (Kegan Paul, London, 1942).

were, to pre-natal conditions.   Once women have become fully-fledged individuals a return to submission is impossible without an irreparable loss of human values.   A remedy cannot be found in undoing the social development, but in attempting to find new adjustments to changed conditions, and to organize social life in a way which satisfies human needs—emotional no less than economic.

REFERENCES

IVY PINCHBECK : *Women Workers and the Industrial Revolution* (Routledge, London, 1930).
Woman's Coming of Age, A Symposium, ed. by S. D. Schmalhausen and V. F. Calverton (Liveright, New York, 1931).
F. MÜLLER-LYER : *The Evolution of Modern Marriage* (Allen & Unwin, London, 1930), translated from *Phasen der Liebe*, München, 1943.
DOROTHY GEORGE : *London Life in the 18th Century* (Kegan Paul, London).
BEATRICE WEBB : *My Apprenticeship* (Longmans, London, 1926).
FRANCES POWER COBBE : *The Life of Frances Power Cobbe as Told by Herself* (Swan Sonnenschein, London, 1904).
R. M. BUTLER : *A History of England 1815–1918* (Home University Library, London, 1928).
J. M. ROBERTSON : *A History of Freethought in the 19th Century* (Watts & Co., London, 1929).
JOHN LANGDON-DAVIES : *A Short History of Women* (Cape, London, 1928).
ESMÉ WINGFIELD-STRATFORD : *The Victorian Tragedy* (1930).
Victorian Sunset (1932).
The Victorian Aftermath (1933) (Routledge London).
JANET E. COURTNEY : *The Adventurous Thirties. A Chapter in the Women's Movement* (Oxford Univ. Press, 1933).
EDWIN A. PRATT : *Pioneer Women of Victoria's Reign* (Newnes, London, 1897).
MARGARET LAWRENCE : *We Write as Women* (Michael Joseph, London, 1937).
ED. T. COOK : *The Life of Florence Nightingale* (Macmillan, London, 1925).
MARY WOLLSTONECRAFT : *Thoughts on the Education of Daughters* (London, 1786).
Vindication of the Rights of Women (London, 1792).
MARY RITTER BEARD : *On Understanding Women* (Longmans, New York, 1931).
ETHEL M. WOOD : *Mainly for Men* (Gollancz, London, 1943).
JOSEPH TENENBAUM : *The Riddle of Women* (John Lane, London, 1939).
A. V. NYEMILOV : *The Biological Tragedy of Woman* (Allen & Unwin, 1932).
FANNINA W. HALLE : *Woman in Soviet Russia* (Routledge, London, 1933).
ERICH FROMM : *The Fear of Freedom* (Kegan Paul, London, 1942).
JOS. KIRK FOLSOM : *The Family, its Sociology and Social Psychiatry* (Wiley, New York, and Chapman & Hall, London, 1934).
ERNEST R. MOWRER : *The Family, its Organization and Disorganization* (Chicago Univ. Press, 1932).
IRENE CLEPHANE : *Towards Sex Freedom* (John Lane, London, 1935).

CHAPTER III

THE BIOLOGICAL APPROACH : HAVELOCK ELLIS

When, more than half a century ago, Havelock Ellis set about planning his main work, *Studies in the Psychology of Sex*, Woman had become so much a topic of discussion, and her properties and rights were obscured in such a maze of conflicting arguments, that before attempting to approach his main problem Ellis found it necessary first to establish scientifically what woman actually was, i.e. which of her traits were founded in her particular constitution and were biologically determined, and what other attributes were the outcome of fashion, habit, upbringing, or superstition.

There was, on the one hand, an age-old tradition of male superiority, rooted in social institutions and upheld by public opinion. There were, furthermore, in late Victorian England, hundreds of conventional restrictions imposed on women's activities, interests and social contacts ; a tight net of prejudices surrounded and hampered all their movements. Women were taught to cultivate " mildness of manner " and " modesty of demeanour ", and the " art of investing little nothings with an air of grace, if not of interest " [1] ; but they were warned : " However learned you may be, avoid conversation upon abstract subjects " and : " if you should be thrown into society where indiscretions (*double entendre*) are perpetrated, never hear, much less understand them." Books of etiquette advised ladies " assiduously to cultivate " a subdued and soft tone of voice and a " courteous mode of expression ", but not to display any conversational talents. They were instructed, as a means of winning affection, to feign interest in any subject that might be broached, but never to be deeply interested in a subject for its own sake. " If you happen to have any learning, keep it a profound secret, especially from men, who generally look with a jealous and malignant eye on a woman of great parts and a cultivated understanding." [2] Lady Mary Wortley Montagu, a very brilliant woman herself, advised girls to hide whatever learning they may possess " with as much solicitude as she would

---

[1] *The Ladies' Pocket Book of Etiquette*, 7th ed., George Bell, London, 1840.
[2] Dr. Gregory : *A Father's Legacy to His Daughters*.

hide crookedness or lameness ".[1]   Their whole upbringing consisted in teaching how to take up the right pose according to
social convention, to simulate or to dissimulate, until, in the
end, women themselves did not know their proper selves.   They
were so often told what kind of behaviour was " unnatural "
and " indiscreet " that they, themselves, did not feel sure about
their own abilities.

On the one hand Feminism was beginning to make headway,
sufficient to leave some imprint on public opinion and political
discussions.   Since the middle of the nineteenth century the
enfranchisement of women had become an ever-recurring subject
in parliamentary debates.   In 1825 William Thompson, socialist
disciple of Robert Owen, had published an " Appeal of One
Half of the Human Race, Women, Against the Pretensions of
the Other Half, Men ".   In the first draft of the Charter of
Rights and Liberties of 1838 the Chartists included the suffrage
of women in their programme, though it was withdrawn later
as likely to compromise their teaching as a whole.   But the
suffrage movement was most materially assisted by the election of
John Stuart Mill as Member of Parliament for Westminster
in 1865.   He, in debates which led up to the Reform Bill soon
after, moved an amendment for the enfranchisement of women,
and in 1869 he published his famous *Subjection of Women*.   In
the same year, 1869, women were given the municipal franchise
by an overwhelming majority of votes, and in the following
year were admitted both to vote for and to sit on the School
Boards then set up, and thus to take part in public affairs.   The
Women's Disabilities Bill, too, passed its second reading in the
House in 1870 with a majority of 33, but was, through Mr.
Gladstone's personal intervention, defeated in the committee
stage.

The equalitarianism of one branch of feminist opinion which
upheld the view that sex was an unimportant accident in human
nature and that seemingly sexual differences were for the most
part merely differences in upbringing and as such could easily
be removed, was opposed by the more moderate view of another
section whose claims to equal rights for women were based on a
theory not of " equality " (in the sense of identity) but of
" equivalence " of both sexes.

It was not surprising, therefore, that the controversy gave

---

[1] Quoted from Irene Clephane, op. cit., 1935.

rise to an absolute fog of contradictory statements in which real facts could hardly be discerned, and that each side tried to win the support of science in attempting to justify its particular view.

The fact that this justification of women's actual or desired position in society was sought mainly in the fields of physiology and biology can be explained in two ways ; in part, it is due to the nature of the subject under discussion, and in part to the rapid development of the natural sciences which had in turn given rise to Positivism, i.e. a philosophy which tried to explain both things physical and things human by the application of the methods and results of natural science.

The most far-reaching ideological influence of the century had, of course, been Darwin's. His Theory of Evolution pervaded not only Natural Science, but gave a new turn to historical, philosophical and sociological thinking and to criticism of theological and classical texts. It was the " decay of old opinions and the agitation that disturbs European society to its inmost depths ", said John Stuart Mill in the preface to his *System of Logic*,[1] which made it imperative to study the question

whether moral and social phenomena are really exceptions to the general certainty and uniformity of the course of nature, and how far the methods by which so many of the laws of the physical world have been numbered among truths irrevocably acquired and universally assented to, can be made instrumental to the formation of a similar body of received doctrine in moral and political science.

Herbert Spencer as well as Auguste Comte were equally imbued with the conviction that the scientific problem of the day was the application of laws, analogous to those established in the Natural Sciences, to social and moral phenomena. And it was the same trend of thought which moved Havelock Ellis to study the biological principles underlying the psychology of sex.

The problem of woman attracted others among his contemporaries, too, to scientific investigation. In the very year, 1894, in which Havelock Ellis first published his *Man and Woman, A Study of Secondary and Tertiary Sexual Characters*, Cesare Lombroso's book *La Donna Delinquente, la Prostitutà e la Donna Normale* was issued in Italy, and Lombroso's collaborator and son-in-law, G. Ferrero, wrote an essay on " The Problem of Woman from a Bio-Sociological Point of View ". Two years earlier Lombroso had read a paper on the " Sensibility of Woman " at an Inter-

[1] Preface to the first edition, 1843.

national Congress of Experimental Psychology in London. The *Nineteenth Century* published an essay on " Mental Differences between Men and Women ", by C. J. Romanes, in May 1887. The next year saw the publication in Holland of a pamphlet *Over de Aequivalentie van Man en Vrouw* by the woman doctor Catharina van Tussenbroek. There is little point in enumerating here the many books published in the following year [1] in many parts of the world, all written with a view to justifying the particular authors' attitude to women with the assistance of scientific theories drawn from physiology and biology. It is sufficient to emphasize two main facts : First, that at the time of Havelock Ellis's work woman had become a topic of discussion ; and second, that under the influence of Positivism there was a tendency to treat the problem not in a speculative but in a practical way ; that is, as an object of natural science.

This latter point deserves stressing because without that influence and the ensuing increase in scientific interest it would be difficult to explain why a man like Havelock Ellis, with his artistic nature and his philosophical turn of mind, should have made it his main purpose to establish " the sure and simple foundations of man's organism " [2] upon which the superstructure of his universe is built. Difficult to explain, too, why he, a man so intensely interested in spiritual problems, should have made the study of sex—of " the serious and vitally important subject to which the best energies of my life should be devoted " [3] —his central problem. " . . . in these as in other matters we cannot know the spiritual facts unless we realize the physical facts of life." [4] " I regard sex as the central problem of life," Havelock Ellis wrote in the general preface to the *Studies in the Psychology of Sex* (1897).

And now that the problem of religion has practically been settled, and that the problem of labour has at least been placed on a practical foundation, the question of sex—with the racial questions that rest on it—stands before the coming generations as the chief problem for solution. Sex lies at the root of life, and we can never learn to reverence life until we know how to understand sex.

His main purpose, therefore, was to study the physical facts on which some of our strongest beliefs and idiosyncrasies are based, and thus by the light of reason to illumine the dark complexity of ideologies.

---

[1] More references will be found in the bibliography at the end of this study.
[2] *The New Spirit*, 1890.   [3] Pamphlet on the Bedborough Trial, 1899.
[4] *Affirmations*, 1898.

His approach to the problem was—again in accordance with the new trends of thought—dynamic. He did not view the physical facts he studied as static traits, fixed once and for all at the time of their creation, but as having gradually developed and as subject to further evolution. His aim was not to describe Woman as she existed, here and now, but to discover those trends in the biological evolution (with special regard to the problem of Femininity and Masculinity) which are constant enough to warrant predictions. To the special field of his investigations he brought an attitude which has become characteristic for the new approach to social problems. In a Fabian essay on Socialism in 1889 it was described in these words :

> Owing mainly to the effects of Comte, Darwin and Herbert Spencer we can no longer think of the ideal society as an unchanging State. The social ideal from being static has become dynamic. The necessity of the constant growth and development of the social organism has become axiomatic. No philosopher now looks for anything but the gradual evolution of the new order from the old, without breach of continuity or abrupt change of the entire social tissue at any point during the process.[1]

Now, viewed from this dynamic perspective what physical facts are there—beyond the primary sexual characteristics—which have been sufficiently well established to be adduced as evidence in arguments about woman's comparative merits and deficiencies ?

After collecting and studying an enormous amount of evidence, Havelock Ellis found a surprisingly limited number of data on which the different investigators agreed. Even in the case of measurable facts the results varied considerably, not to speak of such observations as allow of individual interpretation. Differences of opinion partly arise from generalizations which pay insufficient attention to individual variations and often are based on too small a number of observations. They are partly due to the fact that external causes, such as habits, occupations, traditions, ways of living, and also psychological and social factors which have a strong influence even upon apparently unchangeable elements in the human constitution are valued differently by different observers or not taken into account at all.

Differences of opinion also spring from the inevitable bias in the investigator's mind which, as Havelock Ellis remarks, " has an unfortunate tendency to run on similar lines, so that we gain

[1] Quoted from Beatrice Webb, op. cit.

nothing by putting one observer's results against another observer's results." [1]

There are a host of fallacies which have arisen from one or another of these causes. Havelock Ellis draws attention to two of the more striking examples.

Respiration, for instance, was considered to be constitutionally different in man and woman, man's respiration being abdominal, woman's costal (the chest chiefly moving), until it was found—so Havelock Ellis maintains, but the point is still controversial to-day—that costal breathing was the effect of women's conventional dress. " The evidence clearly points to the conclusion that the sexual differences in respiration found among civilized races are not, as was formerly supposed, natural sexual characters, but merely the result of the artificial constriction of the chest formerly practised by women." [2]

This is one of the many examples which could be quoted (concerning, for instance, " constitutional " adiposity, muscular strength, dexterity, intellectual capacity, etc.) in illustration of the difficulties one has to contend with if one tries to define natural sexual characteristics.

The most striking example of fallacies arising from the investigator's personal bias is the history of opinion regarding sexual differences in the construction and weight of the human brain. It forms, as Havelock Ellis says, " a painful page in scientific annals ". Scientific and unscientific advocates of male superiority based their arguments on the fact that man's brain has a greatly superior absolute weight, and it was emphasized by brain anatomists that the frontal lobes—believed to be the seat of logical thought and of all higher intellectual processes—were distinctly more developed in men than in women.

Until quite recent times it has over and over again been emphatically stated by brain-anatomists that the frontal region is relatively larger in men, the parietal in women. This conclusion is now beginning to be regarded as the reverse of the truth, but we have to recognize that it was inevitable. It was firmly believed that the frontal region is the seat of all highest and most abstract intellectual processes, and if on examining a dozen or two brains an anatomist found himself landed in the conclusion that the frontal region is relatively large in women, the probability is that he would feel he had reached a conclusion that was absurd. It may, indeed, be said that it is only since it has become known that the frontal region of the brain is of greater relative extent

---

[1] *Man and Woman*, 1894, p. 39 of the 8th rev. ed. (Heinemann, London, 1934).
[2] Ibid., p. 54 (all quotations are from the 8th rev. ed., 1934).

in the Ape than it is in Man, and has no special connection with the higher intellectual processes, that it has become possible to recognize the fact that that region is relatively more extensive in women.[1]

Under these circumstances the problem of ascertaining what, apart from the reproductive and related organs, are the permanent physical factors which go to the making of feminine characteristics seems quite insoluble. The difficulty can, however, be overcome if one introduces a constant into the equation —in Havelock Ellis's case the constant quantity of Evolution.

If one assumes the validity of the theory of Evolution it is then possible to separate what is constitutional from what is accidental and acquired. On this basis any trait which is in harmony with the general trend of evolution will be natural and organic ; all other characteristics will be artificial and transient. To give one example : Changes in human constitution which, e.g., would make reproduction difficult or impossible could, as not being in accord with the trend of Evolution, be ascribed to unhealthy living conditions, to bad nutrition, to psychological, social or other extraneous causes. But their symptoms could not be regarded as part of the permanent, " normal " human nature.

Havelock Ellis had a complete, and one might say religious, confidence in Nature and a passionate belief in Man's fundamental unity with the rest of creation.

An exaggerated anxiety lest natural law be overthrown [i.e. by human conduct] is misplaced. . . . The world is not so insecurely poised. We may preserve an attitude of entire equanimity in the face of social readjustment. Such readjustment is either the outcome of wholesome natural instinct, in which case the social structure will be strengthened and broadened, or it is not ; and if not, it is unlikely to become organically ingrained in the species.[2]

The impact of Darwinism on Ellis's ideas is here, as in other places, quite obvious.

His is an attitude of almost Oriental passivity and submission to the supreme law—which, however, is not a divine law, but the Law of Nature. Whatever is in harmony with Nature is beyond good and evil. The rational mind of Havelock Ellis accepts the sentence " Nature has ordained " with the devotion of the faithful who submits to the supreme command of the Lord. " Our supreme business in life—not as we made it, but as it was made for us when the world began—is to carry

---

[1] Ibid., pp. 38–39.　　　　　　　　[2] Ibid., p. 459.

and to pass on as we received it, or better, the sacred lamp of organic being that we bear with us . . ." [1]

This, certainly, is the expression of a deeply religious feeling, however unorthodox, towards organic nature—an attitude which Ellis's biographer, Isaac Goldberg, aptly describes as " rational mysticism ". The religious impulse in Havelock Ellis has been " displaced "—to borrow the psycho-analytical term—and changed into devotion to a supreme Law of Nature and the belief in an essential unity of the universe. One can quite fairly sum up Havelock Ellis's attitude, on the lines of the Mohammed dogma, in the one article of faith : Nature is Great : and Science is her Prophet.

Science brings the True Revelation. It does not destroy but discloses the Mysteries of Life.

The Life thus revealed is the harmonious union of opposites. " Life has been defined as, even physically and chemically, a tension." [2]   " Living is the alternate release and return of tension." [3]   Or, in the terms of the " Psychology of Sex ", life is the alternation of tumescence and detumescence. " All the fine art of living lies in a fine mingling of letting go and holding in. The man who makes the one or the other his exclusive aim in life will die before he has ever begun to live." [4]   " The world is full of apparent contradictions, and every highest truth is the union of opposites." [5]

In a different form we meet here with the Hegelian law of thesis—antithesis—synthesis. Underlying, in either case, is the Romantic pattern of thought, aiming at harmony between two opposing forces. Intellect and emotion ; science and religion ; real and ideal world ; life and art ; action and contemplation ; mind and matter ; they all appear not as separate entities, but as twin aspects of one essential unity. " In the soul the spiritual can no more be subordinated to the material, strictly speaking, than in the water the oxygen can be subordinated to the hydrogen. The old dispute for supremacy between mind and matter no longer has any significance. Both matter and mind are in the end equally unknown . . ." [6]

In Ellis's philosophy life thus manifests itself in opposing tendencies, and the " supreme art of living " consists in the realization of this duality and in the comprehension of an existing harmony.

[1] *The New Spirit.*   [2] Ibid.   [3] *Affirmations.*   [4] Ibid.   [5] *Notes.*
[6] *The New Spirit.*

In a world seen as a totality no part can be called unimportant, common, or unclean. Every particle of creation is sanctified by its participation in the divine process of Life. Only under the aspect of this totality will truth be seen undistorted. The attempt to single out portions of the whole for separate consideration is doomed to failure unless one keeps in mind that essential unity.

Approached from this angle the problem of Man and Woman cannot be a question of the comparative merits of the two sexes. Mankind is one whole ; man and woman are two complementary opposites, forming together one unity. They are the obverse and reverse of one coin—two aspects of one essence. Here the traces of Platonic philosophy are unmistakable. And, as for Plato the equality of Man and Woman was a natural consequence of his idealism, for Havelock Ellis, too, the question of the superiority of either sex cannot arise, just as it does not arise between mind and matter, or hydrogen and oxygen. However different they may be, the two sexes are designed for each other and complementary to each other.

This view reflects, to a certain extent, the contemporary equalitarian claims of women and would, most probably, not have been expressed without the existence, in Havelock Ellis's time, of women who on account of their personal achievements were entitled to equal consideration (such as, for instance, Ellis's great friend, Olive Schreiner). It shows that at least among the progressives of the period woman was beginning to be accepted as an equal partner.

In opposition to one section of feminists who stressed the resemblance of the two sexes, Havelock Ellis sets his view of the bipolarity of life, i.e. that the essence of life is tension between opposing principles. This idea is—like all of Ellis's views—founded on the physical facts of the human organism : " So long as women are unlike in the primary sexual characters and in reproductive function they can never be absolutely alike even in the highest psychic processes." [1]

But to those traditionalists who upheld the superiority of the male Havelock Ellis's reply is that humanity could not exist, far less advance, if there were not an equilibrium between the two opposing forces. As every individual is the product of both father and mother, it would be difficult to imagine how progress could be achieved if one half of humanity were of an inferior kind.

[1] *Man and Woman*, p. 26.

A species in which the maternal half exhibited a general inferiority of vital functions could scarcely survive ; still less could it attain the somewhat special and peculiar position which—however impartially we may look at the matter—can scarcely be denied to the human species.[1]

The sexual adjustment has been proceeding for so vast a period of time, even if we only take Man and his immediate ancestors into consideration, that the sexual balance has become as nearly perfect as possible, and every inaptitude is accompanied by some compensatory aptitude, even if it has not, as sometimes occurs, itself developed into an advantageous character.[2]

This conception of " compensatory unlikeness " is the basic idea and the ever recurring *leit-motiv* of Havelock Ellis's considerations. In reading his study, *Man and Woman*, one comes to imagine him as a sort of Justitia, holding a balance, and for every weight put on one scale producing, with an ever-ready " . . . but . . .", a counterpoise on the opposite scale.

Woman's organism, he maintains, for instance, is more affectable, i.e. more liable to minor oscillations. Owing to the periodic reproductive cycle with its constant changes in physiological balance, to the special disposition of the endocrine glands in women, and to the resulting fact that the vasomotor system of women is less stable and more responsive to stimuli, women are, mentally and physically, more irritable. The more watery consistence of feminine blood, a slight degree of anæmia, which may possibly be regarded as physiological in women, the periodic excessive excretion of calcium during menstruation (calcium compounds being largely responsible for vasomotor stability)— all these are factors which increase affectability and neuro-muscular exhaustibility.

This affectability, however (sometimes termed " irritability ", " plasticity " or " suggestibility ") is in part responsible for the tact for which women are renowned, and for their ability to adapt themselves more easily to unforeseen circumstances. If, therefore, women are more apt to succumb to the influence of momentary surroundings, this peculiarity involves advantages which fully compensate for its drawbacks.

Furthermore, that affectability is counter-balanced by woman's greater " disvulnerability ". Though more subjected to minor oscillations, mental and physical, she has a greater power of resistance to the more serious disturbances.

Whereas " men possess greater aptitude in dealing with the

[1] Ibid., p. 457.   [2] Ibid., pp. 458-9.

remote and abstract interests of life, women have, at the least, as great an aptitude in dealing with the immediate practical interests of life ". Owing to their " suggestibility " they seem, in fact—if we are to believe Havelock Ellis's testimony—to be specialists *par excellence* in the method of successfully muddling through :

> Women dislike the essentially intellectual process of analysis ; they have the instinctive feeling that analysis may possibly destroy the emotional complexes by which they are largely moved and which appeal to them. Women dislike rigid rules, and principles, and abstract propositions. They feel that they can do the right thing by impulse, without needing to know the rule, and they are restive under the rigid order which a man is inclined to obey upon principle.[1]

Havelock Ellis tends to regard these characteristics as organic (although a sociological explanation could also be given for almost any one of them) and " probably correlated with instinctive and emotional qualities." In his view they are due to the primitive and fundamental division of labour which Nature had in mind (if one may say so) when introducing the " comparatively recent device " of Sex. The job of reproduction, which is " Nature's main concern ", has then been divided into two different spheres of action. But there is no reason to restrict woman's activities to this natural function.

> While the woman has no more reason for feeling herself a mere " breeding machine " than the man has for thinking himself a mere " provender machine "—though so many are little but that—yet, reduced to its simple natural elements, to which there is no need to reduce it, that is the naked natural fact, whatever deviations may follow. Woman breeds and tends ; man provides ; it remains so even when the spheres tend to overlap.[2]

Women tend to vary less from type than men. " In men, as in males generally, there is an organic variational tendency to diverge from the average, in women, as in females generally, an organic tendency, notwithstanding all their facility for minor oscillations, to stability and conservatism, involving a diminished abnormality." [3] (The organic conservatism mentioned here does not involve social conservatism ; it is a " zoological fact ".)

As we shall see later, this " variational tendency " has been contested by others, e.g. by K. Pearson, and still seems to be a debatable issue. As seen by Havelock Ellis it produces in man " many brilliant and startling phenomena "—but it " also

---

[1] Ibid., pp. 407–8. [2] Ibid., pp. 447–8. [3] Ibid., p. 439.

produces a greater proportion of worthless or even harmful deviations, and the balance is thus restored with the more equable level of women ". Whereas there are more geniuses to be found among men, there are also among them more idiots and criminals.

In terms of a " variational tendency " compensation is again found for an obvious deficiency—the conspicuous absence of women in the ranks of genius—and the balance of values is restored.

Woman is biologically nearer to Nature and nearer to the child than is man. She " retains her youthfulness for the sake of possible offspring ". Seen biologically :

> We all exist for the sake of our possible offspring, but this final end of the individual is more obviously woven into the structure of women. The interests of women may therefore be said to be more closely identified with Nature's interests. Nature has made women more like children in order that they may better understand and care for children.[1]

It is necessary to point out that here Havelock Ellis is not talking about mental traits but is concerned with the characteristics of woman's physical constitution. This infantility—not to be confounded with infantilism—far from being a weakness has, on the contrary, made woman the leader in the evolutionary process, for the infantile form is " in some morphological respects the most evolutionary advanced form of the species ".[2]

The infant ape resembles more closely the human type than the adult ape which, in comparison, is more bestial. Equally the human infant shows more distinctly the specifically human characteristics—the relatively large head and brain, the small face, the delicate bony system, hairlessness—than the adult or the senile type.

> The Ape starts in life with a considerable human endowment, but in the course of life falls far away from it ; Man starts with a still greater portion of human or ultra-human endowment, and to a less extent falls from it in adult life, moving, though only slightly, towards the Ape. It seems that up to birth, or shortly afterwards, in the higher mammals such as the Apes and Man, there is a rapid and vigorous movement along the line of upward zoological evolution, but that a time comes when this foetal or infantile development ceases to be upward, but is directed to answer to the life-wants of the particular species.[3]

Moving towards senility is a process of degeneration.

The infant ape is higher in the line of evolution than the adult, and

[1] Ibid., p. 457.   [2] Ibid., p. 37.   [3] Ibid., p. 34.

the female ape, by approximating to the infant type, is somewhat higher than the male. Man, in carrying on the line of evolution, started not from some adult male simian, but from the infant ape, and in a less degree from the female ape. The human infant bears the same relation to his species as the simian infant bears to his, and we are bound to conclude that his relation to the future evolution of the race is similar.[1]

Woman, having some average characteristics which are nearer to the infantile type than the corresponding male characteristics, therefore bears more obviously the germs of the superman in herself.

Woman's

conservatism is thus compensated and justified by the fact that she represents more nearly than man the human type to which man is approximating. This is true of physical characters : the large-headed, delicate-faced, small-boned man of urban civilization is much nearer to the typical woman than is the savage. Not only by his large brain, but by his large pelvis, the modern man is following a path first marked out by woman : the skull of the modern woman is more markedly feminine than that of the savage woman, while that of the modern man has approximated to it ; the pelvis of the modern woman is much more feminine in character than that of the primitive woman, and the modern man's pelvis is also slowly becoming more feminine.

We may note also that, as many investigators have found, the student (to whose type the modern man has approximated) occupies, both physically and mentally, a position intermediate between that of women and ordinary men. Throughout the whole course of human civilization we see men following up women and taking up their vocations, with more energy, more thoroughness, often more eccentricity. In savagery and barbarism men have been predominantly hunters and fighters in character, while our phase of civilization has been industrial, that is to say, feminine, in character, for the industries belonged primitively to women, and they tend to make men like women. Even in recent times, and in reference to many of the details of life, it is possible to see the workings of this feminisation ; although, it is scarcely necessary to add, this is but one tendency in our complex modern civilization . . .[2]

It will be understood from what has been said before that this feminization represents in Havelock Ellis's eyes not a degenera-tion—an " effeminacy "—but, on the contrary, a progress. The highest human type, the man of genius, has many child-like traits ; and the ancient Greeks whom we still consider the essence of civilized humanity, have often been compared to children by their less civilized contemporaries. The progress of our race is, as Havelock Ellis says, a " progress in youthfulness ", and women

---

[1] Ibid., p. 445.   [2] Ibid., pp. 454-5.

are, both by their own proximity to the child-type and by their child-bearing functions, " guardians of the progressive youthfulness of the race " ; [1] Havelock Ellis thus gives a new interpretation to the closing words of Goethe's *Faust*. The saying " Das Ewig-weibliche zieht uns hinan " in his eyes represents a " biological verity " which neither its author nor those who quote it may have suspected.

Where many modern authors would note the influence of occupations on mental and physical characters, and the influence of technical inventions and scientific discoveries on occupations, Havelock Ellis is inclined to see the workings of a biological law of Evolution which, as of necessity, embraces all the scientific, technical and consequent practical changes.

According to his cosmic view of the problem, the main feminine traits may be stated briefly as follows :

    1. greater affectability—compensated by greater disvulnerability ;

    2. less variational tendency, i.e. less aptitude to produce either genius or degeneration ;

    3. biological conservatism and infantility—involving leadership in the evolutionary process.

Apart from this general outline which indicates structural tendencies rather than actual character-traits, Havelock Ellis made very extensive and detailed studies of all psychological and physiological processes in women in order to discover definite sexual peculiarities.   But although he collected and investigated a fantastic amount of references on specific points, his conclusions are indefinite.   He is aware of the complexity of each trait, of the questionable starting-point of any investigation (the way questions are put greatly colours their result), and he realizes the extreme susceptibility of all human traits under the influence of external conditions.   Even if he commits himself to such a statement as—activity is an essentially masculine, passivity an essentially feminine quality, based on the different rôles the two sexes have to play in the biological game—he does not omit to say that the relative passivity of civilized women is artificially reinforced by conventions.   Or, defining modesty (" both what may be termed natural modesty, which is more or less shared with the lower animals, and artificial modesty, which depends on social fashion and is easily modifiable ") as a more especially feminine trait and connected with the more

[1] Ibid., p. 446.

passive part in sex activity generally played by the female in nature, he does not fail to indicate : " How modifiable is modesty may be seen by the increasing number of societies established for the practise of what is termed ' Nudism ', whereby men and women in a completely unclothed state are enabled to meet socially without any embarrassment." [1]

The results obtained with regard to the essential characters of men and women are, thus, admittedly of " limited significance ". What is important, however, is the determination of general trends. Single facts are too complex and too mobile to be exact indicators.

The facts, moreover, are so numerous that even when we have ascertained the precise significance of some one fact, we cannot be sure that it is not contradicted by other facts. And so many of the facts are modifiable under changing environment that in the absence of experience we cannot pronounce definitely regarding the behaviour of either the male or the female organism under different conditions. There is but one tribunal whose sentence is final and without appeal. Only Nature can pronounce concerning the legitimacy of social modifications. The sentence may be sterility or death, but no other tribunal, no appeal to common sense, will serve instead. [2]

Havelock Ellis's attitude is, as we have seen, determined by his religious faith in Nature, by his concept of Life as tension, and of Truth as the blending of opposites. It reflects, moreover, the prevailing optimism of his period—its belief, strengthened by unprecedented scientific progress and an undreamed-of increase in wealth, that, if left to themselves, all things will turn out well in the end. It is the same attitude as is expressed, for instance, in the economic *laissez-faire* doctrine of the Liberals.

Ellis's tendency to find compensation for every natural weakness may, in part, spring from a strong sense of justice. But it arises, no less, from his cosmic optimism. It results, moreover, from a special disposition of his character and a consequent attitude towards his own life : namely his ability to turn failures into victories. His way of dealing with the perplexities of human nature is an exact reflection of his characteristic way of settling the difficulties of his own nature, as seen in this autobiographical note : " . . . The weaknesses and defects were overcome, not by any effort of masculine protest to create artificially what was not there, but by accepting the facts of constitution and tem-

---

[1] *Studies in the Psychology of Sex.*   [2] *Man and Woman*, p. 443.

perament as they come from Nature and making of them an act by which failure could be woven into success."[1]

We see here a unity of Life and Work which we could not describe better than Havelock Ellis has done himself when, at the end of his career, he took stock of his life and gave a final account in these words :

As I look back, I seem to see one who was, instinctively and un-consciously, an artist in living, one who used, honestly and courageously, the material of such mixed quality that was put into his hands at the outset and slowly wrought the work that Nature and his own nature —they seemed to him one—had set him to do, together with his own life, into one large and harmonious whole, so that all he lived he wrote and all that he wrote he lived.[2]

REFERENCES

HAVELOCK ELLIS : *Man and Woman, a Study of Secondary and Tertiary Sexual Characters,* 1st publ. 1894, revised ed. (8th ed., Heinemann, London, 1934).

Studies in the Psychology of Sex (F. A. Davis Co., Philadelphia, 1898–1928).

The New Spirit (1st publ., Bell, London, 1890, 4th ed. 1926).

Affirmations (Scott, London, 1898).

A Study of British Genius (Hurst & Blackett, London, 1904).

The World of Dreams (Constable, London, 1911).

" The Synthesis of Dreams ", publ. in the *Psychoanalytic Review,* 1925–6.

The Task of Social Hygiene (Constable, London, 1912).

Impressions and Comments, 3 series (Constable, London, 1914–24).

The Dance of Life (Constable, London, 1923).

Little Essays of Love and Virtue (written for adolescents) (A. & C. Black, London, 1922).

Marriage, To-day and To-morrow (1929).

My Life (Heinemann, London, 1940).

ISAAC GOLDBERG : *Havelock Ellis : a Biographical and Critical Survey* (London, 1926).

JOHN STUART MILL : *The Subjection of Women* (Longmans, London, 1869).

CESARE LOMBROSO : *La Donna Delinquente, la Prostituta e la Donna Normale* (Turin, 1893).

" The Sensibility of Woman " (*Mind*, Vol. I, London, 1892).

G. FERRERO : *The Problem of Woman from a Bio-Sociological Point of View* (Turin, 1893).

CATHERINA VAN TUSSENBROEK : *Over de aequivalentie van Man en Vrouw. Weerlegging van de biologische beschouwing van Dr. W. H. Cox* (Amsterdam, 1898).

[1] *My Life,* 1940, p. 524.   [2] Ibid., p. 524.

CHAPTER IV

A PHILOSOPHICAL APPROACH: OTTO WEININGER

Respect for Life as the world's greatest miracle, love and admiration for the dynamic forces of existence, for growth and evolution, which were such characteristic features of Havelock Ellis's personality, are conspicuously absent in Otto Weininger.[1] It is not the variety of Nature which appeals to him but the constancy of Spirit. His reverence is not for Life, the ever changing, ever recurring, but for the eternal world of Ideas. Empirical life is only accidental ; the realm of ideas alone is essential and real.

In a world of changing social and economic conditions, when traditional moral and intellectual values were first shaken by new ideas and new social experiences, Weininger tried to hurry to the rescue of time-honoured values. Amidst the crumbling ruins of a hitherto apparently stable culture he holds up his shield of eternal ideas and permanent, unchangeable values. For him duration is the criterion of values, and he goes even so far as to consider immutability in itself a value, whatever the form in which it may present itself. " Rigid unchangeability gains respect even if it assumes the form of undying hatred or obstinacy." [2]

Weininger therefore is on the search for the permanent type, not for the passing empirical phenomenon. His method is deductive and, necessarily, speculative. He refuses to ask why things are as they are and whether they could not be altered. He is, in many ways, like Shylock insisting on a hard and fast principle. He has nothing of the reformer who would inquire into the causes and conditions of things with a view to their possible improvement. His genius is brilliant in illuminating the things as they are and will remain, as he tries to ensure by rooting them in the perennial ground of ideas.

I do not talk about it whether things were once different ; this must not bother us [he says with reference to what he considers to be

[1] *Sex and Character*, first German edition, Vienna, 1903. Eng. transl., Heinemann, London, 1906.
[2] All quotations are translated from the German edition by Kiepenheuer, Berlin and Leipzig, 1932.

feminine character-traits], it is like the problem of the Jews ; one says Jews have only become what they are, and once upon a time they were quite different. Maybe : yet we do not know that. Whoever gives Evolution so much credit may believe it : there is no evidence . . . But what women are like to-day, this is what matters. And if we meet with things which cannot possibly have been grafted on to a creature from without, we may confidently assume that this being has remained the same.

One cannot possibly imagine a more radical contrast than that between this and Havelock Ellis's attitude.

It is contrary to the spirit of sociology, too, which endeavours to study the effects of social institutions on human mind and actions. There are, however, several reasons why *Sex and Character* should not be omitted in a sociological study on feminine character-traits—quite apart from its enormous popularity and influence with more than one generation of German youth.

Firstly, Weininger conveys a picture, however distorted by his personal resentments, of woman in a certain phase of her history. It is a portrait, seen through a magnifying glass, of bourgeois woman in his contemporary society. It may be a caricature, exaggerating all weaknesses, but it puts on record her characteristic functions in that specific form of society.

Secondly, there are certain similarities worth noticing between some of Weininger's observations and conclusions and other contemporary psychological theories. The coincidence cannot be accidental, and is even more interesting as it occurred in spite of very different methods and starting-points.

Furthermore, Weininger seems very often extremely close to the crux of the problem, so close in fact, that one would think he only needs to stretch out his hand to grasp the pure truth, but then in the last moment his unfortunate emotional bias always blinds and prevents him from actually reaching this goal.

The case of Weininger also affords an excellent example of how complex a problem the attitude towards women is, and how intertwined it is with a whole system of other attitudes—towards Life in general, and Sex in particular. His book, although called *Sex and Character*, and although seemingly a characterological study on feminine traits, is in fact a treatise on the problem of " Genius and Sex ". In the contest between Spirit and Sexuality, which has been called the " professional disease of genius ", Weininger was too much an interested party to be a fair umpire. Spirit was here fighting with desperate intensity for its independence—and it failed in a most tragic way. The suppressed emotions took terrible vengeance ; entering unconsciously into his reasoning they thwarted Weininger's judgment, deprived it of its scientific objectivity, and thus depreciated the value of his findings. If ever an example was needed for what in psycho-analytic theory is understood by " rationalization ", i.e. for the habit of finding suitable reasons to justify preconceived notions and to satisfy emotional needs, here it is supplied with painful clearness : Weininger's superior intellect and his amazing wealth of knowledge are not used to foster an objective, critical judgment, but to supply more and better arguments in favour of a preconceived view. His former friend, Dr. Hermann Svoboda, says : [1] " If for some personal motive or other an opinion took hold of him, in the twinkling of an eye he had a combination of ideas to justify this view to himself."

Finally, and this is important, in the history of woman's emancipation Weininger's book performed a definite function. At a time when in private and public life women assumed more and more independence and when it became increasingly difficult to keep them in their subordinate position, Weininger hurried to save the face of masculine superiority. At a time when legal and social equality was to be given to women—and it should be emphasized that Weininger himself was in favour of this equality of rights—his work had the object of maintaining the prerogative of male superiority by securing it firmly to a philosophical system of absolute values. The problem is thus raised above the level of political controversy into the realm of eternal ideas. In its essence and seen functionally, Weininger's theory amounts to the assurance : " You may safely give them their legal equality—and, in fact, for the sake of justice and self-respect you ought to do so—but morally and intellectually they can never be our equals ! " L. T. Hobhouse,[2] speaking of civic rights, says :

> Differences can only be justified ethically by the belief in an innate and ineradicable difference in capacity to meet civic responsibility on the part of different classes. In proportion as this belief is dissolved by experience the obligations of citizenship become universal, and the idea of citizenship as an exclusive right merges in that of personality, with rights and capacities which all may share simply as human beings.

As the belief in an innate inferiority of women began in actual practice to crumble in Weininger's time, it could only be restored

---

[1] Dr. Hermann Svoboda : *Otto Weiningers Tod* (Wien, 1923).
[2] L. T. Hobhouse : *Morals in Evolution* (London, 1925).

on a non-empirical and transcendental plane. When the idea of the Rights of Man had already been well established in people's minds, the further refusal to apply it to a hitherto disqualified group of persons could only be maintained by an *a priori* assumption which denied not only these Rights but even a personality to the individuals concerned.

The starting-point of Weininger's investigation is the observation, which had already been made by others, that the physiological fact of maleness or femaleness does not necessarily imply characterological masculinity or femininity, i.e. that sex in itself does not give sufficient grounds for psychological types. As we have seen before, during the second half of the last century more and more people became doubtful about the validity of the usual differentiation between masculine and feminine character-traits. A great number of scientific theories were evolved, and more and more studies are still being written on the subject to-day. They all agree on one point : namely, that the time-honoured distinction of psychological sex characters is artificial and therefore wrong ; and they all endeavour, in different ways, to discover what really are the fundamental psychological characteristics of either sex.

From either the practical method of investigation of Margaret Mead,[1] who went out to New Guinea to find an answer to the problem by comparing the behaviour of different primitive tribes, or from Mathias and Mathilde Vaerting, whom comparative history served in place of a laboratory,[2] or from S. Freud's clinical researches, or, in fact, from any other experimental way of treating the subject, Weininger's method is fundamentally different. He tries to discover not empirical facts but the pure Platonic idea of " the Man " or " the Woman " in themselves.

The object of science no less than of art, he says, is the type. Even empirical sciences, such as physics or chemistry, are concerned not with empirical but typical situations. No circumstance may ever occur in practice which completely corresponds to the conditions given in the law of gravity ; no water ever be found which contains nothing but H_2O. But these abstractions are necessary to establish the general principles on which things work. Weininger is profoundly sceptical with regard to the methods of modern science and its bent for statistics. What

[1] Margaret Mead : *Sex and Temperament* (George Routledge & Sons, London, 1935).
[2] Mathias and Mathilde Vaerting : *The Dominant Sex* (Allen & Unwin, London, 1923).

matters in science is not the average, but the ideal type. Without it a progress of our knowledge is impossible.

Weininger's psychology of types is the application of Kant's Ideas Founded on Reason (" Verstandesbegriffe ") to the sphere of psychology. He conceived of two ideal types, *M* and *W* (the ideal Man and the ideal Woman) as absolute standards for reality. These types have neither real nor metaphysical existence ; they are heuristic constructions set up as an invariable standard of measurement. They are assumed to be present in real individuals in different degrees. Every living individual represents an intermediate form somewhere between these two extremes. Every individual thus is, not only in disposition but in fact, bi-sexual ; its actual sex depends on the proportion of *M* and *W* which together form its make-up. An individual *A* consists of *aM* plus *áW* whereby *a* as well as *á* are larger than nought, but smaller than one.

It may be noted here, as we shall see later, that the bi-sexuality of human beings forms, though in a different setting, an important part in Freud's theory. In C. G. Jung's Psychology of Types,[1] too, complementary parts are assigned to masculine and feminine traits within each individual. Where the " Persona ", or outer character, of a person is feminine, the Soul, or inner attitude, is masculine, and vice versa. To give one example for each theory : The psycho-analyst Paul Bousfield [2] writes :

Masculine and feminine traits are discovered not only in members of both sexes but in the same individual, and the fact is expressed by saying that individuals are bi-sexual ; that is, each individual possesses qualities of both sexes . . . One may say that all men have a potential woman in them and all women a potential man, and that under present conditions what we may call the " masculine " side of the woman and the " feminine " side of the man are repressed, at a sometimes great cost to the personality as well as a loss to society of a part of the psychic energies of individuals.

And C. G. Jung says :

Experience teaches that the soul is wont to contain all those general human qualities the conscious attitude lacks . . . That the complementary character of the soul is also concerned with the sex-character is a fact which no longer can be seriously doubted. A very feminine woman has a masculine soul, and a very masculine man a feminine soul. This opposition is based upon the fact that a man, for instance, is not in all things wholly masculine, but has also certain feminine traits.

[1] C. G. Jung : *Psychological Types* (Kegan Paul, London, 1933).
[2] Paul Bousfield : *Sex and Civilization* (Kegan Paul, London, 1925).

Weininger's conception of intermediate sexual forms (" sexuelle Zwischenstufen ") is both in its origin and in its intention individualistic—as his philosophy on the whole is an apotheosis of the individual human mind. It creates scope for an infinite range of individual possibilities along a gamut extending between *M* and *W*. At the same time it conforms to the scientific aim of reducing qualitative differences to quantitative ones. It opposes those superficial generalizations which label a person characterologically " Man " or " Woman " according to his, or her, primary sex characteristics and without consideration of characterological dispositions. Weininger hoped his philosophy would lay the foundation for a more individualizing education.

Every shoemaker [he says], who takes measurements of feet, must have more knowledge of individual differences than the educators in school and home nowadays, who cannot be made to realize such a moral obligation. For until now all the intermediate sexual forms (especially among women) are educated in such a way as to approximate as closely as possible to a conventional ideal of man or woman ; a mental orthopædy is applied in the fullest sense of a torture. Thereby, not only is much variety lost in this world, but many things are nipped in the bud which might otherwise develop, other things are dislocated to an unnatural position, artificiality and hypocrisy are cultivated. All the time our education has had a uniforming influence on everybody who was born with either male or female sex characteristics. Very soon boys and girls are put into different clothing, learn to play different games, elementary education already is strictly separated, all girls, indiscriminately, learn needle-work, etc. The intermediate forms get the worst of it.

Unfortunately, but through Weininger's own tragic fault, the effect of his work was exactly the opposite to what he intended. It encouraged rash generalizations, for *W*, the Platonic idea of Woman, was itself—not in its intention but in fact—a generalization. In the course of his work Weininger would at least as often speak of women generally as of the absolute, undiluted principle which his conception of *W* was meant to be, and he would confuse the two. He would speak, for instance, of the " organic mendacity of women ", which obviously is a generalization, as well as of the " amorality of Woman ", which may be justified as an abstraction. In the confusion of the two the adoption of an absolute idea proves a useful expedient, for it enables Weininger to fall back to a secure position whenever a generalization becomes untenable, i.e. when it is contradicted by facts. If, for instance, he meets with the objection that some traits which he characterized as typically feminine are conspicuous in the men of some nations, he has recourse to his original conception of intermediate forms, and would reply that in the make-up of those nations, in Englishmen, Chinese, or, more especially, in Jews, the substance W is represented in a higher proportion than in others. However much Weininger hated any theory which would value the individual not for his own sake but for his place in some particular category—a hatred which he, being born a Jew, felt most intensely—his method of creating the Platonic idea of a type is in fact nothing else ; it is a generalization raised on to a philosophic level.

A justification for this violation of principles is implied in Weininger's theory itself : As women are not individualities, have no " intelligible Ego ", no personality, no soul, are not, like men, " Monads ", the making of generalizations which, applied to men, would be quite inadmissible, is thereby vindicated.

Weininger applies the same method of using two standards of measurement when dealing with psychological method. Any real psychology, he says, would have to be transcendental, that is, it would have to assume an ultimate cause of our thinking, will and feeling, as a precondition of all experience. Such psychology would try to comprehend the " intelligible Ego ", the essence of personality. It would have to be a " theoretical biography ", i.e. it would have to be characterology, the science of the permanent structure of personality. Empirical psychology, which confines itself mainly to the observation of single elements of mental life, without trying to understand the more profound unity behind them, is quite incapable of explaining the more complex phenomena of personality, such as, for instance, the problem of a personal style, the desire of immortality, the phenomena of loneliness, nostalgia, hope, repentance, and many others. This empirical sort of psychology is, however, adequate in dealing with women, for women have no personality, no transcendental Ego, and such questions as personal style, desire for immortality, and so on, do not arise in their case.

Women are, thus, something entirely different from men ; they represent the opposite principle.

The dualism of Weininger is philosophically based on the systems of Plato, of Kant, and of Christianity. Psychologically, its rigid application to the particular problem of sex may be explained as a displacement of a " complex of male superiority ". The exaggeration of sex differences is one of the unconscious techniques of the masculine mind to maintain its feeling of dominance undisturbed, when the ideology of feminine inferiority is losing its strength.

The intensity of Weininger's desire for self-esteem and dominance is undoubtedly related to the fact of his Jewish descent. His chapter on Judaism with its poignant and passionate anti-semitism is a fairly certain indication.   The words Fritz Wittels [1] wrote about Freud refer equally well to his contemporary fellow-citizen Weininger : " In Austria he had never been able to escape the sense of inferiority which early affected him, as it does all Jews in German-speaking lands and especially those who move in intellectual circles."   This feeling of inferiority in Weininger's case was compensated for by ambition and by a desire to dominate which expressed itself most strongly in the abysmal chasm which he erected between his own and the other sex.

This psychological explanation, both necessary and interesting, does not, however, exempt one from the obligation to take Weininger's theories at their face value and to discuss them on their own ground.

Weininger accentuates the differences between the two sexes —which he himself, with a suspicious over-emphasis, calls " a 'most enormous, cosmic contrast and an essential difference "— by not opposing man and woman but genius and woman, assuming that in every man there is at least potentially and to a certain degree genius, whereas woman is so entirely bare of it that the idea of a " genial woman " is a contradiction in terms.   There were gifted women—mostly those with a strong dash of masculinity in their make-up—but there never was, and never can be, a woman of genius.

This statement of the self-contradictory nature of the contrast between woman and genius hardly seems to fit in with the theory of intermediate sexual forms.   It is difficult to see how the basic assumption of Weininger's theory, the view that all real persons represent mixed forms of the two abstract principles M and W, can be reconciled with this extravagant contrast of woman and genius.   Here is, it seems, a logical ' hitch ' which hints at the unconscious intrusion of emotions into reasoning. In the light of what has been said before, it will be evident that the logical inconsistency here is a symptom of unconscious wishes which were to be fulfilled by rational argumentation.

[1] Fritz Wittels : *Sigmund Freud*, transl. Eden and Cedar Paul, London, 1924.

Brought out in relief against genius woman has one, only one, quality : she is Sex. Her only interest in life is restricted to sexual activities either in herself or in other persons, although she is not aware of it because she lacks the duality necessary for consciousness. Sexuality is her only end and sense in the universe. It is quite wrong to assume, as many people do, that women are indifferent to sex and that, if they have sexual intercourse, they only yield to masculine desire (which was the typical Victorian ideology). Ideals of chastity and virginity are essentially masculine ideals and are imposed on women. In these as in other matters women conform to masculine standards of morality ; they are capable of doing so owing to their innate receptivity and passivity. Women themselves have no standards of their own, they are a-moral (not immoral). Having to comply constantly with foreign standards accounts almost entirely for the typical feminine ailment of hysteria. It also produces hypocrisy and mendacity, tendencies to which women are organically predisposed.

There are two ideal types of woman (" ideal ", here again not used in the sense of ethical values but of Platonic ideas) : the Mother and the Courtesan. The courtesan is the woman who seeks sexual intercourse for its own sake ; the mother seeks it for the sake of procreation. In reality the two types are intermingled, and any woman may represent both, either at the same time or at different times. Neither of them is very particular in the choice of her mate as long as he serves her purpose. If, however, there appears to be some selection, woman's choice is not determined by the value of the man she chooses but by the value he is able to confer upon her, for woman has no value of her own and is entirely dependent on other people's opinion. (" Es fehlt ihr der Sinn für den Eigenwert der menschlichen Persönlichkeit.") She judges herself and her sister-women by the valuation which men have set on them. For this reason married women are esteemed so much more highly than single ones by other women. Her marriage is considered as a token of the worth a woman has found in Man's eyes, and on that account alone she is thought " worthy ".

A genius, as Weininger describes him, is a personality who embraces the whole world in himself and therefore understands everything and everybody. His memory is continuous and universal—not his ability to remember learned matter, but his memory for his experiences ; and everything means experience to him, for everything is important. His mind is of intense alertness. His thoughts are all articulate and clear ; he has a " universal apperception ". He is the creator of his own moral law. His will is directed towards the realization of values. His feelings, like his thoughts, react to the slightest stimulus, that is, his sensibility equals his intellectual power. He is intensely aware of his uniqueness, and therefore values human personality above all else in others as well as in himself. His universal memory, his all-embracing mind, his soul which, like a monad, reflects the whole world and yet is a comprehensive unit, and his ardent desire for immortality make him transcend time.

Contrasted with the qualities of this superman the list of feminine traits contains nothing but negatives : Woman's thoughts are never distinct and articulate ; they have the form of " henides ", i.e. of unclear, half-conscious images in which thinking and feeling are intertwined. Hence her sentimentality, her mawkish tenderness which, however, never attains the degree of deep emotion. Except for the sphere of tactile sensations her sensibility is poor. Woman's judgment is uncertain. Articulation and lucidity of thought are so much felt to be masculine traits that they are even regarded as tertiary sex characteristics of man. Intellectual superiority is considered to be a criterion of masculinity and has a sensual effect on women. Woman lives unconsciously and only receives her consciousness from man. For this reason alone woman could never be a genius, for genius implies the highest degree of consciousness.

The vague character of woman's thoughts accounts for her lack of memory. She feels no reverence for her own past and no attachment to her own name or to private property—in short, she has no appreciation of permanent values. She has no desire for immortality, at least not for individual immortality ; the propagation of the race is, as we have seen, her special concern.

Her defective memory makes feminine mendacity not a feature of immorality (anti-morality) but of a-morality. She does not do wrong knowing what is right, but she lacks the power of discrimination between true and false because the substance of her thoughts is undefined and her memory is short. Everybody remembers only those things and experiences which are of value to him. The fact that woman remembers only her amorous experiences—but these with great detail—is another proof of the limited sphere and the nature of her interests. Not only has woman no understanding for what is true or false with regard to her own utterances but she does not conceive of the value of truth. She knows neither the moral nor the logical Imperative. She has no relation to Law nor does she know of a duty to herself. She has no intellectual conscience.

Her deficient memory prevents her from having any exact relation to either Time or to its negation, Eternity. She therefore cannot take the proposition of identity, or its contradictory, or the exclusion of the alternative, as axiomatic, nor does she know the principle of conclusive reason. (" Für das absolute Weib gibt es kein Principium identitatis, und contradictionis und exclusi tertii . . . Da W dieses Gedächtnis so wenig als die Kontinuität sonst irgend kennt, so gibt es für sie auch kein principium rationis sufficientis.") In short, the absolute Woman has no Logic.

After this list of negations which, far from being complete, is only a very short summary of the main points, it will not surprise anyone to learn the conclusion that woman has neither Essence nor Existence, that she has no part in ontological reality, and that " she is not, she is nothing ". Translated into plain language this means that woman has only an empirical reality, and that in fact she has no soul. She lacks individuality and an independent will and she is excluded from a higher, metaphysical existence.

It is appropriate to mention here that the problem of medieval theologians : " Habet mulier animam ? " has also been revived in our time by C. G. Jung, who equally replies in the negative. His contention, however, is that, if we speak of the Anima of man, we must rightfully speak of the Animus of woman. Jung thus does not deny woman a soul altogether but states that it is different from the soul of man in so far as it contains those masculine traits which are repressed from the outer attitude of woman, whereas the masculine soul comprises the repressed feminine traits. The two conceptions of " soul " are, however, not commensurable, as, for Jung, it is a psychological notion, for Weininger a metaphysical one.

If, in Weininger's opinion there is no sign of a human soul or of personality in woman, the question seems justified whether, in his view, Woman is a human being at all. To this he would —though as it seems reluctantly—reply that she nevertheless is ; for, first of all, she is the complement to man ; and secondly, there are certain characteristics of humanity in which she shares, as, for instance, language—" the external, if not the internal form of judgment "—or a certain memory, though not a consistent continuity of consciousness. Women do possess substitutes for all masculine traits. It follows that all notions have two different meanings according to whether they apply to men or to women. Masculine vanity, for instance, is desire for value and dignity and the longing of man to see this aim undisputed. (" Männliche Eitelkeit ist eine Emanation des Willens zum Wert, und ihre objektive Äusserungsform, Empfindlichkeit, das Bedürfnis, die Erreichbarkeit des Wertes von niemand in Frage gestellt zu sehen.") Feminine vanity, however, is the delight of woman in her own body and, at the same time, the wish to feel her body the object of desires.

In this way all such notions as modesty, love, fear, phantasy, sensibility, etc., have in Weininger's view two different forms, one for men and another for women. In fact, one might just as well say, there are two different interpretations, according to the benevolence or malevolence of the interpreter.

There is still another problem arising out of Weininger's conception of Woman : if women really are so inferior, how is it possible that they were adored and glorified by the greatest spirits of humanity ? How could a being, devoid of any qualities, be the inspiration of genius in all times ?

To this undeniable fact the explanation is given in Weininger's profound and admirable analysis of Love. Love, as he understands it, has nothing to do with sexuality, but is, indeed, antagonistic to it. Although there is always a sensual element in love, love and desire mutually exclude each other. True love is always Platonic. It is the feeling Dante had for Beatrice, or the devout have for the Virgin Mary. It springs from the desire for perfection and from the knowledge of one's own limitations. It is the great illusion that one can find outside one's own self the ideal which one strives for, but which nobody is ever able to attain. Love is a phenomenon of projection : it makes another individual the bearer of all that one would like to be but never achieves. The word " loveliness " is derived from " love " : beauty exists for the loving subject alone. Love thus creates for man a new woman instead of the real one, as art, the universal love (" die Erotik des Alls "), creates the abundance of forms out of chaos. Love thus is comparable only to religion—or, as Weininger formulates it in Kant's terms, it is a Transcendental Idea. It springs from the same psychological source and has the same elevating and purifying effect.

This sentiment has been expressed in all great poetry of the world but nowhere, perhaps, more beautifully than in Goethe's Marienbader Elegie : [1]

> Dem Frieden Gottes, welcher euch hienieden
> Mehr als Vernunft beseliget—wir lesen's,—
> Vergleich' ich wohl der Liebe heitern Frieden
> In Gegenwart des allgeliebten Wesens ;
> Da ruht das Herz, und nichts vermag zu stören
> Den tiefsten Sinn, den Sinn, ihr zu gehören.
> In unsres Busens Reine wogt ein Streben,
> Sich einem Höhern, Reinern, Unbekannten
> Aus Dankbarkeit freiwillig hinzugeben,
> Enträtselnd sich den ewig Ungenannten ;
> Wir heissen's fromm sein !—Solcher seligen Höhe
> Fühl' ich mich teilhaft, wenn ich vor ihr stehe.

Such a sublime sentiment can, Weininger thinks, have nothing to do with sexuality ; it is its contradiction. Weininger surpasses in this respect even St. Paul. There cannot be anything more wicked, " disgusting, bestial, swinish," he says, than sex, and he would never go as far as to concede that, at least, as the apostle said, " it is better to marry than to burn ". The exaggerated emphasis with which Weininger, over and over again, expresses his disgust, has no doubt very personal reasons—reasons which probably determine his whole attitude to the problem of woman, and which have been the object of much guessing and theorizing. All suppositions put forward, however, are much too hypothetical to serve as a sound basis for a judgment of his psychological motives. However this may be, we can trace in Weininger's philosophical system itself the causes of his abhorrence of sex. And here, we find his extreme individualism to which the idea of the union of two individuals into one unit is repugnant. And, closely connected with it, the view that, while, according to Kant, no human being must ever be used as a means, but is an end in

---

[1] The English translation, quoted from *Goethe and Faust*, by Stawell and Dickinson (publ. G. Bell & Sons, London, 1928) does not seem to convey the same feeling as the original passage. It runs as follows :

> The peace of God, we learn, brings blessedness
> Here upon earth, passing all understanding ;
> And I dare set with it the peace of love
> In the glad presence of the one beloved.
> There the heart rests and nothing alien stirs
> The deepest sense, the sense that he is hers.
> Within the soul's pure places moves a spirit
> Unto a higher, purer and unknown
> Giving itself freely in thankfulness,
> Reading the riddle of Him no tongue can name :
> Goodness we call it ! In that high sweet air
> I feel that I may stand when she is there.

itself—in the sexual act woman is used as a means to satisfy masculine lust or to propagate children. The sexual act, therefore, is a degradation of woman—i.e. of the human being in her —and is therefore immoral.

Here, however, there is another logical fallacy. For if, as Weininger's whole argument sets out to prove, woman is nothing but sex, if she really, as he says, has no other purpose in the universe and no other interest in life, the sexual act would rather seem to be a fulfilment of her own ends than a " misuse " for ends outside herself. Here again, a break in the logical chain of the argument indicates that the theory has the function of wish-fulfilment. Again it proves to be a rationalization of Weininger's instinctive fear of sex rather than a convincing argument.

Weininger's philosophy is a system of consistent dualism : of the antipodes Subject—Object, Form—Matter, Existence—Non-existence, Spirit—Flesh, Something—Nothing, Love—Sexuality, the one is identified with Man, the other with Woman. It is the philosophical and systematic elaboration of a view shared also by Freud who, trying to define the essence of maleness and femaleness, writes : [1] " In maleness is concentrated subject, activity, and the possession of a penis. Femaleness carries on the object and passivity."

This is not the only point of reference between Weininger and Freud. There are several similarities in their theories worth recalling. These similarities are the more striking as they coincide with a certain resemblance of external circumstances to which they may, or may not, be related. Both authors are Jewish intellectuals grown up in the slightly oppressive, though not aggressively anti-semitic atmosphere of Vienna at the end of the nineteenth century, i.e. during the last decades of the Austro-Hungarian Empire. The oppressiveness of anti-semitism was strong enough to develop in its objects a critical spirit, but it was not so strong as to prevent their participation in the dominant culture, nor was it so aggressive as to alienate or frustrate them. It afforded them at least the opportunity to meet the challenge on the intellectual plane.

The somewhat decadent splendour and brilliant morbidity of that epoch has found the most adequate expression in Arthur Schnitzler's work. It culminated in the catastrophe of the first

[1] " Infantile Genital Organization of the Libido," *Internat. Jour. of Ps.-An.*, April, 1924, p. 129.

World War which has been described by that other Viennese Jewish intellectual, Karl Kraus, in his *Die letzten Tage der Menschheit* (The Last Days of Mankind). It was a period of decline in which sensitive minds could anticipate the future fall and become aware of facts which to people in general still remained indistinct and inarticulate. They belonged to a group which by its very structure and mobility made them responsive to the slightest disturbances. All the authors mentioned—and other representative writers of the decaying Austrian Empire, too—have in common that they are Jewish intellectuals with a bourgeois background. They were detached in a twofold sense. As intellectuals they were detached to a considerable extent from their class,[1] as Jews, who only a few generations ago were emancipated from the Ghetto, they were not completely absorbed or assimilated by the society of which they were a part.

The situation all these writers have in common enables them to become articulate about processes which in their contemporaries have not yet reached the level of consciousness.

It is the peculiarity of a culture in a state of decay that, as a consequence of the disintegration of its system of values, facts become visible about which one usually does not speak, and psychological processes are laid bare which normally remain unnoticed. This accounts in part for the sudden emphasis on sex and for the passion to unmask the unconscious mechanisms which is so characteristic of the thought of this epoch and which has, perhaps, been most strongly developed in the Viennese intellectual circles.

The difference between Weininger's and Freud's approach is that whereas in the former Sex assumes the character of an obsession and is dealt with in metaphysical terms, Freud's technique is analytical and tries to unveil the hidden psychological processes connected with the sex instinct. That sex was moved into the focus of attention is due to the circumstance that it was one of the most tabooed subjects in the previous era.

In spite of their revolutionary attitude against a world of taboos Weininger and Freud are still children of the passing age in so far as they accept the relation between the sexes, as it prevailed in their special bourgeois social milieu, as eternally valid. The type of masculine superiority and feminine passivity which they have in mind is linked up with experiences they were bound to have in the world in which they lived.

---

[1] Cf. *Ideology and Utopia*, op. cit.

Apart from these more general traits and external similarities, there are analogies between the doctrines of Freud and of Weininger in details, too.

As we have seen in the beginning, there is common to both the acceptance of bi-sexuality as a physiological as well as a psychological fact.

Though they formulate it differently, both authors agree that there is a relation between memory and will, and memory and valuation. Weininger's theory that we remember only those things which are of either conscious or unconscious value to us, although set in a different context and with different implications, is corroborated by Freud's theories of the mechanism of forgetting.

Weininger's theory is, furthermore, in agreement with Freud's on the point of the—at least partly—sexual nature of the relation between mother and son.

Although Weininger does not elaborate the view to the point of a particular doctrine, he is equally, with Freud, convinced of the ambivalent nature of all feelings ; i.e. while, for instance, hope and fear—or, as Weininger assumes, love and desire—are two contrary feelings, neither of them exists in reality without an element of its opposite. There is no hope without some fear mixed in it, no love entirely without desire.

Finally, there is a certain correspondence of views with regard to art. Art is, for Weininger no less than for Freud, a sublimation of the Eros—only the underlying conceptions of Eros are fundamentally contradictory. Weininger's statement that all genius is essentially erotic, with love directed toward the universe and eternal values, instead of towards woman, would be subscribed to by Freud—though Weininger's Platonic concept of a-sexual love is radically different from Freud's view.

If it is true that Weininger's Ideal Woman really is the exaggerated caricature of woman in a particular phase of her history, it remains now to identify his model. What characteristics of bourgeois woman are left if we abstract all distorting extravagances ?

The picture we thus gain is that of a woman who has but two possible social functions : that of mother and that of prostitute. She is in her spiritual no less than in her material standards entirely dependent on men. Her attitudes and judgments are formed by the men of her surroundings. She is not the master of her own will, and if she wants to obtain something she has to resort to indirect means. Her status is not acquired by virtue of her own individuality, but is conferred upon her by the man on whom she depends for her living. Her field of interests is limited, according to the social functions which she is called upon to perform. Convinced of her inferiority she feels uncertain and self-conscious in all other spheres outside her " own ". But the very sphere which alone is assigned to her is, by Christian standards, considered to be vicious. She lacks the sense of her own value, the dignity which only personal achievements are able to confer.

This is, in short, the essence which we are able to distil from Weininger's doctrine, and it gives a fairly characteristic picture of the typical bourgeois woman of the upper classes in a Christian society with patriarchal traditions.

The analogy between many of her characteristic attitudes and those of Jews, which Weininger extensively elaborates, really exists, though in a different sense from the one he has in mind : it is the effect of a similar social position. Those attitudes are not, as Weininger would have it, innate characteristics, but the result of subordination. Any subject group which for generations has lived in close contact with the dominant class would develop —with variations, of course, according to circumstances and dispositions—similar psychological traits.

If we thus set Weininger's portrait in its correct social background we can only subscribe to his demand for woman's emancipation from" herself ". Weininger himself had assimilated the standards of his own society too well, and was too little willing to give up any of his prerogatives, to understand that this involves not a repudiation of her own " nature ", but a social revolution, i.e. a drastic change in social and cultural institutions and dominant beliefs, and a shifting of power positions and privileges. He failed to see that it is not a renunciation of her sexual function on the part of woman which is necessary for the liberation of mankind, but the bringing to an end of a situation in which these were her only possible functions. He failed to see, too, that the development of a personality depends to a large extent on the opportunities and the experiences available, and that the relation between man and woman is not inherently, by its very nature, a situation in which one partner, the male, is the active, conscious subject, while the other, the female, is the passive, will-less object, but that this relation is the result of attitudes which a cultural tradition has produced. As Weininger knew perfectly well, all objects of perception and all experiences enter our consciousness in the way we see them, i.e. coloured by our subjective view. However much Weininger, as well as Freud, may view the relation of man and woman as a relation of subject to object, the causes of this observation lie in the observer's mind and not in the observed relation itself. The idea of sexual union as the misuse of a woman " as a means instead of an end in herself " is certainly no less revolting to-day than it was forty years ago. But what Weininger was unable to envisage, imbued as he was with Victorian morality, has since become a more or less generally accepted ideal : the union, in a common partnership, of two free individuals, equal in their rights. His intransigent individualism could not find any solution to the problem, because the patriarchal and Christian elements in his approach to sex still entirely dominated his mind. His doctrine, in all its uniqueness, is symptomatic of his position at the dawn of a new culture ; it embodies the struggle of a time-honoured tradition, which through the ages had acquired the compelling force of an instinct, against a still vague presentiment of a change to come and the knowledge of its necessity.

Weininger himself became a victim of this struggle when, at the age of twenty-three, he solved the conflict in his own case by suicide.

REFERENCES

OTTO WEININGER : *Sex and Character*, 1st German edit. (Wilh. Braumüller Verlag, Vienna, 1903 ; Engl. transl. Heinemann, London, 1906). *Ueber die letzten Dinge* (Vienna and Leipzig, 1904).
HERMANN SVOBODA : *Otto Weiningers Tod* (Vienna, 1923).
EMIL LUCKA : *Otto Weininger, Sein Werk und seine Persönlichkeit* (Vienna, 1905).
L. THALER : *Weiningers Weltanschauung im Lichte der Kantischen Lehre* (1935).
C. G. JUNG : *Psychological Types* (Kegan Paul, London, 1933).
PAUL BOUSFIELD : *Sex and Civilization* (Kegan Paul, London, 1925).

CHAPTER V

THE PSYCHO-ANALYTICAL APPROACH : SIGMUND FREUD

The Victorian attitude towards sex, which has loomed so large behind Weininger's philosophy, found another expression in the doctrine which more than any other ideological factor has contributed to dispel it. There is a peculiar irony in the fact that the very theory which was chiefly responsible for a more enlightened outlook in matters of sex and for the disappearance of Victorian morality should have been tinged with its ideology, particularly in its dealing with women. It is probably fair to say that no other single scientific theory has so much affected the outlook of the present generation as psycho-analysis. It has created what W. H. Auden calls " a whole climate of opinion ", and, no matter whether we are aware of it or not, the way we think and the way we feel is coloured by its discoveries. Its imprint is perceptible in contemporary art, philosophy, literature, no less than in psychology, psychiatry, anthropology, sociology and education, and even our every-day commonsense judgments bear the mark of its influence. If we no longer take people's feelings and thoughts at their face value ; if we ask ourselves what function certain attitudes fulfil in the life organization of a person ; if we attribute to unconscious drives the motivation of people's overt behaviour ; if we talk in a frank and matter-of-fact way about sex problems ; if we pay attention to early childhood experiences ; or if we generally attempt to apply a rational system of causation to irrational psychic processes, we proceed on a foundation which Freud has built. His technical terms have become part of our common vocabulary, and even if we criticize him we use the tools which he has supplied. But in doing so we shall at once come into conflict with the orthodox school of psycho-analysts. For in the same way as doctrinaire Marxists regard as " ideological superstructures " all social theories except Marxism, Freudians are inclined to take other scientific theories for " rationalizations " of unconscious libidinal forces, but refuse to have their own system analysed with respect to underlying emotional motives and hidden cultural implications.

In the interest, however, not only of consistency but of

scientific advance it is necessary to apply an equal measure of scrutiny to psycho-analysis itself and to try, as far as this is possible, to show the extent to which it reflects existing trends of thought, prevailing prejudices and unconscious personal senti-ments.   Freud's views on feminine psychology (expressed in many places, but expounded most comprehensively in *The Psychology of Women*) [1] seem to give particular proof of these influences.

The tendency to seek in congenital, constitutional factors the clue to what was considered the characteristically feminine person-ality type, was, as we have seen, common to Freud and his contemporaries.   It is mainly due to the vast progress which biological science had made since Darwin and which gave impetus and direction to the scientific interest of the later nine-teenth century.   It has been reflected in Havelock Ellis's work, and expressed in such books as Lombroso's *La Donna Delinquente, la Prostitutà e la Donna Normale,* P. J. Möbius' *Ueber den physio-logischen Schwachsinn des Weibes* (On the Physiological Imbecility of Woman) or, more recently, in A. W. Nyemilov's *The Biological Tragedy of Woman* and others.   The underlying assumption is summed up in the statement : " Anatomy is destiny." [2]   The interpretation Freud gave to the meaning of this anatomical difference is, however, his own personal contribution to the discussion of feminine psychology, and it is in accordance with his general view on the overruling importance of sexual factors in mental life.

In Freud's view the development of the feminine character is shaped at the outset by one essential anatomical characteristic (typically formulated in negative terms) : the lack of a penis. The difference in external genitals is conceived by psycho-analytical theory as a deficiency on the part of women.   All feminine character-traits, interests, attitudes, emotions and wishes are reactions, in some form or other, to this basic " defect ". Experience with female neurotics has taught Freud that there is among women a widespread, in fact a general dissatisfaction with their sexual rôle.   It is expressed in inferiority feelings, in con-tempt for their own sex, in revolt against their passive rôle, in envy of man's greater freedom, in the ambition to equal man in intel-lectual or artistic achievements, in strivings for independence, in tendencies to domineer over other people, and in all sorts of

---

[1] Chapter XXXIII, " New Introductory Lectures on Psycho-Analysis " (Hogarth Press, London, 1933).
[2] " Some Psychological Consequences of the Anatomical Distinction between the Sexes " (*Internat. Journ. of Ps-An.*, 1927).

devices to make up for the social disadvantage of not being a man. The root of all these grievances and compensatory mechanisms, the key note, so to speak, to which the entire psychology of women is tuned, is, according to Freud, to be found in the early discovery of the girl that she is lacking an essential organ.

As we learn from our psycho-analytic work all women feel that they have been injured in their infancy, and that through no fault of their own they have been slighted and robbed of a part of their body ; and the bitterness of many a daughter towards her mother has as its ultimate cause the reproach that the mother has brought her into the world as a woman instead of a man.[1]

The psycho-analytic theory is, in short, this : At an early age the little girl discovers, by the observation of other children, of brothers, or of her father, that there are other human beings who have external genitals whereas she has none. This discovery comes as a shock to her, " which leaves ineradicable traces on her development and character formation, and even in the most favourable instances, is not overcome without a great expenditure of mental energy." [2] Her envy of man, based on an anatomical difference, has an enormous influence on the mental traits of women. It is responsible for the comparatively greater part envy and jealousy play in their mental life and the consequent lack of a sense of justice. It is at the root of the " greater amount of narcissism attributed by psycho-analysis to women ". " Their vanity is partly a further effect of penis-envy, for they are driven to rate their physical charms more highly as a belated compensation for their original sexual inferiority " [sic].[3] Feminine beauty and " especially that of a woman's face is a substitute to her for the loss of a penis ".[4]

Modesty " which is regarded as *par excellence* a characteristic of women " is, however much modified by civilized conventions, " originally designed to hide the deficiency in their genitals." [5] If women are thought to have " contributed but little to the discoveries and inventions of civilization ", they may at least be found inventors of the technical processes of plaiting and weaving —discoveries which owe their origin to the same impulse : to hide their physical deficiency.

The little girl's attachment to her father, the mature woman's

[1] *Some Character-Types met with in Psycho-Analysis*, Collected Papers.
[2] *The Psychology of Women*, p. 160.   [3] Op. cit.
[4] J. Harnik : " The Various Developments Undergone by Narcissism in Men and Women " (*Internat. Journ. of Ps.-An.*, Vol. V, 1925).
[5] S. Freud : *The Psychology of Women*, p. 170.

desire for a child, the mother's particular satisfaction at the birth of a son, in fact almost all phenomena of feminine psychology, are explained by psycho-analysis as effects of the same basic envy and the endeavour to compensate for an organic inferiority. The woman who comes to the psycho-analyst for treatment is very often, says Freud, driven by the same impulse. " And what she quite reasonably expects to get from analysis, such as the capacity to pursue an intellectual career, can often be recognized as a sublimated modification of this repressed wish." [1]

There are three possible lines of psychological development as a reaction to the basic experience of woman's organic " deficiency ". The one leads to " normal femininity ", i.e. to reconciliation with the feminine sexual rôle, to acquiescence in the passivity that in Freud's view constitutionally goes with it, and to the desire for a child. In less favourable cases the painful discovery of her " castration " may lead to sexual inhibitions and to neuroses, or else it may result in a " modification of character in the sense of a masculinity complex." [2] The term " masculinity complex " is used in psycho-analytical literature in the widest sense, including all shades from open homosexuality to mere " dreams with male tendencies ", or to intellectual interests in normal women. It is conceived so widely that it embraces cases where

the repressed wish to be male is found in a sublimated form, i.e. masculine interests of an intellectual and professional character and other kinds are preferred and accentuated. Femininity, however, is not consciously denied ; they (i.e. women with a " masculinity complex ") usually proclaim that these interests are just as much feminine as masculine ones. They consider it irrelevant to say that the perform-ances of a human being, especially in the intellectual sphere, belong to the one or the other sex. This type of woman is well represented in the woman's movement of to-day.[3]

According to this description the great majority of women in our day would have failed to develop " normal femininity " but would have acquired a " masculinity complex " instead. Why this should be the case, i.e. why in our time the one pattern should prevail over the other, cannot be answered by psycho-analysis, according to which both patterns are individual psycho-logical reactions to the realization of an organic deficiency. However much Freud was aware of the scope of possible variations

---

[1] Ibid, p. 161.   [2] Ibid.
[3] Karl Abraham : " Manifestations of the Female Castration Complex " (Internat. Jour. of Ps.-An., Vol. III, 1922).

he had no doubts about the " norm ". The standards of his own culture he took for unalterable laws and he was convinced that the division of labour in force in the middle class of his period was based on innate sexual differences.

Further and very far-reaching consequences for the psychological development of women result from the different conditions under which the Oedipus complex develops in women and in men, according to their different anatomical structure.

In her first infancy—the pre-Oedipal period—the little girl is, like the little boy, intensely attached to her mother. With the discovery of her own " castration " and, later, the realization that her mother, too, lacks a male genital organ, she turns away from her mother and chooses her father as a love object. " This means, therefore, that as a result of the discovery of the absence of a penis, women are as much depreciated in the eyes of the girl as in the eyes of the boy, and later, perhaps, of the man." (Note the matter of fact way in which the contempt of women is taken for granted !) From her father the little girl expects the male organ which her mother has refused her ; a wish which is later transformed into the wish for a child by the father.

This development is in striking contrast to that of a boy and is used to explain a characteristic mental difference between the sexes. According to psycho-analytical theory every little boy forms an intense attachment to his mother, the Oedipus complex, " in which he desires his mother and wants to get rid of his father as a rival ".[1] Owing, however, to the fear of castration—resulting either from threats or from the observation that there are human beings without external sex organs and the fear lest he may lose · his as a punishment—he represses his Oedipus-complex. The result of this repression is the formation of a " super-ego ", i.e. a rigid system of moral standards and valuations imparting to the individual a striving for perfection.

As we have seen before, the relation of the two complexes (Castration and Oedipus) is completely different in the two sexes. Whereas in the boy they are antagonistic—the one being used to repress the other—in the girl there is no such conflict. Her " castration " is an accomplished fact and no threat of it therefore exists to counteract her libidinal wishes for her father. She feels no urgent need to overcome her Oedipus-complex and she remains in the Oedipus situation for an indefinite period ; she abandons it only late in life, and then only incompletely. The formation of the

[1] *The Psychology of Women*, p. 166.

super-ego must suffer in these circumstances ; it cannot attain the strength and independence which give it its cultural importance, and feminists are not pleased if one points to the way in which this factor affects the development of the average feminine character.[1]

It is due to these circumstances that women have " weaker social interests " than men and that " their capacity for sublimation is less ".[2] Although Freud would not go as far as to ascribe to women an inferior intelligence, he prejudices judgments about their intellectual capacity by the rather axiomatic statement that, owing to their libidinal organization, women have only a limited urge for sublimation. Translated into ordinary language this means that women are, by their organic nature, excluded from participation in cultural and creative activities. The old argument about the intellectual faculties of woman has been transferred on to a different plane ; clad in a new jargon the traditional view of feminine inferiority is here presented afresh.

There is, according to Freud's theory, still another impedimental factor in the psychological development of woman. In her case the transition from infantile to adult sexuality is particularly difficult—again for organic reasons. Libido, " the motor force of sexual life itself is only one for both sexes and is as much in the service of the male as of the female sexual function. To itself we can assign no sex." [3] In its infantile stage it develops much in the same way in boys and in girls. They both pass through the oral, sadistic-anal, and the phallic phase (so called after the organ which at each stage forms the centre of libidinal satisfaction). They both display the same amount of activity and aggressiveness. Any difference that exists is due to individual variations rather than to sex differences.

The organ which in the little girl is the dominant erotogenic zone and centre of masturbatory activity during the " phallic " phase is her " penis equivalent ", the clitoris. In the transition to adult sexuality the girl therefore has to change the centre of sensitivity and to discover, so to speak, a new, hidden organ, the vagina. Thus, with the development of femininity two important changes have to be gone through by the girl to which the boy is not subjected : Change of the love object (the transfer of her attachment from her mother to her father) and, secondly, change of the erotogenic zones. This process is in Freud's view very difficult and complicated and absorbs a great amount of mental energy.

[1] Ibid., p. 166.   [2] Ibid., p. 172.   [3] Ibid., p. 169.

It is our impression that more violence is done to the libido when it is forced into the service of the female function ; and that—so to speak teleologically—Nature has paid less careful attention to the demands of the female function than to those of masculinity. And —again speaking teleologically—this may be based on the fact that the achievement of the biological aim is entrusted to the aggressiveness of the male, and is to some extent independent of the co-operation of the female.[1]

The peculiar Freudian concept of sexual intercourse as a purely masculine act, viewed in terms more or less similar to rape, which underlies the above statement, can be left till later. At the present moment the main concern is with the psychological consequences resulting, in Freud's view, from the constitutional process of maturing femininity. In contrast to the boy for whom puberty means a stage of new intensification of the libido, for the girl it is a period of increased repressions. It is the masculine part of her being which is repressed, coinciding with the transition of the erotogenic zone from the " masculine " counterpart of her genitals, the clitoris, to her feminine organ, the vagina. This repression and the change of centres of sensitivity account for the greater disposition of women to neurosis and particularly to hysteria [2] which in consequence is a kind of functional disease of woman. The absorption of so much mental energy by the process of developing femininity is, moreover, in part responsible for the diminished power of sublimation in women. And it is, according to Freud, due to this process that the psychological development of woman is arrested at a much earlier age than that of man.

A man of about thirty seems a youthful and, in a sense, an incompletely developed individual of whom we expect that he will be able to make good use of the possibilities of development which analysis lays open to him. But a woman of about the same age frequently staggers us by her psychological rigidity and unchangeability. Her libido has taken up its final positions and seems powerless to leave them for others. There are no paths open for further development ; it is as though the whole process had been gone through and remained inaccessible to influences for the future ; as though, in fact, the difficult development which leads to femininity had exhausted all possibilities of the individual.[3]

It did not occur to Freud that under the conditions prevalent in his society a woman of thirty had, in fact, not many " paths open for further development " and not many possibilities to make good use of. At thirty her " final positions " must have

[1] Ibid., p. 169.
[2] " Three Contributions to the Theory of Sex " (*Imago*, London, 1942).
[3] *The Psychology of Women*, p. 173.

either been taken up, i.e. she must have been married, or else she could not have any expectations for the future. This lack of opportunities would in itself suffice to explain the " rigidity " and " unchangeability " which Freud observed in his women patients, without having to resort to biological hypotheses.

Summing up, the characteristic mental traits associated with the constitutional structure of women and mentioned so far are : penis-envy, resulting in a general disposition to envy, jealousy and social injustice ; a greater amount of narcissism as compared with that of men ; a weaker urge and a smaller capacity for sublimation, i.e. for cultural activities. To this may be added a general antagonism to civilization, caused not so much by woman's physiological structure as by the biological purpose which she represents.

Women represent the interests of the family and sexual life ; the work of civilization has become more and more men's business ; it confronts them with ever harder tasks, compels them to sublimations of instinct which women are not easily able to achieve. Since man has not an unlimited amount of mental energy at his disposal, he must accomplish his tasks by distributing his libido to the best advantage. What he employs for cultural purposes he withdraws to a great extent from women and his sexual life ; his constant association with men and his dependence on his relations with them even estrange him from his duties as husband and father. Woman finds herself thus forced into the background by the claims of culture and she adopts an inimical attitude towards it.[1]

The portrait of woman which results if we thus fit together the details expounded in different contexts certainly is far from flattering. It represents an envious, hysterical person with limited intellectual interests and a hostile attitude towards cultural achievements.

The implicit assertion of man's primary superiority, which was in strange contrast to contemporary changes in the cultural rôle of women, has been a stumbling-block to many psycho-analysts and has evoked doubts and divergencies among some of Freud's disciples. Ernest Jones, for instance, said in 1927 : " There is a healthy suspicion growing that men analysts have been led to adopt an unduly phallocentric view of the problems in question, the importance of the female organs being corre-spondingly underestimated." [2]

Karen Horney, too, has taken Freud's interpretation of

[1] *Civilization and Its Discontent*, p. 73, 2nd ed., Hogarth Press, London, 1939.
[2] " Early Development of Female Sexuality " (*Internat. Jour. of Ps.-An.*, 1927.)

feminine psychology as a challenge of " masculine narcissism " and opposed it by an assertion of the feminine point of view within psycho-analytical theory. To confront the two views affords an interesting example of the same set of premises, the same method of investigation and the same scientific terminology being used to defend two divergent standpoints. Karen Horney would agree with Freud that the little girl is in fact constitution- ally at a disadvantage compared with the little boy. Her organic structure makes the gratification of certain (exhibition- istic and masturbatory) tendencies more difficult for her, and the greater ease with which a boy can satisfy his impulse to investigate by examining his own body may be the basis for greater objectivity and for a greater interest in external objects in the man. But—and here Karen Horney is in striking contrast to Freud—" when she reaches maturity a great part in sexual life (as regards creative power perhaps even a greater part than that of men) devolves upon a woman—I mean when she becomes a mother ".[1] Her capacity for motherhood is—so Karen Horney asserts—an " indisputable superiority " of woman and is the cause of intense envy in boys. This envy of feminine productivity is a dynamic factor in masculine psychology and " serves as one, if not as the essential, driving force in the setting up of cultural values ".[2] Karen Horney admits that the cultural productivity has been incomparably greater in men than in women, but, she asks, " is not the tremendous strength in men of the impulse to creative work in every field precisely due to the feeling of playing a relatively small part in the creation of living beings, which constantly impels them to an over-compensation in achieve- ment ? " The penis-envy in women has not found a corre- sponding compensatory expression, " either because it is absolutely less than the envy of men ", or because in normal cases it is transformed into a desire for husband and child and in this way loses its power as an " incentive to sublimation ". If, neverthe- less, a " flight from womanhood " can be observed in women, it

[1] Karen Horney : " On the Genesis of the Castration Complex in Women " (*Internat. Jour. of Ps.-An.*, Vol. V, Jan., 1924).
[2] Karen Horney : " The Flight from Womanhood : The Masculinity Complex in Women as Viewed by Men and by Women " (*Internat. Jour. of Ps.-An.*, Vol. VII, 1926).
  More recently another psycho-analyst, Gregory Zilboorg, equally " inclined to think that it is not penis-envy on the part of woman, but woman-envy on the part of man, that is psychologically older and therefore more fundamental ", has made a new departure in psycho-analytical theory based on the assumption of a basic feminine superiority in his study : " Masculine and Feminine. Some Biological and Cultural Aspects " (*Psychiatry*, Vol. 7, Aug., 1944, No. 3).

is due not to primary instinct but to the experience of real—physical and social—disadvantages. Her sense of inferiority is not constitutional but acquired.

Karen Horney's reply to Freud is an almost exact inversion of his theory. To his masculine claim of superiority she opposes her claim to feminine biological superiority ; his assumption of penis-envy in women she answers with her assumption of " envy of motherhood " in men ; and Freud's contention that sexual activity is a masculine prerogative, and that " the achievement of the biological aim is entrusted to the aggressiveness of the male ", she contradicts with the statement that the greater part in sexual life and actual biological creation devolves upon women.

The whole argument looks like a bid for supremacy between two highly interested competitors. It certainly shows how hard it is to achieve scientific detachment in matters of personal concern. And it bears witness to the competitive spirit that has animated discussions about feminine traits ever since women voiced their claims to consideration as complete individuals and pretenders to the Rights of Man.

Against the rather obvious accusation of masculine partiality Freud defends his position with a gallant gesture towards women which is quite an amusing example of chivalry entering a scientific argument :

> Whenever a comparison was made which seemed to be unfavourable to their sex, the ladies were able to express a suspicion that we, the men analysts, had never overcome certain deep-rooted prejudices against the feminine, and that consequently our investigation suffered from bias. On the other hand, on the basis of bisexuality, we found it easy to avoid any impoliteness. We had only to say : " This does not apply to you. You are an exception, in this respect you are more masculine than feminine." [1]

Freud could not have given away his attitude of masculine superiority more clearly than by this polite bow to the " ladies " and his willingness to distinguish some of them with the order of merit of being " more masculine than feminine ".

As the bisexuality referred to in the above quotation is a corner-stone in Freud's libido-theory it still needs closer examination. The bisexuality of all living organisms is one of the more recent discoveries of biological science. We have met with some of its implications for human psychology both in Havelock

[1] *The Psychology of Women*, pp. 149–50.

Ellis's and in Weininger's theories. It means, in short, that every individual has, at least potentially if not actually, the characteristics of both sexes, but normally develops the one set to a greater extent than the other. There is no clear-cut line between absolute masculinity and absolute femininity, but reality presents us with a mixture of both in different proportions which vary considerably with each individual. It is, in Freud's words, " as though the individual were neither man nor woman, but both at the same time, only rather more the one than the other ".[1]

In order to determine the proportion of the two elements in a given mixture one has first to reduce these to their fundamental essence as, for instance, Weininger has done with the stipulation of two pure types M and W. For Freud the contrast masculine–feminine is, ultimately, the contrast between active and passive ; or, to be more exact : masculinity implies activity, femininity is characterized by a " preference for passive aims ", which is not quite the same as passivity. (" It may require a good deal of activity to achieve a passive end.") [2] In Freud's own words :

Psychoanalysis has a common basis with biology in that it pre-supposes an original bisexuality in human beings (as in animals). But psycho-analysis cannot elucidate the intrinsic nature of what in conventional or in biological phraseology is termed " masculine " and " feminine " : it simply takes over the two concepts and makes them the foundation of its work. When we attempt to reduce them further we find masculinity vanishing into activity and femininity into passivity and that does not tell us enough.[3]

Now, it is a peculiar and interesting phenomenon that in Freud's interpretation " bisexuality " has a distinctly masculine connotation. The period in human life in which bisexuality is most pronounced is, naturally, early childhood, i.e. the time before adult sexuality, secondary sex characteristics, and psycho-logical corollaries intensify the tendencies towards one sex rather than the other. At that age we find children of both sexes developing the same kind of activity and aggressiveness and a sexuality centered on a " masculine " genital. (In girls it is represented by a corresponding but, so to speak, underdeveloped organ—an " inadequate substitute ", as Helene Deutsch calls it [4]—the clitoris.) The auto-eroticism of both boys and girls is masculine in character.

[1] Ibid., p. 146.   [2] Ibid., p. 148.
[3] " The Psychogenesis of a Case of Homosexuality in a Woman " (Coll. Papers, pp. 202–32, London, 1920).
[4] Helene Deutsch : " The Psychology of Women in Relation to the Functions of Reproduction " (Internat. Jour. of Ps.-An., Vol. VI, 1925).

Equally, libido, which as the instinctual source of energy to both men and women is understood to be bisexual, actually, if we keep to Freud's definition of masculinity = activity, is a masculine force. Freud himself remarks that " libido could always be called ' masculine ', no matter whether it appears in man or in woman, in the sense that, as an instinct, it is always active, even if directed towards a passive aim ".[1]

This identification of the masculine with an absolute norm is a remarkable example of the way in which, in a masculine culture, standards of the one sex are generalized and represented as neutral—here called bisexual—and taken as valid for mankind in general, irrespective of sex. Georg Simmel, the German sociologist, has pointed out [2] that the same is true of all the values of our culture : the historical development has been such that all categories of our thinking, all norms of our ethics, all artistic forms and social institutions are based on this equation of masculine and " objective " which transforms a psychological superiority, resulting from a superior power position, into a logical one. In the same way, says Simmel, every government based on subjective force tries to defend its authority by an objective justification and thus to transform might into right. The psychological mechanism by which this generalization of the masculine norm is performed is described by Simmel in a passage which is worth quoting in full :

To take from two opposite notions, which derive their meaning and value from each other, one, and to raise this one to embrace and dominate once more the whole game of give and take and of balance, this time in an absolute sense, is a thoroughly human tendency, presumably of deep metaphysical origin, which has found an historic paradigm in the fundamental sexual relation of Man.

The fact that the male sex is not only considered relatively superior to the female, but that it is taken as the universal human norm, applied equally to the phenomena of the individual masculine and of the individual feminine—this fact is, in many different ways, based on the power position of the male. If we express the historic relation between the sexes crudely in terms of master and slave, it is part of the master's privileges not to have to think continuously of the fact that he is the master, while the position of the slave carries with it the constant reminder of his being a slave. It cannot be overlooked that the woman forgets far less often the fact of being a woman than the man of being a man. Innumerable times the man seems to think purely objectively, without his masculinity entering his consciousness at all.

[1] S. Freud : " Three Contributions to the Theory of Sex " (*Imago*, London, 1942).
[2] Georg Simmel : " Das Relative und das Absolute im Geschlechterproblem " (*Philosophische Kultur*, Leipzig, 1911).

On the other hand it seems as if the woman would never completely lose the more or less vague feeling of being a woman ; this feeling forms the ever-present background underlying all her experiences of life. Because masculinity, as a differential factor, in phantasies and principles, in achievements and emotional complexes, escapes the consciousness of its protagonists more easily than is the case with femininity in the corresponding situation (for within the sphere of his activities man's interest in his relation to the Feminine is not as vital as woman's interest in her relation to the Masculine) expressions of masculinity are easily elevated for us to the realm of a supra-specific, neutral, objectivity and validity (to which their specifically masculine connotation, if noticed at all, is subordinated as something individual and casual). This fact is evident in the extremely frequent phenomenon that certain judgments, institutions, aims, or interests which we men, naively so to speak, consider purely objective, are felt by women to be thoroughly and characteristically masculine.[1]

In generalizing the masculine type and making it a universal norm Freud went further than anyone else : for, to him, even being equipped with male sex organs is part of the general standard, to the extent that the " poverty in external genitals " (in K. Abraham's term) is considered to be an organic deficiency, and that woman is supposed to regard her own biological function (i.e. the ability to bear children) as a compensation for her constitutional inadequacy. It seems plausible to Freud and his school that one half of humanity should have *biological* reasons to

---

[1] In the original the passage is thus :

" Jene durchgehend menschliche, wohl in tiefen metaphysischen Gründen verankerte Tendenz, aus einem Paar polarer Begriffe, die ihren Sinn und ihre Wertbestimmung aneinander finden, den einen herauszuheben, um ihn noch einmal, jetzt in einer absoluten Bedeutung, das ganze Gegenseitigkeits oder Gleichgewichtsspiel umfassen und dominieren zu lassen, hat sich an der geschlechtlichen Grundrelation der Menschen ein historisches Paradigma geschaffen.

" Dass das männliche Geschlecht nicht einfach dem weiblichen relativ überlegen ist, sondern zum Allgemein-Menschlichen wird, das die Erscheinungen des einzelnen Männlichen und des einzelnen Weiblichen gleichmässig normiert—dies wird, in mannigfachen Vermittlungen, von der Machtstellung der Männer getragen. Drückt man das geschichtliche Verhältnis der Geschlechter einmal krass als das des Herrn und des Sklaven aus, so gehört es zu den Privilegien des Herrn, dass er nicht immer daran zu denken braucht, dass er Herr ist, während die Position des Sklaven dafür sorgt, dass er seine Position nie vergisst. Es ist gar nicht zu verkennen, dass die Frau ausserordentlich viel seltener ihr Frau-Sein aus dem Bewusstsein verliert als der Mann sein Mann-Sein. Unzählige Male scheint der Mann rein Sachlich zu denken, ohne dass seine Männlichkeit gleichzeitig irgendeinen Platz in seiner Empfindung einnähme ; dagegen scheint es, als würde die Frau niemals von einem deutlicheren oder dunkleren Gefühle, dass sie Frau ist, verlassen ; dieses bildet den niemals ganz verschwindenden Untergrund, auf dem alle Inhalte ihres Lebens sich abspielen. Da das differentielle, das Männlichkeits-Moment, in den Vorstellungsbildern und Normsetzungen, in den Werken und Gefühlskombinationen, dem Bewusstsein seiner Träger leichter entschwindet, als das entsprechende an dem Weiblichkeitsmoment geschieht—denn für den Mann als den Herrn knüpft sich innerhalb seiner Lebensbetätigungen kein so vitales Interesse an seine Relation zum Weiblichen, wie die Frau es an ihrer Relation zum Männlichen haben muss—so

feel at a disadvantage for not having what the other half possesses (but not vice versa).

The adoption of masculine standards as the absolute norm applicable to mankind as a whole has two equally harmful results for the judgment of women. The one is a mystifying over-estimation of woman by virtue of those qualities which cannot be explained by male criteria. The other is contempt for human beings who fail to live up to the norm.

In Freud's writings we find both attitudes represented : on the one hand the wonder at the " enigmatic " woman, the approach to feminine psychology as a " riddle " to be solved, and a theory which views the development of femininity as a particularly " difficult and complicated process " ; on the other hand there is the contempt—as we had sufficient occasion to see—for her inferior intellectual capacities, her greater vanity, her weaker sexual instincts, her disposition to neuroses and hysteria, and for her constitutional passivity. The latter is, in Freud's view, associated with masochistic tendencies. There is, he says, in feminine psychology " some secret relationship with masochism ".—" The repression of their aggressiveness, which is imposed upon women by their constitution and by society, favours the development of strong masochistic impulses, which have the effect of binding erotically the destructive tendencies which have been turned inward." [1] This contention has been worked out by Helene Deutsch into a theory according to which masochistic wishes to be violated and humiliated—both physically and mentally—are the clue to feminine psychology. Her view of sexual intercourse as a " sadistic act of taking possession " on the part of man, and a " masochistic subjugation " on the part of woman [2] is but the elaboration of an assumption ever recurring in psycho-analytical literature : the view that " sexual activity is essentially associated with the male organ, that the woman is only in the position to excite the man's libido or respond to it, and that otherwise she is compelled to adopt a waiting attitude ",[3]

heben sich die männlichen Wesensäusserungen für uns leicht in die Sphäre einer überspezifischen, neutralen Sachlichkeit und Gültigkeit (denen die spezifisch männliche Färbung, wo sie etwa bemerkt wird, als etwas Individuelles und Zufälliges subordiniert wird). Dies offenbart sich in der unendlich häufigen Erscheinung, dass Frauen gewisse Urteile, Institutionen, Bestrebungen, Interessen, als durchaus und charakteristisch männlich empfinden, die wir Männer sozusagen naiv für einfach sachlich halten . . ."

[1] *The Psychology of Women*, pp. 148–9.
[2] Helene Deutsch : " The Significance of Masochism in the Mental Life of Women " (*Internat. Jour. of Ps.-An.*, 1930).
[3] K. Abraham : " Manifestations of the Female Castration Complex " (*Intern. Journ. of Ps.-An.*, Vol. III, 1922).

that, moreover, the sex instinct in woman is weaker and that she derives only a limited or indirect satisfaction from sexual intercourse. Ferenczi has developed this view into a " Genital Theory " according to which the sexual impulse is ultimately man's wish to return into the mother's womb—a meaning which the sexual act cannot assume for woman, who therefore has no fundamental impulse for, or primary satisfaction from coitus. What pleasure she does derive results partly by way of a " masochistic conversion and partly by identification with the child which she may conceive. These, however, are only compensatory devices ". The feminine attitude towards sex is, like other traits, considered by psycho-analytical theory to be based on organic constitution and biological function and therefore part of the unchanging " human nature ". Evidences to the contrary which are supplied by other cultures are disregarded, although they are numerous. In Hindu books, for instance— such as *Kâmasutrâm* and *Anángaránga*—women's urge of love is reckoned to be " eight times as potent as that of man " ; the code of Manu states that " women are by their very nature experts in the seduction of men, hence man should avoid being found even with his nearest kin in lonely places . . ." ; Ovid, in his *Ars Amandi*, considers woman's uncontrollable passion " ten times fiercer than ours and full of madness " ; in the famous medieval novel *Roman de la Rose* it is said : " A virtuous woman ; Nay, I swear by good St. Denis that this is more rare than is a phoenix " ; and in a seventeenth-century book by Vendette a passage runs thus : " In love-affairs men are mere children in comparison with women ; women have, in such matters, a greater imagination and command more time to dwell on the affairs of the heart ; they are more lascivious and love-sick than men." [1]

It thus appears that judgments on the strength or weakness of the sex impulse in women are not based on organic facts but are in accordance with a cultural pattern, and vary with time and milieu. In Western civilization during the nineteenth and at the beginning of the twentieth century it would have been not only scandalous to admit the existence of a strong sex urge in women, but it would have been contrary to all observation. And although the enforcement of rules of conduct and of so many restrictions was deemed prudent in order to keep up the

[1] Examples quoted from *The Riddle of Woman* (op. cit.) by Joseph Tenenbaum, who gives these and more instances in his chapter on " The Sex Urge in Woman ".

illusion of " innate " feminine virtuousness, it never occurred to our fathers and grandfathers that it was but an illusion and that, had this not been so, the rigorous supervision of their daughters and wives would hardly have been necessary.

Even Karen Horney, the " equalitarian " among the psycho-analysts, would not go as far as to oppose to the masculine sex impulse a corresponding primary feminine sex impulse, but would base her claims to feminine equality on woman's capacity for motherhood. It thus seems that in psycho-analytical theory it is understood that there are two different instincts in men and women : a sex instinct which is masculine, and an instinct of procreation which is feminine.

Underlying this assumption, as well as other psycho-analytical ideas, is the Victorian notion that " sexual activity is lawfully masculine " (this is Freud's term), but that for women sexuality is a matrimonial duty they have to put up with. To admit that from her sexual function a woman could derive an equal amount of satisfaction, pleasure, happiness—and, if it comes to it, even sense of power—with man, would have been shocking to Victorian ideology. The same attitude is also at the bottom of Freud's theory of penis-envy ; it is the inability to understand that woman no less than man has been equipped by Nature with a sex instinct and the means to gratify it, and that, if she has any reasons for envying man, they are not likely to be of a physiological character.

Alfred Adler, who had made inferiority feelings and the " masculine protest " the central ideas of his Individual Psychology, comes nearer to a sociological interpretation when he asserts that in our competitive culture the dichotomy masculine-feminine has assumed a symbolic value, serving as an analogy to more general ideas of socially " superior " and " inferior ", of " above " and " below ". In a society based, like ours, on individual competition, Adler finds two unconscious presuppositions underlying the thoughts of both his men and women patients : first, that " human relations in all circumstances represent a struggle ", and, secondly, that " the feminine sex is inferior and by its reaction serves as the measure of masculine strength ".[1] Therefore the struggle upwards assumes the form of what Adler calls the " masculine protest ", i.e. a fight against those qualities in oneself which by tradition and consent usually

[1] Alfred Adler : *The Practice and Theory of Individual Psychology* (Kegan Paul, London, 1924 (p. 35).

are associated with the feminine sex, such as weakness, timidity, shyness, passivity, prudishness, etc. Adler's " masculine protest " represents all strivings for " strength, greatness, riches, knowledge, victory ", and all " coarseness, cruelty, violence, and activity as such ". As the child grows up into a hard and competitive world it increasingly wants to get rid of those qualities which hamper its struggle for existence.

The normal craving of the child for nestling, the exaggerated submissiveness of the neurotically-disposed individual, the feeling of weakness, of inferiority protected by hyper-sensitiveness, the realization of actual futility, the sense of being permanently pushed aside and of being at a disadvantage, all these are gathered together into a feeling of femininity. On the contrary, active strivings, both in the case of a girl as of a boy, the pursuit of self-gratification, the stirring up of instincts and passions are thrown challengingly forward as a masculine protest.[1]

The terms " masculine " and " feminine " are clearly used here as symbols of a contrasting pair of values : the one implies all positive, desirable qualities, the other one is associated with al negative, despicable characteristics. This analogy is based, Adler says, on a " false evaluation but one which is extensively nourished by our social life ".

Envy of men, refutation of the feminine rôle, attempts to compete with men, or to copy them in order to feel " complete individuals ", contempt for their own inferiority—these are the phenomena observed in their women patients both by Freud and by Adler and occupying a central position in their respective theories. But while Psycho-analysis seeks a biological explanation and regards these attitudes as conscious rationalizations designed to cover up an underlying organic deficiency, Individual Psychology views them as the expression of a striving for power, a power which in our society is associated with the male sex.

It is as well to remind ourselves that the beginning of women's emancipation coincided with the height of capitalist expansion and liberal ideology and that both theories originated at this time. The striving for power which Adler took as the primary motive in human psychology is a typical characteristic of a competitive culture. Women who endeavoured to participate in this culture did so on a competitive basis. Out of their feminine seclusion they came into the open and found all places occupied by men. When they wanted to contend with them on the ground of a philosophy of Human Rights they found

[1] Op. cit. (p. 22).

themselves classified as *hors concours* because of their sex. No doubt this disqualification was resented by a very great number of them, who reacted to it in different ways : with envy, hatred, revolt, inferiority feelings, increased exertions to make themselves acceptable by adopting as completely as possible the rules of the game (Freud's " masculinity complex ") and other reactions listed by Freud under the heading of " penis-envy ". The resentment is likely to find a most acute expression in unbalanced personalities, such as the neurotics who are the patients and objects of the psychiatrist's investigation. There is no doubt that the factual observations made by Freud are correct. They are valid, that is to say, for the class of people who made up his objects of observation : the neurotic persons of middle and upper middle-class origin in the Central-European society of his time. They are also valid, most probably with corresponding modifications, in every society with strong patriarchal traditions. For Freud and his orthodox pupils there was no doubt that the patients they analysed, and the people they met, were representatives of " the " human type. Future research will have to concentrate on defining the specific character of the field of observation on the basis of comparative evidence. A modified Freudian theory will have to include such social and cultural factors as particular influences of the environment, the power of prevailing traditions, ideals and historical institutions.

It was in a sense rather fortunate for psycho-analytical theory that, owing to otherwise very fateful political developments in Central Europe, a great number of its supporters had to go abroad. In foreign countries they came into close contact with divergent cultural patterns and different personality types. In consequence there came into existence—mainly in the United States of America—a new type of psycho-analyst who, while preserving the fundamental achievements of the Freudian school, became increasingly culture-conscious and inclined to a more sociological orientation. This new trend has, of course, not affected all exiled psycho-analysts. Helene Deutsch, for instance, has only recently published a *Psychology of Woman*,[1] in which she restates her former orthodox views. But the number of psycho-analysts with a definite leaning to sociology is large enough to be regarded as a new psycho-analytical " school ". Among these are Karen Horney, Eric Fromm, Clara Thompson and others. (Paul Bousfield has, in this country, expressed similar

[1] Dr. Helene Deutsch : *Psychology of Woman* (Grune & Stratton, 1944).

tendencies.) These people are supported not only by their own experience but by anthropology and sociology—two sciences of a fairly recent development—in their conviction that there is no " universal man " or " universal woman ", but that human beings have to be studied in relation to their milieu—or, to use the technical term, to the " cultural pattern ". The realization that in different societies women fulfil different social functions and accordingly display different attitudes and mental characteristics has shattered the idea of the all-powerful influence of anatomy and biological facts on character-traits. As Clara Thompson has pointed out,[1] it is possible to explain every single trait attributed by Freud to a biologically determined development of the libido (such as all the implications of " penis-envy ", the repression of aggressiveness, passivity and masochism, the narcissistic need to be loved, the rigidity, i.e. prematurely arrested character development of women, the weaker super-ego, etc.) by the influence of " cultural pressures ", that is by the impact of a concrete historical situation on character structures.

To suppose that human beings are born as " tabulae rasae " on which every trait is to be impressed by social and cultural influences of the surroundings would certainly be no less a mistake than to assume that " anatomy is destiny ". The dangers of a one-sided stress on environmental factors, which a purely sociological point of view might entail, has been considerably reduced by the new turn which psycho-analytical theory has been taking, and no doubt, the integration of psycho-analytical with sociological thinking which we are witnessing at present will be most fruitful in its effects both on psychological and sociological knowledge.

REFERENCES

S. FREUD : " The Psychology of Women " (Chapter XXXIII, *New Introductory Lectures*, Hogarth Press, London, 1933).
" Three Contributions to the Theory of Sex " (*Imago*, London, 1942).
Taboo of Virginity, 1918.
Civilization and Its Discontent (Hogarth Press, London, 1930).
Totem and Taboo (Kegan Paul, London, 1919).
The Psychogenesis of a Case of Homosexuality in a Woman (Collected Papers, London, 1920).
" Civilized Sexual Morality and Modern Nervousness " (*Collected Papers*, Vol. 2, London, 1924).
Analysis Terminable and Unterminable (London, 1937).
" Some Psychological Consequences of the Anatomical Distinction Between the Sexes "(*Internat. Jour. of Ps.-An.*, London, 1927).

---

[1] Clara Thompson : " Cultural Pressures in the Psychology of Women ", published in *Psychiatry*, Vol. V, No. 3. Baltimore, Aug. 1942.

K. Abraham : " Manifestations of the Female Castration Complex " (*Internat. Jour. of Ps.-An.*, Vol. III, March, 1922).

Paul Bousfield : *Sex and Civilization* (Kegan Paul, London, 1925).

C. D. Daly : " The Psychology of Man's Attitude Towards Woman " *British Jour. of Medic. Psychology*, Vol. X, 1930).

Helene Deutsch : " The Psychology of Women in Relation to the Functions of Reproduction " (*Internat. Jour. of Ps.-An.*, Vol. VI, 1925).

" The Significance of Masochism in the Mental Life of Women " (*Internat. Jour. of Ps.-An.*, 1930).

Psychology of Woman (Grune & Stratton, 1944).

J. Harnik : " The Various Developments Undergone by Narcissism in Men and Women " (*Internat. Jour. of Ps.-An.*, Vol. V, 1925).

Karen Horney : " On the Genesis of the Castration Complex in Women " (*Internat. Jour. of Ps.-An.*, Vol. V, January 1924).

" The Flight from Womanhood : The Masculinity in Women as Viewed by Men and by Women " (*Internat. Jour. of Ps.-An.*, Vol. VII, 1926).

" The Denial of the Vagina " (*Internat. Jour. of Ps.-An.*, 1933).

The Neurotic Personality of Our Time (Kegan Paul, London, 1937).

New Ways in Psycho-Analysis (Kegan Paul, London, 1939).

Ernest Jones : "Early Development of Female Sexuality (*Internat. Jour. of Ps.-An.*, 1927).

"Phallic Phase " (*Internat. Jour. of Ps.-An.*, 1927).

J. H. W. Van Ophuisen : " Contributions to the Masculinity Complex in Women " (*Internat. Jour. of Ps.-An.*, Vol. V, 1924).

Clara Thompson : " The Rôle of Women in this Culture " (*Psychiatry*, Vol. 4, 1941).

" Cultural Pressures in the Psychology of Women " (*Psychiatry*, Vol. 5, 1942).

" ' Penis Envy ' in Women " (*Psychiatry*, Vol. 6, 1943).

Alfred Adler : *The Practice and Theory of Individual Psychology* (Kegan Paul, London, 1924).

Alice Rühle-Gerstel : *Freud und Adler* (Dresden, 1924).

Das Frauenproblem der Gegenwart (Leipzig, 1932).

Erwin Wexberg : *Individual Psychology and Sex* (Jonathan Cape, London, 1931).

Georg Simmel : " Das Relative und das Absolute im Geschlechterproblem " (*Philosophische Kultur*, Leipzig, 1911).

Gregory Zilboorg : " Masculine and Feminine. Some Biological and Cultural Aspects " (*Psychiatry*, Vol. 7, 1944).

CHAPTER VI

FIRST INVESTIGATIONS IN EXPERIMENTAL PSYCHOLOGY: HELEN B. THOMPSON

It is interesting to note how, in the theoretical discussions of the problem of woman, the terms of reference have changed. Both parties, those advocating male superiority as well as those championing equality of the sexes or even feminine superiority, had for centuries looked to theology to supply them with arguments. The supporters of masculine rule naturally made use of the Bible and of St. Paul's pronouncements, such as : " For a man indeed ought not to cover his head, forasmuch as he is the image and glory of God ; but the woman is the glory of the man. For the man is not of the woman ; but the woman of the man. Neither was the man created for the woman, but the woman for the man." (1 Cor., xi. 7–9.) Or, in Milton's words :

> My author and Disposer, what thou bidst
> Unargued I obey ; so God ordains ;
> God is thy law, thou mine ; to know no more
> Is Woman's happiest knowledge, and her praise.

But the opposition as well, in arguing their point, had recourse to the authority of the Scriptures. In one of the first " feminist " books ever written, *Of the Nobility and Superiority of the Female Sex* (first published in 1505), the author, Heinrich Cornelius Agrippa von Nettesheim, justifies his plea for feminine superiority by an exegesis of his own : " Adam means Earth ; Eve stands for life ; ergo, Adam is the product of nature, and Eve the creation of God. Adam was admitted to the Paradise for the sole purpose that Eve might be created . . ." [1]

It was natural, then, to argue in theological terms, and it was equally " natural " later to discuss the problem in terms of Natural Science. Mainly during the nineteenth century justifications of all points of view on the question of woman were sought in biological tendencies and evolutionary trends. The solutions were sought, so to speak, in the germ plasm.

More recently, the emphasis has again been shifted, and the main attention been directed towards the modifiability of human nature under the impact of personal experience and cultural milieu.

[1] Quoted from Joseph Tenenbaum : *The Riddle of Woman*, op. cit.

This new attitude towards human nature arose at a certain stage in historical development when the quiet flow of tradition was disturbed and changes became drastic and obvious enough to make themselves felt in all walks of life.

The growing restlessness of the middle and lower classes preceding the French Revolution had already produced various plans to cure the ills of society. Babeuf, Saint-Simon, Fourier, Robert Owen, had put forward their schemes of social reconstruction. They, in their turn, followed a number of philosophers whose attention had been attracted to problems of historical evolution by the social development they were witnessing : Montesquieu, Diderot, Condorcet, Turgot, Voltaire, are French examples. David Hume and Adam Smith in this country, Lessing, Herder, Kant and Hegel in Germany, manifest the same trend.

The French Revolution and the growing imprint of industrialization on the most various aspects of the social order further increased the general interest in the social forces at work. Auguste Comte's endeavours, for instance, to establish the principles of an " ordered progress " which would involve " neither restoration nor revolution ", and which resulted in the foundation of Sociology as a science, were the outcome of his profound alarm at the effects of the Revolution. He, as well as others of his contemporaries, felt that in the social sphere evolution was not necessarily identical with progress, and the need for and interest in social reform grew increasingly.

Attention was, moreover, directed towards the mechanisms of change and the pliability of human nature by the closer contact with different social and cultural systems, made possible by expanding capitalism. The study of foreign peoples, their customs and mores, offered a wide field of comparison and numerous objects of meditation.

Finally, migratory movements on a large scale, due to the colonization of other continents, created a kind of social laboratory for new experiments. The immigration to North America, in particular, which gave rise to an integrated national and cultural unit out of racially and culturally most diverse elements, afforded a strong incentive to social study. (To the present day the interest in social sciences is, for this reason, more acute in the United States than it is, for instance, in this country. The number of sociological books published every year, the number of social research institutes and professorial chairs in the U.S.A. are far above the corresponding figures in this country.)

Each of these factors contributed to an attitude which no longer took for granted things as they were, but began to doubt traditional values and institutions. Together they led to an emphasis on change, movement and development, to an atmosphere of relativity and a readiness to overhaul traditional thoughts, beliefs and ideals.

This change of attitude found expression not only in the social sciences, but affected the scientific outlook in general. The " basic thought that the world is not to be comprehended as a complex of ready-made things, but as a complex of processes " (as Fr. Engels said)—the fact that it was no longer static objects but activities which became the centre of interest and scientific investigation—is one of the major events in the development of scientific thought in recent time. The relativist outlook, the emphasis on dynamic processes, and the willingness to re-examine all, even our most elementary concepts and all phenomena of ordinary everyday life itself, are characteristic features of present-day culture. They have found expression in contemporary art no less than in all branches of science. Doubt as a heuristic principle has, from the days of Descartes on, been the foundation and the most distinctive characteristic of Modern Man. Now once more it became active and invaded all departments of thought : Physics found it necessary to reconsider the fundamental notions of time and space ; analytical psychology re-examined under its magnifying glass such elementary emotions as parental and sexual love. Music disposed of the old conceptions of harmony ; modern painting cleared away ancient ideas of form. Sociology, a new science altogether, came into being in order to make an inventory of assets and liabilities, to study the mechanisms of the dynamic social processes and to investigate the underlying principles.

The motives responsible for the new scientific outlook in general, and for the foundations of Sociology as a new science in particular, are the same motives which account in great part, if not exclusively, for the ever increasing interest in our special problem : the psychological traits of woman.

It may be worth recapitulating in this connection the main points, more extensively dealt with in Chapter II.

The most important ideological influence was undoubtedly the ideal of Human Rights, based on a philosophy of " equality " and " liberty " disseminated by the French Revolution. This philosophy implied—even if it did not state expressly—equal rights for women no less than for men. The first publications in support of the emancipation of women were, in fact, the *Declaration des Droits des Femmes*, submitted to the French National Assembly in 1798, and the *Vindication of the Rights of Woman*, by Mary Wollstonecraft, in 1792, in this country. The very wording of these titles testifies sufficiently to their spiritual origin in French Revolutionary ideology. In different ways and various expressions this appeal has made itself heard ever since and has enormously increased both in weight and in volume all over the world.

The decisive economic factor in the rise of the problem of woman was, as we have seen before, industrialization, with the consequent transfer of productive activities from the family to the factory and the creation of an enormous leisure-class of bourgeois women who henceforth strove for improved educational facilities and for re-admission into the economic process.

A further incentive to the study of both the social and psychological aspects of this problem of woman was the growing knowledge of foreign cultures and mainly of primitive peoples. The examination of different institutions afforded the " duality " necessary for adequate judgment. It is impossible to understand and to criticize a situation as long as one is oneself entirely part of it. Only if one has an adequate observation point which ensures a view of things in their proper perspective can one pass a proper judgment. As long as the patriarchal family tradition was undisturbed and no other contrasting patterns were known, whatever was established in social tradition was regarded as part of human nature. As there was only one way of life to be considered, this was thought to be the only possible, the " natural " course. The first perceptible break in that tradition, as well as the background provided by the study of primitive cultures, sharpened critical awareness of established institutions. Such publications as J. J. Bachofen's *Mutterrecht* (1861), L. H. Morgan's *Ancient Society, Researchès in the Lines of Human Progress from Savagery through Barbarism to Civilization* (1877), F. Engels' *Origin of the Family* (1884), E. A. Westermarck's *History of Human Marriage* (1891) and others, increased not only the knowledge of different family systems but the criticism of the existing pattern. The fact that comparisons between contrasting cultural patterns arouse a critical attitude has been known and used by critics of their social system ever since Montesquieu first published his *Lettres Persanes*. But progressing anthropological research has brought this literary technique out of the sphere of imagination and speculation and put it on the firmer basis of established facts. Characteristically, for instance, J. Kirk Folsom uses this device in his sociological study of the family. His book is preceded by a number of pages on which he confronts attitudes and beliefs, held in our Western civilization with regard to various problems of marriage and family life, with respective attitudes towards the same problems in Melanesian society. He thereby succeeds in stressing the peculiarities of our own institutions and in creating an atmosphere of greater objectivity.

More recently, changes in our society have become so marked that comparisons between present and past standards within our own civilization afford bases for comparison similar to those between different cultures. The adoption of a relativistic outlook has consequently been greatly increased.

That woman should have become a problem is therefore due to a set of general changes in the new era : to a new trend in economic development, to a new philosophy of life, and to a new scientific outlook.

But in addition to these general changes, the special interest which the problem of woman has evoked is due to two factors of a specific kind : The first is the development of medicine in general, and the improvement of birth control methods in particular. It had two significant effects on the actual emancipation of woman : relieved from the burden of constant child-bearing she could envisage taking up a career and could compete with men in the economic field on more equal terms. And, secondly, the separation of sex from procreation—in the sense of an inevitable consequence—created a new attitude towards love. It is not our task here to evaluate the revolutionary changes involved in this separation of two hitherto closely linked notions. Our aim is to show that birth-control has, if not fully, at least to a considerable extent, reduced woman's dependence on what Nature seemed to have destined for her, and it enabled her to choose and to accept the responsibility for her love-life (as men have always done). Both in work and in love, therefore, woman became a more equal partner to man.

The other important specific factor contributing to the scientific interest in Woman was the changing attitude towards the problem of Sex.

Introduced by Havelock Ellis and furthered mainly by Sigmund Freud and his school, sex has increasingly become a subject of scientific interest. Unpleasant as the reminder of this connection may be to the emancipated woman, who thinks of herself first of all as an individual and not as an object of merely or mainly sexual interest, the fact must not be overlooked that the scientific interest in the personality of woman developed alongside the scientific interest in sex. Only when sex ceased to be considered a sin could woman be regarded as a human being and not as either a " temptress " or as the incorporation of a necessary evil. In this light Weininger's statement that women are first of all interested in matters of sex is correct, though not in the sense Weininger meant it. Only after society had been freed from an ideology which regarded sex as sinful in itself could women be seen as individuals in their own right instead of as instruments of the devil. This has nothing to do with an " inherent sexual nature " of women but is the natural outcome of a man-made culture in which women of the upper and middle classes were excluded from all but those social functions directly or indirectly connected with sex. With the development of science and the growing influence it exerted on the public mind a number of religious taboos lost their original strength, the taboo on the discussion of sex among others.

An interesting light on the way in which primitive taboos linger on persistently in the form of prejudices and social habits until, in the end, they are dispelled by the more enlightened attitude created by modern science, is thrown by the example of menstruation. The primitive taboo attaching to woman's " uncleanness " lived on in feelings of shame and physical inferiority on the part of women, and in numerous myths, such as the belief that a menstruating woman cannot make butter " set " in the churn, or preserve fruit or jam, that she should not touch meat in a pickle tub nor flowers in a pot for fear they would decay. Many of these and similar superstitions still survive in the popular mind. Even medical science used to treat the problem of menstruation with awe as a kind of mysterious disease and regarded women as " naturally invalid ". " Women ", said Galiani in his *Dialogue sur les Femmes*, " only have intervals of health in the course of a continual disease." More recently, however, doctors are inclined to regard it as a normal process in healthy women and not as an illness and to attribute a great part of the pains and nervousness connected with it to psychological causes, such as, for instance, the " expectation of troubles ".

The mischief [says a report by the Hygiene Committee of the Women's Group on Public Welfare in 1943] [1] is, however, far more serious owing to the survival, in an atmosphere of mystery which surrounds the subject, of the tribal outlook upon it. Women themselves are generally unaware of the extent to which this function is present in the minds of responsible persons in judging of their capacity to enter fresh fields, but startling light was thrown upon it when the alleged incompetence of women in menstruation to be trusted with the lives of passengers was made the ground for refusing to grant them the Pilot's B Certificate for flying. A committee of women doctors had to be set up to contest this decision, which they did successfully.

The all-round progress of the sciences has produced a critical attitude towards institutionalized habits and traditional prejudices. It opened the way for a study of the feminine character which was released from the emotional bonds of religious taboos and was, in its intention at least, objective.

The research was carried out along two main lines. One was the attempt first to establish in a scientific way and to ensure what characteristic mental differences of sex are to be found, here and now, without enquiry into their origin.

The other approach was mainly concerned with the problem of causation, biological, psychological, social, etc., and has produced a great number of varying theories. Sociology is, first of all, interested in the possibilities and limits of social conditioning, that is, in the problem of the extent to which the character structure of modern civilized woman is the result of a certain mode of existence, of social institutions, traditions, and ideologies. It is based on the assumption that, notwithstanding the conditions of his physical and intellectual equipment, man is to a large extent a product of his surroundings, and that—even after allowance has been made for the limits imposed on a man's variability by his constitution and innate tendencies—the margin within which his nature is alterable is still wide enough to be of essential interest and to call for special investigation.

So far, three different lines of approach to the problem of feminine character have been examined, all of which were concerned with causal explanations in terms of innate dispositions

---

[1] *Our Towns. A Close-up* (Oxford University Press, 1943).

and biological functions. Before going on to theories representing a more sociological outlook, we have to consider now some of the attempts to measure existing mental differences of sex without raising the question of their conditioning.

The first scientific attempt to apply experimental methods to the investigation of mental sex differences was carried out in the psychological laboratory of the University of Chicago by Dr. Helen Bradford Thompson during the years 1898 to 1900. Its results were published under the title of *The Mental Traits of Sex* in Chicago in 1903. It is a report of a series of experiments and tests applied to a selected group of twenty-five college men and twenty-five college women, all students of the (co-educational) University of Chicago. They were all of one age-group and came from more or less the same social background. In this way the number of variables was reduced to a minimum, but Miss Thompson herself makes the following comment :

> In order to make a trustworthy investigation of the variations due to sex alone, it is a pre-requisite to obtain individuals for comparison who are near the same age, who have the same social status, and who have been subjected to like training and social surroundings. The complete fulfilment of these conditions, even in the most democratic community, is impossible. The social atmosphere of the sexes is different from the earliest childhood to maturity.

Miss Thompson tries to take this obvious source of error into account as much as possible. The main objection which may be raised against the method of her enquiry is the limited number of individuals subjected to examination and the resulting danger of too rash generalizations and too little allowance being made for individual differences. Confronted with the choice between a thorough investigation of a small number of cases and a necessarily more or less superficial study of a great number of individuals, she preferred to sacrifice the volume of her research to its intensity and exactitude. Being a pioneer she had not yet at her disposal a perfected method of mental testing which would have enabled her to deal with great numbers equally or more thoroughly.

Comparisons were made between the measured aptitudes in men and women of motor ability, skin and muscle senses, taste and smell, hearing, vision, affective processes, of such intellectual faculties as memory, association and ingenuity, and of their general knowledge in English, history, physics, mathematics, biology and science.

The careful measurement of all those faculties shows some slight difference between men and women which, however, are strikingly small and resolve themselves, in the light of Miss Thompson's investigation, mainly into differences in attitudes towards the problems in question and not into innate differences of abilities.

There is, for instance, a certain feminine superiority in association and in memory, both with regard to the rapidity of memorizing and to duration, and a masculine superiority in ingenuity.

The question is [as Miss Thompson puts it] largely one of the distribution of attention. A large part of a boy's attention goes towards his activities—the learning of new movements, the manipulation of tools, the making of contrivances of various sorts. A girl's less active existence must be filled with some other sort of conscious process. The only possibility is that sensory and perceptual processes should be more prominent.[1] [And she goes on] : On the more purely intellectual level it is only natural that in the absence of a sufficient social spur toward originality and inventiveness they should depend more upon memory for their supply of ideas.

The measurable differences in ingenuity on the one hand, memory on the other, are in Miss Thompson's view expressions of two different social ideals : The ideal of manliness which encourages individuality, independence in thought and action, and readiness to experiment ; and the ideal of femininity which breeds a spirit of obedience, dependence and deference. According to these contrasting ideals different characteristics are developed which are, however, only different manifestations of one psychic energy.

This assumption is corroborated by more recent sociological theories which regard the individual's social rôle and his conception of his rôle as among the most important factors in the shaping of personality.

Miss Thompson can find no difference according to sex in the total amount of general information possessed by men and women who have had the same course of education, and no marked difference in the character of affective processes, in the strength of emotions, in the form of their expression, or the degree of impulsiveness in action. There seems to be, however, a greater tendency in women to inhibit the expression of their emotions.

[1] Op. cit., p. 180.

The tendency to introspection, as well as the clearness of thinking, are found to be the same in both sexes. In intellectual interests, and what are considered the easiest and hardest branches of study, and in methods of work, there are only trifling divergences.

Miss Thompson discards the view, which occupies such a prominent place in Havelock Ellis's theory, of a universally greater variability in men than in women. She thinks it necessary to discriminate between normal and abnormal variations. " A class," she says, " which presents the greatest number of abnormalities in character might not be the class which displays the widest normal variations of that character." Her view is based on the extensive studies on variations by the statistician K. Pearson,[1] who draws attention to the need for measurement of variability around the average and who calls the principle that men are more variable than women a " pseudo-scientific superstition ".

More recently L. S. Hollingworth has also contested Havelock Ellis's assumption of a greater variability in males.[2] She points out that the smaller number of feeble-minded women found in institutions is due to the fact that many feminine occupations are of an uncompetitive character and therefore render the detection of mental defectiveness in women more difficult. On a mental level which would make men liable to detention, women are able to live outside institutions with their families or to earn their livelihood with domestic work or prostitution. Thus, although there may be more mentally defective men inside institutions, more feeble-minded women are living outside. In order to rule out environmental influences Hollingworth, moreover, collected a great number of physical measurements of infants at birth [3] and could not find any consistent sex difference in variability. Mental differences, however, which are the main point in the controversy about the differential variability of the sexes, cannot be measured at that age, and this contention of Hollingworth's therefore does not seem relevant.

Summing up the general result of her investigation Miss Thompson says :

[1] K. Pearson : " Variations in Man and Woman " in *The Chances of Death*, Chap. VIII (E. Arnold, London, 1897).
[2] L. S. Hollingworth : " Differential Action upon the Sexes of Forces Which Tend to Segregate the Feeble-minded " (*Jour. Abn. Psych.*, No. 17, 1922).
[3] L. S. Hollingworth and H. M. Montague : " The Comparative Variability of the Sexes at Birth " (*Amer. Jour. Sociol.*, No. 20, 1914–15).

The point to be emphasized as the outcome of this study is that, according to our present light, the psychological differences of sex seem to be largely due, not to difference of average capacity, nor to difference in type of mental activity, but to differences in the social influences brought to bear on the developing individual from early infancy to adult years. The question of the future development of the intellectual life of women is one of social necessities and ideals, rather than of the inborn psychological characteristics of sex.

Miss Thompson's findings are, of course, open to the objection that the principle guiding the selection of individuals for her experiment led her to study a very particular, unrepresentative group of persons. Women who in the eighteen-nineties, in spite of conventional prejudices and the generally inimical attitude towards " blue-stockings ", took up university studies must be considered the exception rather than the rule. They represented an *élite* with regard to their intellect as well as with regard to their character. The results obtained in a study of twenty-five university women prove nothing more nor less than the fact that there are women—whether many or only a few cannot be judged from the data—who equal masculine standards. Miss Thompson's research, therefore, interesting as it is as a beginning, is only of limited value.

Her work was, however, only the first of its kind and was followed by an increasing number of similar studies. The development of psychometric methods on the one hand, and social changes which brought women into the sphere of masculine occupations on the other, led to an intensified study of psychological sex differences.

During the First World War, women were called upon to play an important part in many fields of action and they acquitted themselves beyond all expectations. This fact greatly strengthened their social position and earned them political rights in many countries. The impoverishment of the middle-classes which followed that war, and which increased during the years of economic crisis, brought to middle-class women a share in the economic life of society. The ˙coincidence of economic crisis with woman's entry into the economic field was, in many respects, unfortunate. Although the critical economic situation was, as we have seen, a pre-condition of woman's liberation in the sense that it prepared the ground for her development and allowed her to disentangle herself from the tight grip of tradition, it was, at the same time, a danger to woman's emancipation.

The atmosphere of uncertainty, restlessness, and general dissatisfaction, caused by the economic crisis, was in many minds
associated with the fact that women now had jobs, and in women
themselves it aroused doubts as to the value of a liberation
purchased, as they saw it, at the price of security and happiness.
The fact that millions of men were out of work and family life
was upset, while, at the same time, women provided cheap
labour, created in many people a longing for the " good old
times ", when women had no rights but certain privileges, and
it made them wonder whether woman's place was not the hearth,
after all. A movement " back to the home " spread and it
was particularly marked in Germany, where it became one of
the strong-points of Nazi ideology.

As a consequence of these circumstances the centre of gravity
of the problem was shifted. The question was no longer one of
capability but became one of social expediency. It was increasingly evident that in a highly mechanized economy, such
as ours, which necessitates a huge administrative apparatus,
there were very many jobs which could be done as well by
women as by men and which women were willing to perform.
The problem, as it presents itself to us to-day, is no longer the
question : What are women able to do ?, but : What are the
limits to which society can go in granting women equality,
without endangering its continued existence and the happiness
of individuals ? From an enquiry into causes the problem
became an enquiry into the effects. This is another instance
to show how the way a question is put in the Social Sciences
depends on the social configuration in which it originates. At
a time when women crash-dive in combat-planes or present
themselves to a not even surprised public as record-breaking
snipers, the question has ceased to be one of qualitative differences. Instead, it has become one of ends and means. The
ends being a successful and well-functioning human society,
the change undergone with regard to our specific problem reflects
the change in progress in the social structure at large. The
problem of women presents only one particular instance exemplify-
ing the transition from the individualism of a liberal society to
the organization of a planned society.

Before the development of Individualism the problem of
woman's emancipation and, concurrently, the enquiry into her
aptitudes, could not arise ; after its decline and the move towards
a society which thinks primarily in terms of social welfare, it

could, in its original form, not survive. Only a liberalistic ideology, with its emphasis on individual achievement, created an atmosphere in which the question was primarily focussed on psychological abilities. Such ideals as the utmost development of the individual's faculties or " equal chances for everybody " bred an attitude of curiosity as to the peculiarities and possibilities of human character. This attitude was very typical for the era of expanding capitalism and it is largely responsible for the enormous progress of scientific psychology within the last decades.

REFERENCES

HELEN B. THOMPSON : *The Mental Traits of Sex. An Experimental Investigation of the Normal Mind in Men and Women* (Chicago Univ. Press, 1903).

K. PEARSON : " Variations in Man and Woman " in *Chances of Death* (E. Arnold, London, 1897).

L. S. HOLLINGWORTH : " Differential Action Upon the Sexes of Forces Which Tend to Segregate the Feeble-minded " (*Jour. Abn. Psych.*, No. 17).

L. S. HOLLINGWORTH AND H. MONTAGUE : " The Comparative Variability of the Sexes at Birth " (*Amer. Jour. Sociol.*, No. 20, 1914–15).

ANNE ANASTASI : *Differential Psychology* (Macmillan, New York, 1937).

CHAPTER VII

PSYCHOMETRIC TESTS : L. M. TERMAN AND C. C. MILES

The interest in assessing the characteristics of women grew steadily as time went on and was expressed in an ever-growing literature on feminine traits, abilities and attitudes. At the same time the technique of measurement reached a peak of development as a consequence of large-scale industrialization in which the need to deal with mass phenomena has put a premium on a quantitative approach. The number of books and studies published on the subject of psychological sex differences is legion. From the bibliography attached to this study it will be seen that they were particularly numerous in the nineteen-twenties and early thirties, coinciding with the increased penetration of women into the economic field. Special investigations and experimental studies have been made of almost any particular ability one can think of, extending from sex differences in mathematical aptitude to those in walking a tight-rope. Much valuable material has been obtained.

One of the most interesting and comprehensive attempts to establish the scale by which sex temperaments can be measured is *Sex and Personality : Studies in Masculinity and Femininity*, by Lewis M. Terman and Catherine Cox Miles.[1] This exhaustive experimental study of masculine and feminine personality traits does not try to solve the problem of the origin of those traits, nor does it attempt to fit them into a scheme either of nature or of society. Even less does it aim at establishing Platonic ideals of masculinity and femininity, eternally immutable types of Man and Woman. The authors proceed from the fact that there exists in our society a more or less universal belief in the essentially different characteristics of man and woman—although " there is much difference of opinion as to the differentiæ which mark them off "—and they attempt to discover, by the application of psychometric methods, the facts which form the basis of such opinions.

Its scientific intent is to free the concepts of masculinity and femininity from the irrelevancies and confusions which have become

[1] L. M. Terman and C. C. Miles : *Sex and Personality : Studies in Masculinity and Femininity* (McGraw-Hill Book Comp. Inc., New York and London, 1936).

attached to them as the result of superficial consideration of everyday behaviour. It is necessary to go back to the individual's attitudes, interests, information and thought trends which constitute the real personality behind the front presented to his fellows.[1]

The study tries to establish a reliable scientific measure, arrived at by experimental investigation, of the masculinity-femininity types, i.e. of whatever differences may in fact exist in present-day Western civilization. It aims at finding a measure which " can be applied to the individual and scored so as to locate the subject, with a fair degree of approximation, in terms of deviation from the mean of either sex ".

The principle of the investigation and the method adopted remove the danger, threatening most studies of such complex personality traits as masculinity and femininity, of easy generalization. Its purpose is to make possible in a purely empirical way " a quantitative estimation of the amount and direction of a subject's deviation from the mean of his sex, and to permit quantitative comparison of groups differing in age, education, interests, occupation and cultural milieu ".

The method used is a pencil and paper test of the questionnaire variety, composed of 910 items in two equivalent forms (form A consisting of 456 items, form B of 454) and applied to more than 5,000 persons. It consists of :

(1) a word association test ;
(2) an ink-blot test (which is another type of association test, trying the ideas evoked by differently shaped ink-blots on paper) ;
(3) a general information test, aiming at the measurement of factual differences in the repertories of men and women ;
(4) a test of emotional and ethical attitudes (confined to responses in anger, fear, disgust and pity, and in ethical censure) ;
(5) a test of interests ;
(6) a test of opinions ; and
(7) a test of introvertive response.

The tests of interests and attitudes proved to be the most valuable of the lot inasmuch as they helped to differentiate several types of population. The purpose of the investigation was concealed to the informants behind the title " Attitude–Interest Analysis " so as to arrive at more accurate results. (It is interesting to note that in the case of 31 college students to whom the purpose of the test was revealed beforehand, the mean for the

[1] Op. cit., pp. 453–4.

men was 3·6 points more masculine than the norm, that of women 5·1 points more masculine than the norm—a fact which shows the superior value attributed to a masculine ideal both by men and women.) The composition of the questionnaire was decided upon in a purely experimental way. It owes its origin to a test of interests in and practice of plays, games, and amusements, made by Professor Terman, and applied to gifted and to a control group of school children. From this study it became apparent that there was a definite dichotomy of interests between girls and boys. Those questions revealing the most striking differences were sorted out and formed the basis of the masculinity–femininity test, which was constantly sifted and amplified by a sort of trial-and-error method until its final form was arrived at. By elimination of questions which afforded only insignificant answers, by alterations and additions, the final M–F test was constituted which was applied to groups of seventh- and eighth-grade students, high school and college students, and to non-academic adults. The scoring was done by the use of stencils so as to obtain the most objective results.

" The test is based, not upon some theory as to how the sexes may differ, but upon experimental findings as to how they do differ, at least in the present historical period of the Occidental culture of our own country."

With this important restriction in view, the sexes were found to differ numerically in their preferences for particular kinds of games, colours, books, school subjects, occupations, literary styles, historical characters, and ideals. They were found to differ in the degree of introversion (this is in contrast to Miss Thompson's findings), dominance, inferiority feeling, conservatism, emotional stability, sense of humour, religious attitudes, and other traits. Men were proved, generally, to have a more distinctive interest in exploits and adventure, in outdoor and physically strenuous occupations, in machinery and tools, in science, physical phenomena and inventions. Women on the other hand " evinced a distinctive interest in domestic affairs and in æsthetic objects and occupations ; they distinctly prefer more sedentary and indoor occupations, and occupations more directly ministrative, particularly to the young, the helpless, the distressed ". Of all the special abilities the most distinct difference is a marked superiority in verbal, or linguistic, abilities in females of all age-groups, and a mechanical superiority in males. The authors go as far as to characterize mechanical interest as the outstandingly masculine trait, domestic activity as the typically feminine one.   It is probably outside the scope of their work to investigate —as Miss Thompson certainly would have done—whether these are not two different forms of the same kind of interest.   The difference between the interest in handling hammer and nail may not be so essentially different from the interest in handling a sewing machine ; and mixing ingredients for a food-dish might be only another variation of activities normally carried out in a chemical laboratory.   Here again, the outstanding masculine, and the outstanding feminine interest may be two manifestations of one psychological trend ; but the authors of this study are concerned with those manifestations only and not with the under-lying principles, as is natural in a study the object of which is the measurement of existing polarities between the sexes, and not an inquiry into their origin.   At school, girls tend to get better grades.   " Perhaps," says C. C. Miles,[1] " they are more docile in learning assigned lessons ; apparently they are industrious, and more readily identify their interests with a new purpose than men do."   She assumes that there are probably sex differ-ences in " innumerable personality traits, including humour, self-sufficiency, dominance, introversion, and perhaps especially neurotic tendency ".[2]

Moreover, differences were found in emotional disposition and direction.

Men manifest greater self-assertion and aggressiveness, they express more hardihood and fearlessness, more roughness of manners, language and sentiments . . .   Women express themselves as more compassion-ate and sympathetic, more timid, more fastidious and æsthetically sensitive, more emotional in general and more expressive of the emotions considered [this again in contrast to Miss Thompson], severer moralists, yet admit in themselves more weaknesses in emotional control and (less) in physique.   Compassion and sympathy are per-sonal rather than abstract, less a principled humanitarianism than an active sympathy for palpable misfortune and distress.   In disgust, in æsthetic judgment, and in moral censure the evidence is rather for the influence of fashion and of feeling than of principle and reason.

With regard to the reasons for this contrast the authors of the research are careful not to commit themselves to any definitive statement.

[1] Catherine Cox Miles : " Sex in Social Psychology ", in *Handbook of Social Psychology*, ed. Carl Murchison, (Worcester, Mass., & Oxford Univ. Press, London, 1935).
[2] *Sex and Personality*, op. cit., p. 448.

Masculinity and femininity are important aspects of human personality. They are not to be thought of as lending to it merely a superficial colouring and flavour ; rather they are one of a small number
of cores around which the structure of personality gradually takes
shape. The masculinity–femininity contrast is probably as deeply
grounded, whether by nature or by nurture, as any other which human
temperament presents. Certainly it is more specifically rooted in a
structural dichotomy than the cycloid–schizoid or the extrovertive–
introvertive contrasts . . . Whether it is less or more grounded in
general physiological and biological factors than these remains to be
seen . . . The M–F dichotomy, in various patterns, has existed
throughout history and is still firmly established in our mores. In
a considerable fraction of the population it is the source of many acute
difficulties in the individual's social and sexual adjustment, and in a
greater fraction it affords a most important impetus to creative work
and happiness.[1]

It is interesting to contrast this view with that of A. H. Maslow [2] who has taken dominance feelings as the point of reference
in contrasting personality types. (Maslow distinguishes between
dominance-feelings, dominance-status, and dominance-behaviour,
which are three different phenomena. By dominance-feelings he
means a complex psychological state determined by a person's
evaluation of his self.) He classifies people into high-dominance
and low-dominance types and regards this contrast as more
significant for personality development than the sex difference.
Most of the traits which, according to Terman and Miles's scale,
would be rated feminine are, in his view, correlated to low
dominance feelings. Self-consciousness, inferiority feeling, conventionality, introversion—which in many cases is a psychological
defence technique—social suggestibility, modesty, poor sense of
humour, are more consistently related to low dominance feelings
than to the feminine sex. Leadership, strength of social purpose
and of character, emancipation from trivialities, lack of fear and
shyness, self-reliance and a certain robustness and heartiness of
tastes—traits usually considered " manly " in our culture—are
found in many women to-day and are in direct proportion to
dominance feelings. These feelings are determined by cultural
factors, such as status, education and social ideal, and are only
indirectly linked to sex, inasmuch as those factors act differently
upon the two sexes. Masculinity and femininity are, in Maslow's
view,

---

[1] Op. cit., p. 451.
[2] A. H. Maslow : " Dominance, Personality, and Social Behaviour in Women "
(*Jour. of Social Psychology*, No. 10, 1939).

unsatisfactory concepts as a dimension of personality. A high dominance woman is more like a high dominance man than she is like a low dominance woman. This is, of course, not true for anatomical and physiological make-up and the external details of social conventionality, e.g. clothes, training, etc. If we speak of inner personality, however, we must conclude that it is better either (*a*) to describe as masculine both high-dominance men and women, and as feminine low-dominance men and women, or (*b*) to drop the terms altogether because they are misleading.[1]

Some of the implications of this study become obvious in Terman and Miles's research, too. And its main significance does not lie in the fact that it supplies a quantitative measurement by which the relative masculinity or femininity—within the framework of our own contemporary culture—of individuals or of groups can be scored ; nor does its chief interest rest upon its disclosure of the wide range of possible individual variations and of a considerable margin within which the two sexes overlap.

Between the two extreme scores of a young male athlete at the one end, and of an aged housewife at the other end, there is an almost infinite scope of intermediate gradations. At the centre of the scale the most masculine group of women, that of college women athletes, and the most feminine scoring group of males, that of passive male homosexuals, overreach each other.

The most interesting aspect of the investigation is the study of the correlation between the M–F score and such influences on personality as domestic milieu, education, age, occupation, abilities and interests, and such psychological factors as, e.g., cross-parent fixation. All these factors are found to have definite effect on the M–F score. The comparisons are no less interesting where they reveal no relationship, as, e.g., between the M–F score and physical measurements, health or intelligence.

Very roughly summarizing the findings one can say : There is a very marked influence of occupation on the M–F score. Mechanical occupations have a masculinizing effect, social or humane pursuits, culture and philanthropy, concerns of the spirit —as contrasted with material objectives—have a profoundly feminizing influence. High scholarship students, for instance, whose interests generally are more cultural than mechanical or athletic, score more feminine than low scholarship students ; religious groups are interesting examples for extremely feminine scores among men ; " Who is Who " men are found to be less

[1] Op. cit., p. 18.

masculine than other men of equal educational level. "Culture tends to make men's minds resemble women's ; intelligence and education to make women's minds resemble men's." [1]

Age expresses itself in increasing relative femininity of score in both men and women.

There is a definite relationship between the M–F score and both intensity and direction of interests. "Masculinity in women is associated with more intense positive interests, mental femininity is expressed in less intense interests—and these are directed toward the arts of home and social life—in indifference to the active, scientific and, in the better educated, intellectual interests."

Domestic milieu is found to have a strong correlation to the M–F score. Not only do parents, their character, work, mutual relation, etc., influence the score of their children, but vice versa, children, their number and sex, influence the score of their parents. "Highly masculine females seem especially likely to have a father who is an engineer or has otherwise displayed an interest in mechanics. The daughters, perhaps also the sons, of ministers or other religious workers seem more often than others to score highly feminine." The number of brothers and sisters, their relative age—all these are environmental factors positively related to the M–F score.

Naturally, education is one of the most marked influences on the M–F score, for it stimulates specific interests and directs them into certain channels, it fosters some attitudes and discourages others, and it forms the basis of most valuations in later life.

External influences on the M–F score of female occupational groups have been found in the following order of their importance :

(1) educational-intelligence influence (apparently quite generally operative) ;

(2) leadership influence (although related to the first trend it appears to have additional constituents) ;

(3) influence of the world of business and interests outside the home. (This "broad interest trend" is operative in both married and unmarried women who carry on activities in business or in the world of ideas . . . The influence of occupation tends to be larger than the influence of home duties after marriage. Women are more apt to score with their occupational group than with their housewifely group) ;

(4) marital influence (operating opposite to the three influences enumerated above).[2]

[1] Op. cit., p. 223.　　　　　　　　　　　　　　　　[2] Op. cit., p. 183.

In spite of this comprehensive evidence of the influence of environmental factors on the formation of a social character, the study is not a contribution to the discussion of the nature-nurture problem which has been the core of the dispute about the feminine character.

Certainly we do not have enough evidence to exclude the gross physiological differences between the sexes from any part in determining the distinctive preferences of the male for heavy muscular work and of the female for less active occupations, or in determining her greater sympathy for the young and weak or her greater interest in home life, with the relegation of outside interests to the male. To actual or anticipated childbearing and motherhood—differences physiologically determined—we have found no reason to deny a part in determining differences in overt habit and emotional dispositions. And in the present state of our ignorance it would be even more rash to deny the possible influence upon sex temperaments of the manifold differences between the sexes in their endocrine equipment and functioning . . . Whatever our view as to the innateness of the distinctive tendencies . . . our experimental evidence is inconclusive.[1]

The authors, however, stress the point that

singularly powerful in shaping our development are other people's expectations of us, past and present, as shown by their practice and their precepts . . . At any rate society in the shape of parents, teachers, and one's own fellows of whichever sex, expects these differences between the sexes, and literature reflects them. Irresistibly each sex plays the rôle assigned, even in spite of its own protests.[2]

To what extent are these different social rôles of men and women determined by physical constitution, by psychological and social factors ? This question cannot be answered by experimental evidence. What a psychometric research like that of L. M. Terman and C. C. Miles can do is to supply a kind of barometer on which the present state of the weather can be read in terms of exact figures ; and it may also make possible, with a fair degree of probability, predictions as to the very near future. But it does not give information about the nature of the traits it measures, and it does not differentiate between those trends which are " instinctive ", i.e. organically determined, and those which represent an adjustment to cultural norms. The measure it applies is taken from those very qualities it intends to measure. Its findings, therefore, owing to the nature of its method, are confined to establishing a mean of existing characteristics and to relating individual observations to that average. The practical

[1] Op. cit., p. 448–9.   [2] Op. cit., p. 449.

value of this method is undisputed. It is comparable to an elaborate and refined public opinion poll and serves the same purposes ; it gives information on a temporary state of affairs and on existing relations between single factors of the total situation. It supplies useful knowledge to educators, social welfare workers, politicians, industrialists—in fact, to all those interested in the reactions of the public. But it does not, and cannot, elucidate the essential nature of Masculinity and Femininity. It is a static approach. Sociologically speaking it corresponds to the attitude of those people in our society who unconsciously wish to stabilize the social and psychological states as they find them. Even if it is admitted that measurements only record differences as they exist at the time, in its ultimate effect such an investigation limits the horizon of the enquiry instead of broadening it. The dynamic potentialities in the transformation of sex characteristics can only be revealed by a dynamic approach which is bound to be historical in its method.

REFERENCES

Lewis M. Terman and Catharine Cox Miles : *Sex and Personality ; Studies in Masculinity and Feminity* (McGraw-Hill Book Comp. Inc., New York and London, 1936).

Catherine Cox Miles : " Sex in Social Psychology ", in *Handbook of Social Psychology*, ed. Carl Murchison, Worcester, Mass. and London, 1935.

A. H. Maslow : " Dominance, Personality and Social Behaviour in Women " (*Jour. of Social Psychology*, No. 10, 1939).

CHAPTER VIII

AN HISTORICAL APPROACH : MATHIAS AND MATHILDE VAERTING

More light is thrown on the character, origin and variability of those observed traits by the use of a kind of laboratory technique which separates the constant from the accidental factors by changing the variables. In the social field this means that we have to view each trait against different types of social and cultural background. The variety of feminine attitudes and traits which we shall find in this way will enable us to discriminate between the permanent, congenital characters and those which are part of a cultural pattern and the result of social tradition. This discrimination has been the central problem of the question of woman from its very beginning to the present day.

What is now called the nature of women [wrote John Stuart Mill in 1879] [1] is an eminently artificial thing, the result of forced repression in some directions, unnatural stimulation in others. It may be asserted, without scruple, that no other class of dependents have had their character so entirely distorted from its natural proportions . . . In the case of women a hothouse and stove cultivation has always been carried on of some of the capabilities of her nature . . . Men with that inability to recognize their own work which distinguishes the unanalytic mind, indolently believe that the tree grows itself in the way they have made it grow, and that it would die if one half of it were not kept in a vapourbath and the other half in the snow.

Although, to-day, we no longer agree with John Stuart Mill, who apparently assumes that, while woman grows up in an unnatural atmosphere, man is the free master of his, and her, destiny, independent of " unnatural " influences—the main problem is still the same. We have come to think of human beings generally as conditioned by their surroundings and moulded by the specific culture in which they grow up. Nevertheless, the controversy about the respective parts played by constitution and by social milieu in the formation of character is more acute in the case of women than of men. Generally speaking, the discussion about the influence of environment on the development of characters and ideologies is more violent when it deals with subjected or degraded groups of society than it is with ruling

[1] *The Subjection of Women* (London, 1879).

groups.   The *élite* does not doubt that it is *born* an *élite*, and it takes its qualities for granted.   Moreover, it is this class which sets the standards prevailing in a community and has sufficient prestige to enforce them upon the other groups.   Those groups in an inferior position, however, such as the working class, the Jews, Negroes, etc., justify their claim to equal rights by an emphatic reference to the impact of cultural conditioning.   The influence of milieu and history on the character of Jews is a constant topic of discussion.   The theory of the determinative effect of the economic and social " sub-structure " on the " ideological superstructure " forms the centre of Marxist ideology, and affords one of the strongest justifications to socialist claims. In this sense the origin of the sociological approach is strictly connected with the aspirations of rising groups, although it would be wrong to say that sociology, in its later development, is confined to them.

Of those socially subordinate classes women are the largest and most universal group.   The very obvious differences in physical structure and physiological function, moreover, and the very strong emotions linked up with this problem, have made their case even more controversial than that of other groups. Evidently men and women represent two biologically different types.   At the same time social organization has provided for them two different sets of behaviour and of attitudes, two different social rôles have been thought appropriate for them.   These social rôles vary in different cultures.   They are, therefore, institutional rather than physiologically conditioned.   Why one custom prevails in one society and not in another, and why the division of labour between the sexes is different in various social systems, or why some social habits have developed in certain cultures and not in others, all this cannot be explained by physiological differences between the sexes.   " What distinguishes societies and individuals is the predominance of certain attitudes over others, and this predominance depends . . . on the type of organization which the group has developed to regulate the expression of wishes of its members " (R. E. Park and Herbert A. Miller : *Old World Traits Transplanted*, New York, 1921, quoted by E. T. Hiller).[1]   Hiller adds : " In other words, attitudes correspond in the main to the established social structure.   The lines of cleavage between groups, whether of super-ordination or sub-

[1] E. T. Hiller : *Principles of Sociology* (Harper Bros., New York and London, 1933).

ordination, of amity, hostility, etc., are marked by distinctive attitudes ; and this is true also of the relations between the members within each group." [1]   However " natural " a social system may appear to the people concerned, and however much their division of labour and the respective attitudes of the two sexes may seem to be based on innate faculties, the fact that one set of attitudes and one type of behaviour is thought appropriate for women in one society and a different set in another society, is sufficient evidence of the social origin of the prevailing standards of behaviour.   The comparison of different cultures, of their social institutions and prevailing attitudes, thus proves to be the most effective means for the study of feminine character with a view to discriminate between traits of physiological and social origin.

Mathilde and Mathias Vaerting [2] chose the ancient civilizations of Egypt, Libya and Sparta as their main sources of material. This choice was determined not only by the fact that these were the matriarchal societies for which the greatest amount of historical evidence was available, but even more, it seems, by the consideration that, by taking highly civilized and reputed ancient cultures as examples, one could obviate an objection which is so easily made with reference to studies of primitive societies.   This objection is that, whatever different social systems other peoples may have developed, the fact that they did not succeed in creating great cultures was in itself sufficient proof that the patriarchal system and the particular division of labour between the sexes upon which our western civilization is based were preconditions of cultural achievement.   The authors refer to other matriarchal societies as well—such as the Cantabri, Chameros, Iroquois, Lycians, Kamchadales, Nicaraguans and others, but their main body of evidence is taken from the highly developed civilizations of Egypt and Sparta, and they view it in terms of the dominance and subjection of either sex.

The proposition of this study on sex differentiation is that any psychological comparison between men and women must be incorrect as long as it draws a parallel between two psychological types with very different social status.   The usual comparisons are made between dominant males and subordinate females, and they are bound to be unfair because they exclude

---

[1] Ibid., chap. V., pp. 70–1.
[2] Mathilde and Mathias Vaerting : *The Dominant Sex.   A Study in the Sociology of Sex Differences*, transl. (Allen & Unwin, London, 1923) from the German *Die weibliche Eigenart im Männerstaat und die männliche Eigenart im Frauenstaat* (Karlsruhe, 1923).

the influence of inferior status on the minds and attitudes of women and the influence of power on the mental and characterological development of men.   Thus they omit to consider a very important, maybe decisive factor in the formation of the intellectual, moral, and to some extent also the physical make-up of human beings.   A correct judgment on psychological types would have to take the social status and its impact on human character into consideration, and a just comparison can only be made between subjects of equal rank.   It would have to compare men in a dominant social position to women in an equally dominant position, and subordinate men to subordinate women.   This is the task the Vaertings have set themselves in studying the social rôles and corresponding attitudes of men and women in matriarchal societies.

It may facilitate the understanding of their theory to point out, before examining their findings, that at the bottom of their speculation—even if never referred to, nevertheless unmistakable —lies the Marxist philosophy of history.   Their doctrine is an application of Marx's concept of history, as the history of class struggles, to the special problem of women who, in their view, represent a suppressed class of our society.   Like Marx they regard ideologies, i.e. the sets of attitudes, beliefs, ideals, and rational choices prevailing in a community, as the expression of the economic and social structure.   In their interpretation of ancient history they have—like Marx—to struggle against the fact that all recorded history is written by people with the " master-class bias ".   In their special case this means that all history has been recorded by men brought up entirely in patriarchal traditions and incapable of understanding the fundamentally different organizations and ideologies of matriarchal societies.   In addition to this inability to understand divergent systems the Vaertings accuse historians of conscious as well as unconscious misrepresentations of facts.

Making allowance for those misrepresentations the Vaertings believe they have found sufficient documentary evidence for the statement that in a society in which women rule there was a complete reversal of the relative positions of the sexes, accompanied by a complete reversal of social attitudes.   " The canons whereby feminine peculiarities are determined in contemporary civilization are, in all their details, a pure product of the Men's State . . .   There is not a single masculine quality which cannot be paralleled as a ' feminine ' quality in the history of one race or another." [1]   Monosexual dominance thus creates, in the Vaertings' view, a typical mentality in the dominant sex which in a Men's State would be called " masculine ", in a Woman's State " feminine ", and a contrasting mentality for the subordinate sex (either masculine or feminine, as the case may be). Where inequality of the sexes exists, the division of labour, the rights of property, differential sex ethics, and the psychology of love and marriage—all favour one, the ruling sex.   The division is the same, no matter which of the two sexes is dominant.   The differentiation between the sexes, however much it may apparently be based on biological qualities, thus boils down to the expression of different power positions.

The domination of one sex is expressed in terms of (a) the legal position (including property rights), (b) the division of labour, (c) ideologies (including moral codes, religion, sex ethics, ideals of beauty, etc.).

(a) *Legal Position* : Where women rule—so the Vaertings assert—man contributes the dowry which becomes part of the woman's property of which she has the sole right to dispose. The husband adopts the name and nationality of his wife. Woman alone has the right to divorce her partner, should he no longer please her.   Children are called after their mother and inherit from her.   Their social position depends on that of their mother.   Girl children are considered of more value than boys, and where infanticide is practised at all, it is practised on boys. It is incumbent on women to care for their aged parents and to provide for their husband.   (The ancient Egyptian word for woman is identical with " the one who clothes her husband ".)

(b) *The Division of Labour* is, in the Vaertings' view, entirely dependent not on specifically sexual peculiarities, but upon the dominant social position of either sex.   " The division of labour between the sexes originates in this way that the dominant sex tries to stabilize its power and to secure greater freedom for itself by providing food for the subordinate sex." [2]   Where women rule they carry on the occupations outside the home, whilst the men " look after the household and care for the family ".[3]   " The dominant sex, male or female, as the case may be, tends to restrict the subordinate sex to work in the home and to family cares. The behaviour of dominant woman in this respect is exactly like the behaviour of dominant man."   Household duties, nursing, care of the babies, are considered typically masculine

[1] Ibid., p. 24.   [2] Ibid., p. 77.   [3] Ibid., p. 64.

occupations. The Vaertings refer to the testimony of Hero-
dotus, of Sophocles (*Oedipus at Colonus*) and to the Talmud,
for the fact that in Egypt women did men's jobs, and vice versa.
Of the Kamchadales it is said : " For these men home is the
world. When away from home they cannot feel at ease without
the protection and the company of their wives." [1] Equally, all
prestige is connected with women's work in the Women's State.
" Not even a promise of high pay could induce a Kamchadale
woman to undertake sewing, laundry-work and similar services," [2]
because these " men's jobs " would be considered beneath
woman's dignity. The peculiar custom of the couvade, still in
sway in some primitive societies, is explained by the Vaertings
as a token of the obligation in the Women's State of the father
to care for the new-born infant.

(*c*) *Ideologies*. Dependent on the state of legal and economic
supremacy is the psychological attitude of the sexes to each other.
" Dominance in married life runs strictly parallel with dominance
in the State." [3] Where woman rules, it is she who takes the
active part in courtship and wooing. Testimonies of this practice
appeared to the minds of later periods—biassed, as they were,
by the ideology of the man-state—as signs of such obscenity that
they were systematically censured and suppressed. There are
love poems probably written by women, full of admiration of
male grace and beauty. Subordination to the marriage partner
is in the Women's State the part of the husband. In Egyptian
marriage contracts handed down to us " the husband has expressly
to pledge himself to obey his wife ". [4] Chastity and conjugal
fidelity are demanded from man, and his unfaithfulness is often
severely punished. The double standard of sexual morality,
which always develops under mono-sexual dominance, runs in
favour of the dominant sex: the obligations of the wife in the
Women's State are less exacting than those of her husband.
" The dominant sex, whether male or female, has sexual freedoms
which are sternly forbidden to the subordinate sex by custom, the
moral code, and in many instances by law." [5] " Even the
monogamic principle proved impotent to hinder the development
of a duplex sexual morality." In Sparta, e.g., in spite of a monogamous marriage system polyandry was practised, and Plutarch
reports that the infidelity of women was even somewhat glorified

[1] Ibid., p. 70.
[2] Ibid., p. 71, quoted from Meiners' *Geschichte des weiblichen Geschlechts*.
[3] Ibid., p. 28.   [4] Ibid., p. 28.   [5] Ibid., p. 35.

there. In Egypt " the obligation of conjugal fidelity was not imposed upon women " and no stigma was attached to either the mother of an illegitimate child or to the child itself.

The methods used by the subordinate men to get their own way are very much like those considered to be typically feminine in our society. " Among the Kamchadales a husband never secured anything from his wife by force," Meiners reports, " but achieved his ends only by the humblest and most persistent petitions and caresses."

The relative age of husband and wife is reversed in the Women's State.

Far from being dependent upon biological and psychological sexual differentiation the relationship in the matter of ages is simply a consequence of monosexual dominance. The supremacy of either sex tends to establish a particular age relationship between husband and wife, the rule being that in marriage the member of the dominant sex is in almost all cases considerably older than the member of the subordinate sex . . . The chief determinant here is the duty of providing for the spouse, inasmuch as this duty devolves upon the dominant sex.[1]

There is a one-sided valuation of early marriage in the subordinate sex : In the Women's State unmarried men are regarded with contempt and ridicule, just as in our society spinsters are the one-sided subject of derision. In Sparta bachelors were even deprived of their civic rights.

Modesty is the rôle assigned to the subordinate sex ; it is a womanly virtue in the Men's State, a specifically masculine quality in Women's State. (The lack of modesty in Spartan women shocked the rest of Greece. Euripides reports with horror and disgust that in Sparta naked women wrestled with men.) It is imposed on the subordinate sex as a guardian of its chastity, and, in the wooed person, it acts as an incitement to the wooer. Moreover the dominant sex is always inclined to regard the other sex predominantly as sexual beings and its own members as sexually neutral. That is why, under monosexual rule, " the subordinate sex is the main topic of erotic art ; for works of art are exclusively produced by members of the dominant sex ".[2] For the same reason the phallus cult, traces of which are found in many primitive cultures, is associated with feminine rule.

The subordinate sex, i.e. the sex which plays the passive part in courtship and which, as a consequence of its restriction to home duties, has more leisure than the dominant sex, displays the greater

[1] Ibid., p. 43.   [2] Ibid., p. 107.

tendency to bodily adornment and finery.   Uniformity in dress and hair style are characteristic of the dominant sex.

> From the 4th Dynasty to the 18th, the women of Egypt, princess and peasant women alike, continued to wear the same sort of dress —a simple garment without folds [quoted from Erman].

Leisure increases erotic susceptibility.   Since the members of the other sex have less leisure, the pent-up erotic passion of the house-keeping sex seeks an outlet in the practice of bodily adornment—which was primitively regarded (and is unquestionably still regarded to-day) as a preparatory love-act.   There may also contribute an impulse to please the members of the other sex who are the objects of sexual desire.

The more absolute the dominion of one of the sexes, the more vigorously does it maintain its monopoly of extra-domestic avocations. As a consequence, it becomes increasingly overburdened with work, with a concomitant decrease in leisure and a decline in interest for sexual matters.   Wherewith the main motives for bodily adornment disappear and its practice tends to be discarded as superfluous and as merely a nuisance.[1]

Finally, monosexual dominance expresses itself not only in institutions, customs and attitudes, but even in the bodily development of the sexes and, accordingly, in the prevailing ideals of beauty.   Outdoor occupations, freedom of movement and an active life have as a consequence greater stature and muscular strength.   " It is home work, in especial, that impairs bodily fitness." [2]   " The members of the subordinate sex always exhibit a comparative obesity, no matter whether they be men or women." [3]   The ruling sex always possesses superior physical capacity.   Bachofen says :

> It is well known that the physical strength of women grows proportionally with the decline in the physical strength of men.   If to this there be superadded the ennobling influence which the consciousness of power and its exercise have upon them, whilst men are burdened by a sense of enslavement and are depressed by the performance of servile tasks, it is natural that the disparity between the two sexes should soon become more prominent.   A physical degradation of the men and an increasing physical fitness of the women are the necessary outcome of such condition.

While muscular strength and physical fitness are attributes of the dominant sex, beauty is considered as characteristic of the subordinate sex.   This may be connected with the fact that the dominant looks upon the other sex as the embodiment of sexual

---

[1] Ibid., p. 92.   [2] Ibid., p. 76.   [3] Ibid., p. 85.

qualities of which beauty is a prominent one, and that the point of view of the ruling sex dominates the outlook of the entire community. These physical differences, and the superior intelligence generally associated with the dominant sex, are always regarded as innate qualities connected with the bodily constitution of men and women. It is interesting to note that Isis, the female deity, was the legislator and the embodiment of intellectual functions, whereas Osiris, the male deity, was the benefactor, the symbol of affection and sympathy,[1] the exact reversal of the qualities thought characteristic for the two sexes in our own culture.

To sum up, the psychological traits thought typically " feminine " in our society, but found by the Vaertings to be attributes of subordination in either sex, wherever there is an institutionalized inequality of the sexes, are the following :

Passive part in love-making ;
Obedience and submission, tendency to submit to commands and rules ;
Dependence on the spouse ;
Fearfulness ;
Modesty ;
Chastity, bashfulness, " maidenly " reserve ;
Love of home, restricted interests outside ;
Tender care for babies (commonly called " motherliness ") ;
Relatively more monogamous inclinations ;
Interest in bodily adornment, love of finery.

From the extensive quotations given it will be clear that the picture with which we are presented by Mathilde and Mathias Vaerting is rather a sketch drawn in black and white. To be more precise : notwithstanding their use of historical examples in support of their theory the Vaertings deal, like Weininger, with " ideal types ", not with historical realities. The tendency to reduce all the psychological differences of sex to one single principle—the principle of " monosexual dominance "—makes for oversimplification. The proposition of the " Dominant Sex " is, that human nature is only one, but that it manifests itself in two psychological types whose development depends on the relatively dominant or subordinate rôle which a group is called upon to play in society. This theory is a very important step

[1] Ibid., p. 115.

towards a functional view of psychological traits. It is a first attempt to see attitudes and behaviour patterns not in themselves but in their dependence on specific social organizations of which they are expressions. But the Vaertings overlook, firstly, the almost unlimited number of possible variations in social patterns and in psychological types. They think in terms of a contrast between the personality of the two sexes such as exists in their own society, and they simply reverse it in their application to matriarchal societies. But nature, and in this case human nature, is much richer than the Vaertings conceive, and it has provided innumerable variations of social patterns and personality types. " Human cultures do not fall into one side or the other of a single scale," says Margaret Mead in her criticism of the Vaertings.[1]

In expecting simple reversals—that if an aspect of social life is not specifically sacred, it must be specifically secular ; that if men are strong women must be weak—we ignore the fact that cultures exercise far greater licence than this in selecting the possible aspects of human life which they will minimize, overemphasize, ignore.

Secondly, Mathilde and Mathias Vaerting overestimate the part of power in the making of personality. No doubt, the fact that an individual belongs to a ruling or a suppressed group greatly colours his outlook and affects his character. But it certainly is a mistake to think of dominance as the only deter-minant factor of personality. Among the many influences which society exercises upon the formation of character the fact of a relative power-position is only one and must be seen in its right proportions. The attempt to single out one aspect and to use it as a sort of master-key that opens all the secret doors to person-ality-traits, leads to a distortion of facts and to an undue simplifica-tion. Neither is power the only constituent of personality, nor is society divided into two groups of Haves and Have-nots along a line which marks the division of the sexes. It becomes evident that the Vaertings, free as they are from the " master-class bias " of which they accuse other historians, have fallen victims to a servant-class bias which is only a reversal of it. Their theory reflects no less a class ideology for being in opposition to prevailing ideas.

Thirdly, by making simply everything sociologically con-ditioned (apart from the strictly physical aspects of reproduction) they hardly leave anything as a distinctive feature of the feminine sex. They deny altogether the possible influence of physiological

[1] In *Sex and Temperament*, p. xix.

differences on the mind, instead of gradually restricting their significance to what is provable from carefully selected evidence.

It is fairly apparent that the authors started their work with a certain conception, fixed *a priori*, which they set out to prove, and they selected their material to fit into their theory. Their method, therefore, is very often deductive. Such statements as, e.g. : " The absence of prostitution where women rule is therefore a self-evident phenomenon (*sic*), a necessary outcome of the working of the law of reversal," [1] is a conclusion which already takes for granted the principle which they are only about to prove. It is not our task here to criticize the value of the Vaertings' anthropological evidence. Our main concern is to reveal the ideological basis underlying scientific research. And there the framework of the Vaertings' study seems to be set beforehand, as already stated, by the acceptance of a theory which is a modification of Marx's philosophy of history. We find Marx's doctrine that ideologies are the superstructure of the economic conditions of a society transformed into the Vaertings' theory that so-called " masculine " and " feminine " traits are psychological manifestations of an either dominant or subordinate social position. We recognize Marx's concept of history in terms of class-struggles in the Vaertings' assumption of a pendulum movement between female and male domination. In their view evolution went from an original state in which women ruled, to a state of masculine domination, passing through a transitory phase of sex equality (in which, for instance, the Teutons were found at the time of Tacitus) ; the Vaertings see, to-day, the pendulum swinging back and, at the present stage, approaching again an intermediate state of equality. They think that the change was a necessary consequence of the abuses to which any hegemony ultimately leads owing to its inner laws—just as Marx thought capitalism would work itself out and change, more or less automatically, into a socialist state.

Finally, like Marx, the Vaertings conceive of a utopian state of a " classless " society in the future which, in terms of their study, means a society in which neither sex dominates and in which sex differences are reduced to the physiologically unavoidable minimum. In that society everyone, no matter whether man or woman, will be valued as an individual, according to his or her personal merits, and not as a member of any defined group. " Equality of rights will bring the golden age of the highest

[1] *The Dominant Sex*, p. 52.

possible development of individuality and the highest attainable sexual happiness. It will bridge the gulf which monosexual dominance opens between the sexes, the gulf across which spiritual and sexual harmony can today so rarely be established." [1] In their description of the ideal state of the future, which will bring a " climax of intimacy and happiness " into family life,[2] the Vaertings let themselves be carried away by their enthusiasm and become almost lyrical. It is here that the emotional trend underlying the study becomes most obvious.

The parallel with Marx is, however, not complete : it does not go as far as to include a dictatorship of women as the necessary preliminary stage to the ideal " classless " society. For Mathilde and Mathias Vaerting hope that we may be able to stabilize the pendulum at the moment when, on its way back, it has again reached the point of a complete balance of power between the sexes.

The stress on the connection between the Vaertings' theory and Marxism may have given the impression that the " Dominant Sex " was an " Equalitarian Manifesto " rather than a scientific approach to the problem of sex differences.

To a certain extent this may, in fact, be the case. But though the enquiry is based on thinking which, in many respects, seems wishful rather than scientific, it has the merit not only of supplying some striking evidence for their case, bound to have an enormous appeal to all those who sympathize with the Women's Cause, but mainly of being an attempt to see the psychological traits of masculinity and femininity in their social context, as functions of the social structure, and not as static qualities. This dynamic conception of human traits represents a valuable contribution to true sociological thought. In the history of thought new methods of looking at things nearly always present themselves first in exaggerated terms which are used in order to stress their differential point of approach. It is then left to later discussions to develop the qualifications under which the new observations are valid.

REFERENCES

MATHILDE AND MATHIAS VAERTING : *The Dominant Sex. A Study in the Sociology of Sex Differences*, transl. (Allen & Unwin, London, 1923) from *Die weibliche Eigenart im Männerstaat und die männliche Eigenart im Frauenstaat* (Karlsruhe, 1923).

E. T. HILLER : *Principles of Sociology* (Harper Bros., New York and London, 1933).

J. J. BACHOFEN : *Mutterrecht und Urreligion* (1st. publ. Stuttgart, 1861).

---

[1] *The Dominant Sex*, p. 188.   [2] Ibid., p. 190.

CHAPTER IX

THE ANTHROPOLOGICAL APPROACH :
MARGARET MEAD

This attitude of taking a functional view of things has been widely adopted in the social sciences. It is one of the essential characteristics of sociology ; it finds expression in modern anthropology ; and now it is being applied to psychology as well.

Modern anthropology has gone a step further than the Vaertings. It tends to regard each culture as a complete entity of which social characters, the attitudes of its members, and the prevailing behaviour patterns are just as much a part as its laws, customs and institutions. The Vaertings selected one fundamental principle common to all societies—that of social power —and related it to certain sets of psychological traits. They picked out one specific phenomenon, " monosexual dominance ", and traced it in different social systems, leaving out of account all other aspects which together compose a culture. This method is sufficient to prove their case, namely that there is a connection between certain character-traits, usually termed " masculine ", and domination, and between other traits, commonly called " feminine ", and social submission. This procedure has all the advantages, but also all the limitations of an abstraction. It is as if, for instance, a psychologist were to study single elements of the human mind (for instance memory, attention, intelligence, etc.), but should disregard the total aspect of personality. This is, in fact, what psychologists have done for a very long time, and they have produced a a wealth of very necessary knowledge and most valuable observations. These studies of particular details form, so to speak, the bricks of which the edifice of psychology is composed. More recent schools of psychology, however, have adopted the view that one cannot do justice to human personality by the observation and summing up of single traits. Living organisms generally, and human beings in particular, are more than the sum total of single elements. The same psychological trait may have very different causes and different meanings in various individuals. Those statistical methods which describe persons in terms of their measured abilities have proved to be inadequate for the understanding of human character and personality. It is the merit of Freud and the various psycho-analytical schools to have emphasized the necessity of studying a person's life-history, his particular circumstances and experiences, in order to understand what part single features play in the total make-up of personality. Gestalt-theory, too, has maintained that the whole gives meaning to its parts and therefore has precedence over them. The fact of being part of an integrated unit imparts a special quality to each and all elements which therefore cannot be understood disconnectedly.

A similar view has been adopted by modern anthropology with regard to human societies. (It is worth noting that, here again, changes in the scientific outlook have become apparent in different branches of knowledge more or less simultaneously.) It arose as a natural reaction to the dangerously increasing specialization of the sciences during recent decades. Contemporary anthropology views individual cultures in the same way as contemporary psychology views individual persons : as unique and integral entities. " Each culture creates distinctively the social fabric in which the human spirit can wrap itself safely and intelligibly . . . Each people makes this fabric differently, selects some clues and ignores others, emphasizes a different sector of the whole arc of human potentialities." [1]

This total and comprehensive aspect of society opens new ways of understanding social organization as well as human character. In an integrated culture each part has a certain function. Behaviour patterns and human attitudes are no less part of the social mechanism than codes, rituals, customs and mores. In a cultural system all these parts are in harmony. The whole rhythm of culture would be upset unless all the parts were in tune with each other. The chaos we are witnessing in our contemporary civilization bears out the truth of this fact. The disharmony between technical and moral development, between science and religion, and between contradictory ideals and beliefs, has created a state of confusion which is apparent no less on the objective side of our culture, i.e. in the field of economics and social institutions, than in its subjective sphere, in the personality structure of contemporary man.

A functional view of culture implies that attitudes and feelings are not only in a high degree moulded by the social climate in which they develop (this being the Vaertings' assumption), but

[1] Margaret Mead : *Sex and Temperament in Three Primitive Societies*, pp. xiii–xiv (George Routledge & Sons, London, 1935).

that they have an active part to play in the smooth functioning of a society.   They are one of the instruments by which a society regulates its activities—and a very powerful instrument at that. Attitudes and beliefs, being largely rooted in the subconscious sphere of personality, are more compulsive than laws and regulations.   The attitude of submissiveness, for instance, cultivated in women, was a far more effective means of their subjection than marriage laws and church precepts.

This does not mean that culture exercises a systematic pressure on human attitudes in order to use them as " instruments " for certain purposes.   If the use of the term instrument gives this impression it would be inexact.   The fact that human attitudes are a powerful and stabilizing factor in any culture must not be confused with the question of their origin.   It is true that society could not function if its subjective side, as expressed in human attitudes, beliefs and opinions, were not a counterpart of and in accord with its objective, factual conditions.   But the attitudes arise spontaneously by the psychological fact that physical data are given to the human mind in the form of values. The objects constituting our experience are not just " natural " things independent of any valuation, but by their contact with the human mind they accept a certain meaning and evoke a subjective standpoint, i.e. an attitude.[1]   Thus social reality presents itself under two aspects correlated with each other : in the objective form of values and the subjective form of attitudes. Only if we keep this in mind are we able to understand the social mechanism.

The fact that culture creates and gives sanction to certain standards of personality, i.e. the fact that society to a considerable extent directs the feelings and attitudes of its members in the same way as it regulates their behaviour—not only by rules but by consent, example and education, has long been generally accepted in the history of literature.   It is a very peculiar phenomenon that a fact established and taken for granted in òne department of human knowledge should have failed to penetrate general consciousness, and moreover, that the acceptance of its implications should have met with considerable psychological resistance.   The tenacity with which many of the psychologists even to-day cling to their abstraction of the " Normal Man " is, in fact, astonishing.

[1] Viz., the excellent methodological notes in W. I. Thomas' and Florian Znaniecky's *The Polish Peasant in Europe and America* (Knopf, New York, 1927).

Anyone familiar with the history of European literature is aware of the fact that changes of style are more than mere expressions of a new sense of literary form.   They are symptoms of a change in the socially approved pattern of personality.   The biologically determined " human nature " had not changed when the sagacious, stoic and cool sage of the eighteenth century gave way to the sentimental, passionate type of Rousseau's time. There were periods of " Storm and Stress " in which impetuosity and a revolutionary temperament were just as much part of the style as long hair and fluttering ties, and they alternated with times in which disappointments in love caused innumerable young men to share the sufferings of Werther.   On the same soil the same human race has produced in series temperamental types as widely different as visionary mystics and Babbitts.

The implication which psychologists have been reluctant to recognize is that, within the wide range of human possibilities, under the impact of culture, people develop some characteristics and neglect others, and that they live up to certain standards set for them by their society.   Organic nature sets the limits to the range of cultural forms.   But within those limits the number of variations is almost infinite.   Biologically determined human nature is a *condition* of the development of personality traits, not the *cause*—as psycho-analysts contend.   To have sufficiently adequate material is a necessary condition of building a house ; the reasons why we build it, and why we build it in a certain way, may be manifold and are a different proposition altogether. Trying to single out any one reason why a culture should develop a certain character type would be an oversimplification.   The fact of a literary style, and concomitantly of a characterological fashion, cannot be explained by any single factor, be it the state of economic development, the political situation, historic events, new scientific discoveries, or the imitation of eminent examples. The concurrence of all these, and probably many other, circumstances is responsible for the creation of a fashion.

In the same way a society attributes different social rôles, sets different standards, for men and women, rich and poor, old and young, at a given time.

The enormous impact socially sanctioned patterns have on the development of human abilities is well illustrated by a striking example given by Margaret Mead : among the Mundugumor people of New Guinea to be born with the umbilical cord wound round one's neck is considered to be the sign of a future artist.

The association in the minds of those people of a specific and very exceptional manner of birth with the ability to paint is so strong that as a psychological consequence " only those who are so born can paint good pictures, while the man born without a strangulating cord labours humble and unarrogant, and never attains any virtuosity ".

Margaret Mead is convinced that of the thousand and one innate differences between men and women insisted upon in our society " there are many which show no more immediate relationship to the biological facts of sex than does ability to paint to manner of birth ".[1]

In order to get to the root of the problem and to investigate the connection between the mental traits and biological facts of sex—or, as Margaret Mead puts it, in order to discover " the cultural plot behind human relations " [2]—Margaret Mead went to New Guinea and studied three different primitive societies : the mountain-dwelling Arapesh, the river-dwelling Mundugumor, and the lake-dwelling Tchambuli.

The reasons for choosing primitive cultures for the study of social problems are obvious : These primitive societies offer examples of social organizations in their simplest form. They are the nearest possible approach to the ideal laboratory condition of reducing complex phenomena to their simple basic elements. " . . . here we have the drama of civilization writ small, a social microcosm alike in kind but different in size and magnitude ".[3]

In contrast to the Vaertings' book this is a field-study based on first-hand observation and research. It, furthermore, differs from the Vaertings' work inasmuch as Margaret Mead did not set out to prove a certain theory fixed beforehand. The conclusions which she drew from her study were not made to conform with her preconceived ideas. It is true that when she decided to investigate the cultural roots of sex temperaments she started with a certain bias in favour of social conditioning of character traits. But she was convinced, as she admits in the introduction to her book, that there was such a thing as a " natural sex temperament ". Different cultures would present us with different deviations from the normal, and the task of the scientist would be to distil, so to speak, that " natural sex temperament " from all cultural accessories by a process of comparative analysis. To discover this " natural sex temperament " Miss Margaret Mead set out on her journey. She came back with the conviction that

[1] Ibid., p. xvi.   [2] Ibid., p. xviii.   [3] Ibid., p. xvi.

the object of her enquiry was but a phantom—" that the temperaments which we regard as native to one sex " are instead " mere
variations of human temperament to which the members of either
or both sexes may, with more or less success in the case of different
individuals, be educated to approximate ".[1]   Her conclusion, in
other words, is that the biological facts of sex difference are
irrelevant to the social characters of men and women, and that
these are merely arbitrary constructs.

Does, then, Margaret Mead confirm the Vaertings' assumption that the personality-traits of either sex are the function of
their relative social position ?   Emphatically not.   " While every
culture has in some way institutionalized the rôles of men and
women, it has not necessarily been in terms of contrast between
the prescribed personalities of the two sexes, nor in terms of
dominance or submission." [2]   Margaret Mead goes on to say :

No culture has failed to seize upon the conspicuous facts of age and
sex in some way, whether it be the convention of one Philippine tribe
that no man can keep a secret, the Manus' assumption that only men
enjoy playing with babies, the Toda prescription of almost all domestic
work as too sacred for women, or the Arapesh insistence that women's
heads are stronger than men's.   In the division of labour, in dress,
in manners, in social and religious functioning—sometimes in only a
few of these respects, sometimes in all—men and women are socially
differentiated and each sex, as a sex, forced to conform to the rôle
assigned to it.   In some societies, these socially defined rôles are mainly
expressed in dress or occupation with no insistence upon innate
temperamental differences.[3]

The reason inducing Margaret Mead to adopt such radical
relativism with regard to sex temperaments was the observation
that among the three primitive societies which she investigated
one, the Arapesh, displayed homogeneously a temperament which
we, according to our conceptions, would call feminine ; the other,
the Mundugumor, showed uniformly characteristics which we
should attribute to men only ; whereas the third society, that of
the Tchambuli, has institutionalized contrasting sex temperaments for men and women which, however, represent a complete
reversal of the sex attitudes of our own culture—and this in spite
of the existence of formal patrilineal institutions.

Both among the Arapesh and the Mundugumor there is

no idea that men and women are different in temperament.   They
allow them different economic and religious rôles, different skills,

[1] Ibid., p. xxii.   [2] Ibid., p. xix.   [3] Ibid., pp. xix-xx.

different vulnerabilities to evil magic and supernatural influences . . .
But any idea that temperamental traits of the order of dominance,
bravery, aggressiveness, objectivity, malleability, are inalienably
associated with one sex, as opposed to the other, is entirely lacking.[1]

Among the Arapesh—a tribe living in a poor, mountainous
country on primitive agriculture and the raising of pigs—both
men and women are co-operative, unaggressive, contented,
responsive to the needs of others, " maternal " in their attitude
towards children, unaware of a powerful sex drive in either sex.
They belong to one human type undifferentiated with regard to
either birth or rank or age or sex. Such attitudes traditionally
ascribed to women in our culture, as " passivity, responsiveness,
and the willingness to cherish children ", are set up as a pattern
for both men and women alike in the Arapesh society.

In contrast, this " feminine " character type is " outlawed
for the majority of women as well as for the majority of men "
in the society of the Mundugumor, a head-hunting tribe, who
are—women as well as men—a violent, jealous, suspicious people
of " ruthless aggressive, positively sexed individuals, with the
maternal cherishing aspects of personality at a minimum ". This
society, too, has only one standardized pattern for all its members
without distinctions as to rank, age, or sex (the sole exception,
mentioned at the beginning, being the class of artists, a category
apart, segregated by the fact of being born with their umbilical
cord round their necks).

Utterly different from either of these tribes is the culture of
the Tchambuli, a lovable people, dedicated to the pursuit of
religious and artistic occupations. In this society women are,
in fact—by custom rather than by institutions—the managing,
dominating part. They represent a robust, practical, possessive
type, impersonal in outlook, definite in their plans, concerned
with the organizing " businesslike " side of life. They provide
the food supply for the community by fishing, and they produce
the principle article of trade, mosquito bags, which, like the fish,
are bartered for other commodities with neighbouring tribes.
They are " actively sexed and willing to initiate sex relations ".

In contrast, men are delicate and responsive, emotionally
dependent, playful and unpractical, coquettish and rather timid
in matters of sex, shy of meeting with refusal. They are chiefly
engaged in artistic and other non-utilitarian pursuits, in dancing,
painting, carving, and the elaboration of their decorative costumes.

[1] Ibid., p. xxi.

They are treated by their women with a kindly tolerance, like big children.

This evidence suggests that such qualities as aggressiveness, courage, independence, sexual activity, emotionality, gentleness, responsiveness, passivity, and many others which we are used to call either " masculine " or " feminine ", are " as lightly linked to sex as are the clothing, the manners, and the form of head-dress that a society at a given period assigns to either sex ".[1]

The evidence is overwhelmingly in favour of the strength of social conditioning. In no other way can we account for the almost complete uniformity with which Arapesh children develop into contented, passive, secure persons, while Mundugumor children develop as characteristically into violent, aggressive, insecure persons. Only to the impact of the whole of the integrated culture upon the growing child can we lay the formation of the contrasting types. There is no other explanation of race, or diet, or selection, that can be adduced to explain them.

Margaret Mead is convinced that " the same infant could be developed into a full participant in any of these three cultures ",[2] provided the child was settled there very soon after birth, for the training of a personality type starts in early childhood.

The means by which a society enforces the acceptance of a selected pattern are manifold. " This choice is embodied in every threat of the social fabric—in the care of the young child, the games the children play, the songs the people sing, the structure of political organization, the religious observance, the art, and the philosophy." [3] Culture creates a coherent background, a mould into which characters grow and by which they are shaped.

Societies do not usually institutionalize only one character pattern, as in the case of the Arapesh or the Mundugumor. More elaborate social organizations will standardize more and different types. From the rich material supplied by nature in the shape of various temperaments, endowments, intellectual and emotional traits, culture may either create one model, " blending them together into a smooth but not particularly distinguished whole " or " it may isolate each type by making it the basis for the approved social personality for an age-group, a sex-group,

[1] Ibid., p. 280.   [2] Ibid., p. 281.   [3] Ibid., p. 284.

a caste-group, or an occupation group ".[1]   Among the Samoans, for instance, aggressiveness is a trait thought appropriate for middle-aged men of a certain rank.   It is regarded as unseemly in young people, and any child who displayed aggressive traits would be " punished with opprobrium ".   Our own society has in the same way selected single traits and institutionalized them in different classes, sects, occupational groups, sexes, etc.

An instance given by Margaret Mead is the characteristic behaviour pattern expected from a doctor.   " Bed-side manners " are, as Margaret Mead says, " the natural behaviour of some temperaments, and made the standard behaviour of the general practitioner in the medical profession ".[2]   The physician must either naturally, i.e. by temperament, be fitted for this pattern or must try to learn it and adopt, at least, its outward characteristics.

Similarly, Quakers display a certain attitude and certain temperamental traits which are " not necessarily innate characteristics of many members of the Society of Friends ", but have been institutionalized by the sect.

The same is true of the social personality of the two sexes, with the one essential qualification that a person temperamentally unfitted for the behaviour pattern demanded, for instance, by the code of the medical profession, would most probably not become a doctor.   In the sphere of occupations the individual in our society is more or less free to choose the profession most suitable to his endowments—or, at least, to avoid those for which he is unsuited by nature.   With regard to the patterns provided by culture for the two sexes this is unfortunately not the case ; a person is irrevocably born into one of two groups and has to adopt, once and for ever, the standards provided for it.

The traits that occur in some members of each sex are specially assigned to one sex and disallowed in the other.   The history of the social definition of sex differences is filled with such arbitrary arrangements in the intellectual and artistic field, but because of the assumed congruence between physiological and emotional endowment we have been less able to recognize that a similar arbitrary selection is being made among emotional traits also.[3]

If a society finds it useful, such is the argument of Margaret Mead, to establish a certain character pattern for a group of its members it will do so without regard to their actual qualities,

[1] Ibid., p. 285.   [2] Ibid., p. 285.   [3] Ibid., p. 286.

and it will, in almost all cases, succeed in shaping their personalities to its intents and purposes.

If a society insists that warfare is the major occupation for the
male sex, it is therefore insisting that all male children display bravery
and pugnacity.   Even if the insistence upon the differential bravery
of men and women is not made articulate, the difference in occupation
makes this point implicitly.   When, however, a society goes further
and defines men as brave and women as timorous, when men are forbidden to show fear and women are indulged in the most flagrant
display of fear, a more explicit element enters in.   Originally two
variations of human temperament, a hatred of fear or willingness to
display fear, they have been socially translated into inalienable aspects
of the personalities of the two sexes.   And to that defined sex-person-
ality every child will be educated, if a boy, to suppress fear, if a girl,
to show it.[1]

There are, of course, persons constitutionally unfitted to accept
a standard prescribed for the group into which they are born.
A very strong innate disposition in a direction opposed to the
norm of his group may not allow an individual to " wear perfectly
the garment of personality that his society has fashioned for
him ".[2]   He then will become an outsider, a maladjusted person,
unable to fulfil the functions provided for him by society, and
liable to become either a crank or a criminal.   Apart from those
" deviants which are physiologically inadequate, have defective
organs, glands, intelligence " there are, in addition, cultural
deviants, " individuals who are at variance with the values of
their society.   A type of unadjusted persons whose failure to
conform does not rest upon his own weakness and defect, nor to
accident, or to disease, but to a fundamental discrepancy between
his innate disposition and his society's standards ".[3]   Thus, a
violent, assertive temperament would make a person an outcast
in the Arapesh society.   The qualities which are the norm among
the Mundugumor—ruthlessness, aggression, strong sex drive—
would, if found in an Arapesh, make him a maladjusted, thwarted,
and probably utterly unhappy individual.   Vice Versa, a kind-
hearted, contented, or timid nature would among the Mundugumor bring a person into an outcast position comparable to
that of our village idiot.   Among the Tchambuli the possessive,

[1] Ibid., p. 287.
[2] Ibid., p. 289.
[3] Ibid., p. 292.   Margaret Mead is here in accordance with Ruth Benedict,
who, in Patterns of Culture, exposes a very similar theory (Houghton Mifflin Co.,
Boston, and Routledge, London, 1934).

dominating, practically-minded male and the timid, delicate, responsive female would be the maladjusted types. The more rigid a society is, and the less variations of personality-patterns it admits, the greater is its liability to create a class of outcasts, i.e. of socially useless, unhappy, sometimes even dangerous, individuals. The richer a society is in possible variations, and the less standardized the attitudes of its members are, the greater is the chance of every individual to develop his innate faculties in the highest degree. The chances of happiness for the individual increase with the increasing complexity of society— " by the mere existence of values different from those ' appropriate ' to one's own group, a compensation is offered which makes life more bearable ".[1] At the same time society would gain immensely by the recognition of many individual differences in temperament and endowment.

Where writing is accepted as a profession that may be pursued by either sex with perfect suitability, individuals who have the ability to write need not be debarred from it by their sex, nor need they, if they do write, doubt their essential masculinity or femininity . . . We must recognize that beneath the superficial classifications of sex and race the same potentialities exist, recurring generation after generation, only to perish because society has no place for them.[2]

The aim is, not to press individuals into categories fixed for them beforehand, but, instead, to shape our educational institutions in such a way as to enable the development of all existing abilities, however particular, and to encourage every child on the basis of its actual temperament.

No skill, no special aptitude, no vividness of imagination or precision of thinking would go unrecognized because the child who possessed it was of one sex rather than the other. No child would be relentlessly shaped to one pattern of behaviour, but instead there should be many patterns, in a world that had learned to allow to each individual the pattern which was most congenial to his gifts.[3]

This is idealism in the best liberal tradition. If one tried to fix a label to the ideology behind Mrs. Mead's study, it would be " Democratic Planning ". The study shows social science at the cross-road : on the one hand it has discovered the mechanism of social processes ; on the other it realizes the immense dangers of putting those instruments into the hands of sorcerer's apprentices. The knowledge that attitudes and personality traits are

[1] Ibid., p. 315.   [2] Ibid., p. 321.   [3] Ibid., p. 321.

socially produced—the basic conclusion of Margaret Mead's book —is a magic formula for anyone who "looks forward to a planned order of society". But everything depends on who uses it, and to what purpose it is used. In the hands of a totalitarian sorcerer this formula would be used to produce uniformity, rigid control, a short-termed and one-sided efficiency, and endless monotony and frustration. That is why Margaret Mead hastens to explain that her formula, the key to social planning, can, if used wisely, produce the ideal of the Greatest Happiness of the Greatest Number for an indefinite time. Plan for Variety ! Or : Plan for Democracy !—that is the moral to be drawn from her study.

Applied to the case of woman there are two wrong ways of planning, as opposed to one right way. The system prevailing until recently was the standardization of two sex temperaments as two " clearly contrasting, complementary, antithetical " personality types. All institutions of society were modelled to convey and to impress this dual standard, to the detriment of the many intermediate types which did not find enough scope within the prescribed standards to express their particular tendencies. Many thwarted personalities of either sex are the victims of this dualism.

An at least equally harmful procedure would be the abolition of distinctions altogether, entailing a " sacrifice in complexity ". This danger is particularly acute in times of a changing tradition. The gradual admission of women into a man-made society involves the risk of the universal adoption of one, the masculine, pattern. Society would gain nothing, but, on the contrary, would become considerably poorer, if in the process of women's emancipation all those qualities traditionally regarded as feminine were to be outlawed altogether. " The dangerous standardization of attitudes that disallows every type of deviation is greatly reinforced if neither age nor sex nor religious belief is regarded as automatically predisposing certain individuals to hold minority attitudes." [1]

Society needs, for its own progress and for the benefit of its members, opportunities for expressing as many " minority attitudes " as there are differences in temperament and native endowment.

Historically our own culture has relied for the creation of rich and contrasting values upon many artificial distinctions, the most striking

[1] Ibid., p. 315.

of which is sex. It will not be by the mere abolition of these distinctions that society will develop patterns in which individual gifts are given place instead of being forced into an ill-fitting mould. If we are to achieve a richer culture, rich in contrasting values, we must recognize the whole gamut of human potentialities, and so weave a less arbitrary fabric, one in which each diverse human gift will find a fitting place.[1]

It would be easy to produce a long list of examples from history and literature in support of this thesis of Margaret Mead. But to do so would be outside the framework of this study. Its object is to introduce the speakers and to try to trace their ideological background—not to enter into discussion or to supply examples in support of their cause. There is, however, one case in point which is worth quoting as an illustration of what Margaret Mead has stated in general terms. The particular instance is that of Virginia Woolf, who is said to have written the finest English prose of her time and who was tormented by the conflict of being a woman, i.e. expected to conform to a set pattern of behaviour and attitudes—a pattern which she in one of her essays labelled " the Angel of the House "—and, of having, what is called a " masculine mind ". This dilemma occupied a dominant place in her thoughts and was constantly on her mind, though at the same time she was aware that it was

fatal for anyone who writes to think of their sex. It is fatal to be a man or woman pure and simple ; one must be woman manly or man womanly. It is fatal for a woman to lay the least stress on any grievance ; to plead even with justice any cause ; in any way to speak consciously as a woman. And fatal is no figure of speech ; for anything written with that conscious bias is doomed to death.[2]

This is, as Virginia Woolf sees it, one of the main reasons why Fascism has not been able to produce any work of poetry or fiction worth mentioning. The one-sided stress on virility, on " unmitigated masculinity ", produces a ground unfruitful for art. " Poetry," she says, " ought to have a mother as well as a father." The blame for a great deal of sterility in literature—and equally in the other arts—rests upon " all who have brought about a state of sex-consciousness ", that is upon conditions which, by assigning certain character-traits to certain biological classes, create conflicts and inhibitions in those who do not fit

[1] Ibid., p. 322.
[2] This and the following quotations are taken from the final pages of *A Room of One's Own* (Hogarth Press, London, 1929).

into the character-pattern provided for the group to which they, physiologically, belong.

All this pitting of sex against sex, of quality against quality ; all this claiming of superiority and imputing of inferiority, belong to the private-school stage of human existence where there are " sides ", and it is necessary for one side to beat another side and of the utmost importance to walk up to a platform and receive from the hands of the headmaster himself a highly ornamental pot.   As people mature they cease to believe in sides or in Headmasters or in highly ornamental pots . . .   So long as you write what you wish to write, that is all that matters . . .   But to sacrifice a hair of the head of your vision, a shade of its colour, in deference to some Headmaster with a silver pot in his hand or to some professor with a measuring-rod up his sleeve, is the most abject treachery, and the sacrifice of wealth and chastity which used to be said to be the greatest of human disasters, a mere flea-bite in comparison.

Here we have, applied to one particular department of culture, the case put forward by Margaret Mead in general terms.   In either case we meet with the claim of a person to be judged on his or her own, individual merits instead of being included under a general heading and subjected to collective judgment.   This is a claim common to all minority groups against whom there exist discriminations in a society, whether it be on racial, religious or other grounds.   It is characteristic that the protest against the inclusion under a general sex type should come from women although, obviously, it must be equally hard for some men to live up to the masculine standards of personality, and although—as both Margaret Mead and Virginia Woolf point out—the loss to society of valuable talent and character could be expected to be equally great in either case. But, naturally, those who are confined within spacious mansions do not feel the limitations imposed upon them as strongly as those interned within the four walls of a small room—though either group would benefit by free movement in open space.

Both Margaret Mead and Virginia Woolf do more, however, than merely put forward a claim for justice.   Their argument is not so much a problem of ethics, but of psychology.   They are less concerned with the protection of the weak—though this may be assumed to be implied in their proposition—but with the psychological ill-effects of arbitrary restrictions on the development of individuals and with the resulting evil consequences for the advance of culture.   They both agree that freedom from standardization is a necessary condition for the self-fulfilment of individuals, and that complexity of culture is the only guarantor of its progress.

There is, it seems, one objection to be made against Margaret Mead's interpretation of the social forces at work shaping the character patterns of personality. Margaret Mead appears to be somewhat inclined to personify " Culture ". As she conceives it, Culture becomes a sort of independent being which, at its own discretion, creates various forms out of the human raw-material at its disposal. Just as a painter distributes colours on his canvas, sets a stroke of red here, a point of blue there, following only the laws of his imagination, so culture, in Margaret Mead's description, arbitrarily distributes temperaments on the huge canvas of human society. But Culture is too complex a phenomenon to be taken as *prima causa*. The problem remains : Who created the Creator ?

It is probably true, as Margaret Mead says, that no " explanation of race or diet or selection " could account for the characterological differences between the three primitive peoples she investigated. But this does not preclude the possibility of other explanations. We may well wonder, for instance, whether the " bedside manners " which we associate with members of the medical profession are—as Margaret Mead assumes—the " natural behaviour of some temperaments ", selected and institutionalized by culture as the " standard behaviour of the general practitioner ", or whether they are not rather the result of centuries of practice in the medical profession which have developed a type of behaviour in accordance with the best interest of the practitioner as well as of the patient. It is equally questionable whether, in Margaret Mead's words :

We have assumed that because it is convenient for a mother to wish to care for her child, this is a trait with which women have been more generously endowed by a carefully teleological process of evolution. We have assumed that because men have hunted, an activity requiring enterprise, bravery, and initiative, they have been endowed with these useful attributes as part of their sex temperament.[1]

It would rather seem as if it were not only convenient for us to assume that a certain relation between a given occupation and a corresponding type of character existed but, more likely, that certain situations, particularly if repeated in many generations, result in developing certain definite psychological characteristics.

[1] *Sex and Temperament*, p. 286.

This means that, even if we agree with Margaret Mead that " Nature " may not have predestined men to be hunters and have fitted them particularly with certain psychological traits to carry out the job, we do not agree with her that " Culture " has arbitrarily associated the characteristics of " enterprise, bravery and initiative " with the profession of hunters, just as the colours of a flag are associated with a certain regiment. The connection between psychological traits and occupational types is not as superficial as that. We therefore cannot admit her concept of " arbitrary selection among emotional traits " and would not concede such an important rôle to chance.

True, one must not expect science to have rational explanations ready for everything. Even such old and well-established systems as those of the Natural Sciences have to-day come to a point where their protagonists frankly admit that, for all our systematic knowledge and experience, there is still a residue of phenomena which they cannot—and perhaps will never be able to—explain. This is even more true of the newer sciences, such as psychology and sociology, which, apart from being young and lacking a body of traditional knowledge, have the additional disadvantage of dealing in a field in which the objects of study are identical with its subjects. All solutions sociology can offer to-day are of a more or less tentative character and will have to be borne out by later investigations and methodical research. But it seems that the attempt, at least, at a rational explanation should be made—with all caution and with the willingness to revise one's own solution if and when a better one is found. That means that one should in the field of sociological theory adopt a sort of trial and error method, because only in this way can one hope to build up a system of knowledge and to approach nearer to truth.

The hypostasis of one single principle, the stipulation of any one " first cause ", has carefully to be avoided. The temptation to make this kind of simplification is very great as it is based on the structure of human intelligence itself. To crave for an explanation of the complex universe in terms of a few fundamental causes is a characteristic feature of the human mind which derives a particular satisfaction from any theory assuming one single and perennial principle as the basis of all empirical phenomena. The search for the one basic principle underlying the diversity of experience can be traced from the historical beginnings of philosophy and science to the present day. The first systems of thought handed down to us are attempts at finding one primary substance (either water, or air, or the " Infinite ") or one primary principle (the Number of Pythagoras, the " Nous " of Anaxagoras, etc.) as the basis of all existence. Monotheism is an expression of the same psychological tendency in the sphere of religion. Underlying all those systems in the endeavour to find one common denominator for all the rationally inexplicable facts.

The development of science has, by supplying more and more rational explanations, gradually decreased the realm of irrationality and thus restricted the domain of religion. The enormous progress which natural science made, mainly in the nineteenth century, and the vast expansion of control over hitherto undefinable forces which it involved, created an enthusiastic optimism as to the power of science to find rational explanations for everything. The attitude generally adopted during the last decades of the nineteenth century, and still prevalent to-day, is a " common readiness to extend an excited welcome to explanation whether of species or social phenomena by general laws " (Morley). In the enthusiasm of this " excited welcome " the fact that the new theory is only a secularized form of religion— the fact that it only covers with a new name the old " residue of irrationality "—is frequently overlooked. But a name is not yet an explanation and the supersession of God or Providence by such other elementary principles as Nature, or Economic Substructure, or—in Margaret Mead's case—Culture, does not greatly add to our knowledge of the universe as long as it is presented as a final cause. As such it merely substitutes one name for another and its acceptance is equally based on an act of faith. It is different if submitted as a working hypothesis, i.e. as a point of view which draws attention to one chain of causation among various others, without falling into the mistake of a cultural determinism. But, as R. E. Park said, he who explains everything by one thing explains nothing.

The culture-pattern approach is a valuable addition to our knowledge if it is considered one of the many " perspectives " (to use the term of K. Mannheim's *Sociology of Knowledge*), revealing one segment of reality to which, however, the others have to be added, or, better, with which the others have to be confronted in order to complement each other in a more comprehensive view.

REFERENCES

MARGARET MEAD : *Sex and Temperament in Three Primitive Societies* (George Routledge & Sons, London, 1935).

Growing Up in New Guinea (New York and Routledge, London, 1934).

Coming of Age in Samoa (Cape, London, 1929).

RUTH BENEDICT : *Patterns of Culture* (Houghton Mifflin Co., Boston and New York, and Routledge, London, 1934).

VIRGINIA WOOLF : *A Room of One's Own* (Hogarth Press, London, 1929).

W. I. THOMAS AND FL. ZNANIECKY : *The Polish Peasant in Europe and in America*, (A. Knopf, New York, 1927).

CHAPTER X

A SOCIOLOGICAL APPROACH: W. I. THOMAS

Sociology, in its application of a causal system to social processes, is based on the assumption that society as a whole, and man as part of it, forms, in any given situation, the final point of an infinite chain of cause and effect.

This notion, that man is the result of a long dynamic process and not of an instantaneous creation, has been the basic concept of modern science. At first, it was understood only in a phylogenetic sense, but it is now applied to historical evolution as well.

To discover the rules and the system of this development in terms of natural, not supernatural, causation, has been the aim of all sciences concerned with human beings—biology, anthropology, psychology, sociology, etc.—for well over a century now. Man, therefore, as seen by science, is not the product of an act of creation—be it by God, or Nature, or Culture—but has become what he is in a slow, gradual development the principles of which are the sole object of scientific study.

It is rather unfortunate that the development of science presents us with a history of a kind of class-struggle between new and old theories. In the clash of ideas everybody has to take sides for one party and against the other, and when an older theory is thrown overboard the kernel of truth which it contained is very frequently discarded with the rest. For Natural Selection against Divine Creation (or vice versa) was one stage of the struggle. For Nature against Nurture is another stage. Biologists were the champions in the former fight, and after they had survived the combat against the theologians, sociologists entered the arena and the struggle went on—this time about the preponderant influence of either heredity or environment in the conditioning of human beings. As the conflict is fought with so much passion as well as intellectual power and scientific evidence, it has become more and more difficult to distinguish the respective merits of either case. " The spirit of oppugnancy " does only too often take " command of the process of truth-seeking ".[1]

[1] J. M. Robertson : *A History of Freethought in the Nineteenth Century*, Vol. 2 (Watts, London, 1929).

The increasing specialization of science has, moreover, added to the confusion, and to-day we have come to a stage where, for instance, such a psychological phenomenon as mother-love is explained by biologists as a natural instinct, by biochemists as dependent on the supply of manganese,[1] and by some anthropologists as a behaviour pattern conditioned by culture and traditional habit.

Anyone who shall be able to co-ordinate those factious views and to adjust them to each other, will render a great service to science. He will enable us to make a fair judgment as to the extent to which the happiness of an individual depends on the experiences of early infancy, on the absence of sexual repression, on calcium and phosphorus, or on social conditions favouring self-expression. As long as this effort of co-ordination has not been made, all our knowledge remains but fragmentary.

Within the scope of our particular subject one of the books least coloured by partisan bias is William I. Thomas's *Sex and Society.*[2]

Summed up in a single sentence its basic assumption is that we are the heirs of our forefathers both in our innate and in our acquired qualities. The society in which we live is the product of a long evolution during the course of which every stage has been wrought upon the preceding one. The atmosphere which we breathe and in which we grow up is the sum total of all previous experiences. The heritage which has come down to us contains the ingredients of all our past—including the portion bequeathed by our animal ancestors. This animal inheritance forms the nucleus around which successive generations have built their way of life, their habits, their ideas, and their beliefs, each generation adding its contribution to the bulk transmitted. Transformed, refined, sublimated, the elements, fused together into that amalgam Modern Man, are still alive, the basic structure is still recognizable. To give one example [3] : in the mental pattern of modern man we still trace the essential animal interest, pursuit. The physical mechanism of the animal which is characteristically adapted to motion and pursuit (as contrasted to

---

[1] Maintained by one of the leading nutrition-experts of our time in : *Newer Knowledge of Nutrition,* by Dr. E. N. MacCollum, E. Orient-Keiles and H. G. Day (Macmillan, New York, 1939).

[2] W. I. Thomas : *Sex and Society, Studies in the Social Psychology of Sex* (Chicago University Press, and T. Fisher Unwin, London, 1907).

[3] Taken from W. I. Thomas' essay on " The Persistence of Primary Group Norms in Present Day Society and Their Influence in our Educational System ", published in *Suggestions of Modern Science Concerning Education,* (Macmillan, New York, 1918).

the lower organisms) has been sublimated into an intellectual interest. The original scheme has been preserved, and no activity appears to us interesting unless it follows the " hunting pattern ". Mechanical activity automatically performed is dull and felt as drudgery. Modern division of labour has forced a great majority of people into work of this mechanical kind and has robbed them of the spontaneity and interest connected with those occupations which follow the pursuit scheme. This pattern underlies such favoured occupations as scientific research, business enterprise, legal and medical callings [1] and it is expressed in various games. The enormous appeal all sorts of sport have for modern man can be explained as being a means of satisfying the " pursuit interest " of masses of people otherwise deprived of this essential stimulus. The alertness which is vital to animal life and is a preparatory stage to pursuit, becomes, in man, curiosity and " a desire for new experience in the abstract, enabling the mind to take an acute interest in any problem whatever ".[2]

However, it is not only the kernel which has remained more or less intact in the mass of our inheritance : later additions are also clearly perceptible in its structure. Many institutions, taboos, habits, and fears, of primitive man have, in some modified form or other, come down to us without our being aware of their primitive origin. They have survived the context in which they were born and quite irrationally linger on to-day under much changed circumstances. Primitive taboos, for instance, persist in the general attitude toward women at the present day ; and a division of labour which came into existence at a period when the greater physical mobility of man and his superior muscular strength were the decisive factors in building up the social organization, is still valid at a time when changed techniques have largely obliterated the differential mobility between men and women, and when legal machinery as well as technical contrivances have eliminated the disabilities of inferior physical strength.

In order, therefore, to understand present psychological characteristics properly it is best to go back to the prehistoric starting-point and to try to trace the evolution of single traits as they develop in the continuous interaction of traditional

---

[1] Cf. Virginia Woolf's definition of a " highbrow " as a " person galloping across country in pursuit of an idea " (In *The Death of the Moth*, London, 1942).
[2] W. I. Thomas : *The Persistence of Primary Group Norms in Present Day Society* . . ., op. cit,

ways of life and changing circumstances. The problem is therefore to find out, first of all, what is the apparatus with which we have been endowed to meet the vicissitudes and adversities of life ; and, secondly, how have the changing fortunes affected and modified that apparatus.

In formulating the problem in this way we meet again, right from the outset, with the crucial question : how can we distinguish between congenital characters and those which have been acquired as the result of social developments ?

In the search for the fundamental organic differences between men and women W. I. Thomas believes he has found sufficient evidence to establish as his main proposition that males are more katabolic, while women are more anabolic. All further differences can, in the main, be reduced to this fundamental one : Man consumes energy more rapidly, woman is more conservative of it. Man therefore is fitted for feats of strength and bursts of energy, whereas woman shows more stability and endurance. Man's structural variability is mainly towards motion, the variational tendency of woman is towards reproduction. There is conclusive evidence of an association of high specific gravity of blood, plentiful haemoglobin, and the katabolic constitution of the male. " The fact that women undertake changes more reluctantly than men, but adjust themselves to changed fortunes more readily, is due to the same metabolic difference." [1]

For the rest, Mr. Thomas's views on biological sex differences are mainly based on Havelock Ellis's theories and therefore need not be repeated here.

W. I. Thomas considers the constitutional differences between the sexes—those just mentioned, and those more immediately connected with reproduction and childbearing—significant enough to play a decisive part in primitive social organization and division of labour and to have left their mark, both directly and indirectly, on the development of human character.

With regard to the social structure it may be said that on account of the more stationary condition of women and the greater mobility of men " earliest groupings of population were about women rather than males ". Women formed the social nucleus of primitive organization, that fixed point to which men returned from their exploits and around which children grew up. The necessities of childbearing and of caring for the young made

---

[1] *Sex and Society*, op. cit., pp. 35-6.

woman the stable element of society. Her need of protection
for herself and her offspring inclined her to more permanent
unions. W. I. Thomas, furthermore, asserts that " woman
enjoyed a negative superiority by the fact that her sexual appetite
was not so sharp as that of the male. She exercised the right
of choice more arbitrarily than has usually been recognized ".
Whether this statement is warranted seems questionable in view
of the very varying opinions held on the subject of woman's
sex urge in different cultures. To believe King Solomon, for
instance—

> There are three things that are never satisfied,
> Yea, four things say not ; " It is enough " :
> The Grave ; and the barren womb ;
> The earth that is not filled with water ;
> And the fire that saith not, " It is enough."
>
>   (Proverbs xxx. 15, 16.)

The manifestations of the sex instinct, no less than the views
held on it, seem to be more subject to cultural influences than is
usually believed.

We are on more certain ground, however, with the assumption that woman was, more than man, identified with the process
of reproduction and with the raising of children. The child
was hers and remained a member of her group. She did not
go to her husband's family after marriage. The house which
she built was hers. " The germ of social organization was,
indeed, the woman and her children and her children's children."

This was valid as long as society was stable. The rôles
changed when needs of food supply made migration necessary.
" The primitive movements of population necessitated by climatic
change, geological disturbances, the failure of water, or exhaustion
of the sources of food were occasions for the expression of the
superior motor disposition of the male and for the dislodgment
of the female from her position of advantage." [1] To meet this
new situation men were better fitted not only by their greater
mobility but by their superior muscular strength which came
to play an ever-increasing part in the trials of migration, insofar
as it involved clashes with other tribes. Migration and expansion made collisions with the former occupants of territories
unavoidable and necessitated the development of an aggressive
spirit as well as of a military organization.

Military organization and battle afford the great opportunity for
the individual and mass expression of the superior force-capacity of

[1] Op. cit., p. 92.

the male. They also determine experimentally which groups and which individuals are superior in this respect, and despotism, caste, slavery, and the subjection of women are chronic expressions of this trial.[1]

In this way a new social technique brought about a new stratification of society and new standards of valuation. " When chronic militancy developed an organization among the males, the political influence of the female was completely shattered. At a certain point in history women became an unfree class, precisely as slaves became an unfree class—because neither class showed a superior fitness on the motor side." To-day, " each class is regaining its freedom because the race is substituting other forms of decision for violence ".

Organic sex differences made themselves felt not only in matters of primitive social control, but also in the division of labour in primitive society. Generally speaking, " men engaged in activities requiring strength, violence, speed, and such craft and foresight which follow from the contacts and strains of their motor life. Woman's part are the slow, unspasmodic, routine and stationary occupations ". As a consequence of her bodily habits and the presence of children, women's attention was mainly directed to objects lying closer at hand and her energies found expression in connection with these objects. Thus, women developed constructive and industrial activities connected with the house, with food, clothing, etc. They were the first agriculturists, potters, basket-makers, weavers, dyers, tanners, etc. " There is no doubt that the labours of early women were exacting, incessant, varied and hard, and that, if a catalogue of primitive forms of labour were made, woman would be found doing five things where man did one." [2] It is perhaps worth noting that this comparative dispersion of energies into many different channels went on through the ages and is still characteristic of women's work to-day. It may account, in part, for the absence of great achievements on women's record, for concentration is one of the essential necessities for creative activity.

In early society women wielded the main sources of wealth, they were the owners of the house, the producers of food, they provided shelter and security. Economically therefore man was dependent on woman. " The withdrawal of woman from labour is a fairly recent development, conditioned by later considerations," among which the social prestige connected with wealth

[1] Op. cit., p. 93.   [2] Op. cit., p. 124.

played an important part. Early societies, however, did not possess that economic surplus to allow exemption from labour to any group ; also the lower classes of our own society, which do not possess it either, do not exclude women from the productive process.

" Through her identification with the industrial process woman became a property-owner. This and the maternal system (referred to above) were the result of her bodily habit and the social habits resulting from it." [1]

Quite apart, however, from the structural differences of men and women, psychological moments played their part in the establishment of a definite division of labour as a permanent institution.

Primitive division of labour between the sexes was not an arrangement dictated by men, but a habit into which both men and women fell, to begin with, through their difference of organization . . . There is, moreover, a tendency in habits to become more fixed than is inherently necessary. The man who does any woman's work is held in contempt, not only by men, but by women.[2]

Thus, we see that human attitudes, from the beginning, were a regulating and stabilizing factor in the social order. The force of habit is enhanced by the ready support of emotions. In small groups the strength of inner solidarity and cohesion is overwhelming and makes dissent almost impossible. In " face to face groups " the power to enforce standards and social habits and to discourage deviations rests on such subtle methods as public disapproval or derision, gossip and sneer, praise or blame, and on immediate example—on what W. I. Thomas calls, " the definition of the situation ".

This " definition of the situation " is the essential mechanism making for stability in society. It transmits habits and customs and interprets the world to the growing child in a way which makes it almost impossible to perceive it differently. This social technique " is begun by parents in the form of forbidding and information and is continued in the community "[3] by the methods just mentioned, among others. Its agencies are public opinion, unwritten laws, legal codes, and religious commandments. " When the code has been defined, no matter what its content, its violation provokes an emotional protest from society designed to be painfully felt by the offender, and it is so felt, owing to

[1] Op. cit., p. 141.　　　　　　　　[2] Op. cit., p. 140.
[3] From *The Persistence of Primary Group Norms.*

the dependence of the member on society for safety and recognition." [1]   In such small groups as we must assume primitive communities to be, the " emotional unanimity " can be considered almost complete.   It is this unanimity, with its opprobrium for any divergence, which makes mental as well as social progress so difficult, for progress is only achieved by the breaking of norms.

There is still another emotional factor which makes for continuance of the division of labour along the lines indicated above, and that is the sensational and rather spectacular character of the work which fell to man's part owing to his peculiar physical capacity for rapid destruction of energy.   The very nature of man's exploits in that primitive society, in which men were fighters and hunters, and women the agriculturists and industrialists, was of an emotional type.   Man had to dare, to risk his life, to display courage, skill and energy in the course of his dangerous pursuits.   By this emotional character and by the vital importance of those fighting qualities for the survival of the group, man's work got all the social attention of the community.   In contrast, woman's work was unsensational and more in the nature of drudgery—persistent and hard labour, regular, uneventful and prosaic—and she " got her excitements as spectator and approver " of man's activities.   " It can hardly be denied, therefore, that man both enjoyed his exciting kind of performance more than the labours which women were connected with, and that the women justified him in refraining from doing many things he could have done perfectly well without constitutional hurt." [2]   Men thus had the triple benefit of the more emotional and inherently interesting work, of social attention for it, and of the privilege of being exempted from the dull routine work of everyday life.

It would be a mistake to conclude that this division of labour was imposed on women, or that it was a sign of their inferior status.   On the contrary, as has been seen before, woman enjoyed economic independence and undeniable social advantages.   But the struggle for life was hard enough in primitive society to make this kind of division of labour convenient for all parts. This will, perhaps, best be illustrated by the story, recalled in John Langdon-Davies' *History of Women*,[3] of the primitive woman

[1] According to W. I. Thomas's theory human acts are motivated by wishes which he classifies into four groups : (1) Desire for new experience ; (2) desire for security ; (3) desire for response (love) ; and (4) desire for recognition (status).
[2] *Sex and Society*, p. 133.   [3] Jonathan Cape, London, 1928.

who, questioned by Europeans why she carried heavy loads while her husband walked unburdened, answered : " What would I do if we met a lion and my husband were carrying a load ? "

It is interesting to note that the social prestige of masculine work, arisen under primitive circumstances as the natural outcome of the epic character of man's occupation, is still in force to-day, when neither lions threaten us nor hidden enemies lie in wait behind street corners, and when a great deal of men's work is unexciting, monotonous routine work. The prestige which in primitive society was connected with the *quality* of the work is now linked to the superior *social position* of men. Here again, sentiments and attitudes survived the actual conditions which evoked them and became gradually attached to substitute phenomena. (This process of substitution is by no means uncommon. Similar substitutions can be observed, although upon a completely different plane, in psycho-analysis. An original drive can be altered through the processes of " displacement ", of " transference ", and of " sublimation ".) This phenomenon involves the psychologist in untold difficulties. If he would understand a particular sentiment he has to understand the underlying original drive, as opposed to the object it is ostensibly attached to.

When exhaustion of food stores compelled man to enter the sphere of hitherto feminine occupations he had, in the course of his previous hunting and fighting exploits, acquired two important techniques : organizing capacity, and " technological skill in fashioning force-appliances ". Both these capacities, " developed in connection with his violent ways of life, he now transferred to labour ". His " long-continued attention in devising and manufacture of weapons " [1] had trained him in the use of mechanical tools, in short, he brought a new and different mentality to bear on the agricultural process. This grafting of a different outlook upon a traditional method proved to be an enormous success— as frequently is the case when outsiders enter a specialized field ; they widen the outlook and revolutionize existing methods. The plough drawn by oxen is, as Mr. Thomas shows, a result of man's training in the use of weapons and his familiarity with animal power. This combination of weapon-technique plus animal-force introduced a far more productive method into agriculture than was hitherto in use.

[1] *Sex and Society*, p. 142.

When large game began to be exhausted, man found himself forced to abandon his destructive and predacious activities, and to adopt the settled occupation of woman. To these he brought all the inventive technique and capacity for organized action which he had developed in his hunting and fighting life, with the result that he became master of woman in a new sense. Not suddenly, but in the course of time, he usurped her primacy in the industrial pursuits and through his organization of industry and the application of invention to the industrial processes he became a creator of wealth on a scale before unknown. Gradually also he began to rely not altogether on ornament, exploits and trophies to get the attention and favour of women. When she was reduced to a condition of dependence on his activity, wooing became a less formidable matter ; he purchased her from her male kindred, and took her to his own group, where she was easier to control.[1]

The final " subjection of woman " thus is not due to superior muscular strength, but to a more highly developed technique of production, and to the wealth produced thereby.

" In unadvanced stages of society, where machinery and division of labour and a high degree of organization have not been introduced, and even among our own lower classes, woman still retains a relation to industrial activities and has a relatively independent status." [2] We therefore find even in our own society a type of woman which differs considerably from the standard of upper and middle-class woman generally taken as the representative of the whole sex.

The heavy, strong, enduring, patient, often dominant type, frequently seen among the lower classes, where alone woman is still economically functional, is probably a good representative of what the women of our race were before they were reduced by man to a condition of parasitism which, in our middle and so-called higher classes, has profoundly affected their physical, mental and moral life.[3]

It is, by the way, noteworthy that among the working classes, as Mr. Thomas points out, the matrimonial value of a woman consists rather in her economic efficiency than in her physical beauty and that, for the same reason, mature women are not infrequently preferred as wives to young girls.

In what way has the " parasitism " of middle- and upper-class women affected their " physical, mental and moral life " ? It has done so in a positive and in a negative way, and the negative has been by far the more effective. By " positive " is meant here the setting up of a feminine ideal—the beautiful,

[1] Op. cit., pp. 230–1.   [2] Op. cit., p. 231.   [3] Op. cit., p. 232.

gracious, virtuous lady of leisure—and the establishment of a peculiar moral code differing from the masculine code of honour. In contrast to the " contractual " morality of men, the code of morals for women is concerned with her personal and bodily habits. Her virtues are chastity, constancy, reserve and devotion, and " while man is merciless to woman from the standpoint of personal behaviour, he exempts her from anything in the way of contractual morality, or views her defections in this regard with allowance and even with amusement ". Whereas man's morality was formed by his contacts in public life, in commercial, political, professional activities, the feminine code was dictated by the one aim and final necessity—to please men. " And— always with the rather definite realization before her of what a dreadful thing it is to be an old maid—she has naïvely insisted that her sisters shall play within the game and has become herself the most strict censor of that morality which has become traditionally associated with women."[1]

It is in the nature of the secluded and circumscribed life which woman lived that the situations which she normally met with during her life-time were " defined " for her by the " primary group ", that is, by a social unit bound together by ties of emotional solidarity and inner cohesion. Her rules of conduct were prescribed by family and church, i.e. by those institutions which, owing to their strong hold on the emotions of their members, are more powerful influences in the life of the community than any others. Because of the satisfaction of her emotional needs which family and religion supplied, she had no occasion to dissent ; and she had no opportunity to form other ties, as men have, by virtue of common work, common loyalties, or equal interests. Her ideas were not shaped by the hard realities of the world but by her immediate surroundings to which she was bound by affection and on which she depended for security, response and recognition. Her economic security, her emotional response and her social status were conferred on woman by the family—and by the family alone—the same agency which provided her with the definitions of all the situations she was likely to meet. She was excluded from chance acquaintance with such experiences or such different environments as could have upset her conception of the world, or would have promoted criticism. Woman thus lived in a kind of organization comparable to the small and spatially isolated communities of

[1] Op. cit., p. 233.

earlier times.   Here the " influences were strong and steady and
the members became more or less habituated to and reconciled
with a life of repressed wishes ".[1]   And while, in this primary
group organization, " certain new experiences were prohibited
and pleasure not countenanced as an end in itself, there remained
satisfactions, not the least of which was the suppression of the
wishes of others ".[2]   The inhibitive influence of early habit,
example and suggestion is strong enough to make a revolt almost
impossible ; to upset even part of this system would mean to
renounce all chances of happiness.   It occasionally happens
that the whole system of inhibitions in some individual girls
collapses as soon as they are removed from the direct influence
of family and community and the pressure of control relaxed,
as is often the case with country girls coming to town for work.

The loosening of the specific kind of feminine morality which
we are witnessing in our time is directly related to the weakening
of primary-group ties owing to modern technical and social
developments.   The increased size and number of large cities,
new methods of transport, the disappearance of the patriarchal
family as an industrial unit in which several generations lived
and worked together, modern techniques of amusement and
information, are among those factors which brought about a
decline in community sense and primary group control.   And,
among others—

the modern revolt and unrest are due to the contrast between the
paucity of fulfilment of the wishes of the individual, and the apparent
fullness of life around him.   All age levels have been affected by
the feeling that much, too much, is being missed in life.   This unrest
is felt most by those who have heretofore been most excluded from
general participation in life—the mature woman and the young girl
. . .   The world has become large, alluring, and confusing . . .
Social evolution has been so rapid that no agency has been developed
in the larger community of the state for regulating behaviour which
would replace the failing influence of the community and correspond
completely with present activities.[3]

While modern man practically lives in a universe, there is
no universally accepted body of doctrines and practices to guide
him.   But even if such a body of doctrines and practices existed,
they would probably not have the direct emotional appeal of
precepts and examples operating within the tightly knit unit of
family, neighbourhood, village, or religious community.

[1] From W. I. Thomas : *The Unadjusted Girl* (Little, Brown & Co., Boston, 1931).
[2] Ibid.   [3] Op. cit., p. 72.

The negative, or we might perhaps better say unintentional, effect of seclusion within the family group on the mind and character of woman was overwhelming.

Because their problem is not to accommodate to the solid realities of the world of experience and sense, but to adjust themselves to the personality of men, it is not surprising that they should assume protean shapes [1] and develop an " adventitious character ".

Under a system of male control, where self-realization is secured either through the manipulation of the man or not at all, her intelligence expressed itself in the form of cunning, a typical characteristic of disqualified persons.

Cunning is one of the forms which intelligence takes in a fight. And in general people become cunning when they are oppressed or do not participate on an equal footing in their society . . . the " racial " cunning of the Jew has the same origin as the particular cunning in this case—exclusion from recognition and participation.[2]

Difference in natural ability is in the main a characteristic of the individual, not of race or sex.[3]

Those differences in intellectual expression which we observe in whole groups of people, in nations, races, sexes, are due to different experiences of the mind, different stages of culture, and

adventitious circumstances which direct the attention to different fields of interest. The direction of attention and the simplicity or complexity of mental processes depend on the character of the external situation which the mind has to manipulate. If the activities are simple, the mind is simple, and if the activities were nil, the mind would be nil. The mind is nothing but a means to manipulate the outside world. Number, time and space conceptions and systems become more and more complex and accurate, not as the human mind grows in capacity, but as activities become more varied and call for more extended and accurate systems of notation and measurement.[4]

The great superiority of man above all other organisms rests exactly on this adaptability of the human mind to the demands of various situations. The variability of this instrument of mastery is a general human characteristic and there is no innate difference of intellectual capacity between races, sexes, or classes.

The world of white civilization is intellectually rich because it has amassed a rich fund of general ideas, and has organized these into specialized bodies of knowledge, and has also developed a special technique for the presentation of this knowledge and standpoint to the young members of society, and for localizing their attention in special fields of interest. When for any reason a class of society is

---

[1] *Sex and Society*, p. 238. [2] *The Unadjusted Girl*, p. 194.
[3] *Sex and Society*, p. 271. [4] Ibid.

excluded from this process, as women have been historically, it must necessarily remain ignorant.[1]

In other words :

The fundamental explanation of the differences in the mental life of two groups is not that the capacity of the brain to do work is different, but that the attention is not in the two cases stimulated and engaged along the same lines. Wherever society furnishes copies and stimulations of a certain kind, a body of knowledge and a technique, practically all its members are able to work on the plan and scale in vogue there, and members of an alien race who become acquainted in a real sense with the system can work under it.[2]

Thus the " differences in mental expression between the lower and the higher races " and equally between men and women, " can be expressed for the most part in terms of attention and practice ".[3]

These assertions—as we have seen in a previous chapter—are borne out by statistical research and psychometric tests. From Helen B. Thompson onwards to the present day almost all investigators of mental sex differences have agreed that the psychological differences between men and women are in the last resort differences of interest and not of capacity. They are due to a different distribution of attention, not of innate ability. Persistent champions of the innateness of mental sex differences will probably argue that the divergence of interests is constitutional. To them Mr. Thomas would answer that attention is called for by external circumstances and is not directed by inward impulses. If human interests were, in fact, dictated by innate instincts, they would barely exceed the minimum necessary for conservation and reproduction of life. These instincts, moreover, are equal in all human races and would not admit of any explanation as to the differences existing between their mental development. But " at present we seem justified in inferring that the differences in mental expression between the higher and lower races and between men and women are no greater than they should be in view of the existing differences in opportunity ".[4]

If women to-day have not fulfilled all the expectations which this theory of equality of achievement on condition of equal opportunity would seem to justify, it must be borne in mind, first, that a complete equality of opportunity still does not exist, and secondly, that it is impossible, on the part of women, to do

---

[1] *Sex and Society*, p. 301.   [2] Op. cit., p. 282.   [3] Op. cit., p. 291.
[4] Op. cit., p. 312.

away within one or two generations with shackles which have a tradition of centuries.

There is not only a reluctance on the part of men to admit women to their intellectual world, but a reluctance—or, rather a real inability —on their part to enter. Modesty with reference to personal habits has become so ingrained and habitual, and to do anything freely is so foreign to woman, that even free thought is almost of the nature of an immodesty to her.[1]

It will presumably take a considerable time, and the building up of a new tradition, before women will be able to rid themselves of the inhibitions which are no longer imposed on them by custom, but now by their own inner attitudes.

One of these inhibitions is produced by the sense of inferiority evoked in women by the fact that, although for some time now they have been allowed to compete with men on more or less equal terms, they have not yet achieved more than average results. They are deluded by the new sense of equality and do not sufficiently realize that the conditions under which they are allowed to compete cannot at one stroke do away with the disabilities naturally arising from lack of tradition.

Even the most serious women of the present day stand, in any work they undertake, in precisely the same relation to men that the amateur stands to the professional in games. They may be desperately interested and may work to the limit of endurance at times but, like the amateur, they got into the game late, and have not had a life-time of practice, or they do not have the advantage of that pace gained only by competing incessantly with players of the very first rank. No one will contend that the amateur in billiards has a nervous system less fitted to the game than the professional . . .[2]

Another, maybe even more important source of inhibitions is connected with the inner conflict between emotional and intellectual interests which at some time or other almost every " emancipated " woman has to face. Whether it presents itself as a conflict between the desire for independence and the need for affection, or as a dilemma between professional interests and family duties, or again, between such divergent social ideals as individual achievement and devotion to home and family, it is always due to the fact that the " emancipation " has hitherto been limited to the professional and economic sphere and has hardly touched yet the emotional side of family life. The contemporary amusement industry presents us over and over

[1] Op. cit., p. 302.   [2] Op. cit., p. 306.

again, obviously in response to public demand, with one successful type of heroine : the secretary who marries the boss and, once arrived in the secure haven of marriage, " naturally " relinquishes her business activities. The woman with a career of her own still has no emotional appeal for the general public. And, in fact, the cases where women are able to carry on their business activities after marriage are rather the exception than the rule. It is therefore not surprising that women accept their professional activities half-heartedly, either as interim jobs before they marry, or in case they will not be able to marry. Under these circumstances they cannot be expected to perform first-rate achievements.

" Women may and do protest against the triviality of their lives, but emotional interests are more immediate than intellectual ones, and human nature does not drift into intellectual pursuit voluntarily, but is forced into it in connection with the urgency of practical activities . . ." [1]

All that has been said in this connection does not apply to the working-class woman who for lack of time, opportunity and money is not confronted with the problem of intellectual development, and for whom the question of remunerative work is decided by economic necessity. It is a problem chiefly affecting middle- and upper-class women who are not pressed into work by practical need and who are, on the contrary, actively discouraged from devoting themselves seriously to intellectual pursuits by a chivalrous code of manners.

The result of this state of affairs is diminished efficiency on the part of women, irritation—caused by the constant " playing on by stimulations without the possibility to function " [2]—and personal unhappiness.

The remedy [says Mr. Thomas], for the irregularity, pettiness, ill-health and unserviceableness of modern woman seems to lie on educational lines. Not in a general and cultural education alone, but in a special and occupational interest and practice for women, married and unmarried. This should be preferably gainful, though not onerous nor incessant.[3]

It should be added perhaps that the " emancipation of women " would have to be followed by an " emancipation of men " from their notion of a dependent, domesticated and receptive wife. Men would have to get used, more readily than they generally do now, to accept the idea of marriage as a partnership of two

---

[1] Op. cit., p. 303.   [2] Op. cit., p. 240.   [3] Op. cit., p. 243.

fully developed individuals in their own right. And society would have to be organized in a way that makes household work less enslaving. The technical means are at its disposal. What is still lacking is the willingness to use them because, notwithstanding all changes we have undergone in our convictions, subconsciously we are still full of old resentments and emotional habits.

" Sex and Society " is not a history of woman and its merits do not lie in completeness of description. Mr. Thomas has, for instance, no word on religious influences on the position and character of women. He does not deal with the effects of primitive fertility magic and sex taboos or with the enormous influence of Christianity on the status of women. Some of his biological theories are disputable or have been refuted by newer discoveries. Nevertheless, W. I. Thomas's contribution to the discussion of the problem of women has been considerable. Its value lies in the sociological method of his approach and the clear distinction between the different social and psychological factors at work in the shaping of the feminine character. His method, which shares with both the Vaertings' and Mead's theories the common characteristic of regarding personality traits as functions of social conditions, does not commit the same fallacies : neither does he, like the Vaertings, oversimplify the relation of the individual to society by a reduction of all his characteristics to the one cause of dominance ; nor does he, like Margaret Mead, assume a hypostasized " Culture " which arbitrarily selects and institutionalizes certain traits and rejects others. His concept is more dynamic. Personality, in his view, is the outcome of a long process of interaction between social factors and a highly plastic original nature. The social influences, communicated to the individual by way of " definitions of the situation " through parents, friends, teachers, in fact, through all kinds of social contacts—are innumerable. They may consist in social status, in the division of labour, in methods of production, in the values a community sets on a certain conduct or certain attitudes, in the opportunities it affords to its members, in the stimulation of attention in a certain direction, in folkways, beliefs, literary traditions, and many others. Whether one belongs to a small or a large nation, whether one is a member of a suppressed class or not, whether one comes from a family with a professional tradition, are factors, among others, which determine one's outlook. " Warfare makes men warlike and Churches

make men religious. Culture precedes particular individuals,"
says Ellsworth Faris. In John Dewey's somewhat pointed
formulation : " The instincts do not make the institutions, it is
the institutions that make the instinct." [1]

The assumption that the outlook, sentiments, and even the
personal preferences of the individual are so coloured by his
social experience that personality may be described as the subjective aspect of culture, is the basic concept of a new socio-
logically-minded psychology. " The world in which men live
is, on the whole, the world in which they have learned to live.
Things take form and substance as we learn how to behave
towards them. Our habits and our attitudes are the subjective
aspect of the world we know. What things mean for us is
determined, in the final analysis, by the events in our personal
history." [2] In contrast to individual psychology, the main
subjects of which are psychical states of more or less universal
permanence, social psychology is chiefly concerned with
" attitudes ", a concept implying a direction towards something.

The term " attitude ", used by W. I. Thomas to denote an
acquired predisposition to act—or, " a process of individual
consciousness which determines real or possible activity of the
individual in the social world " [3]—has been widely accepted in
social psychology. [4] Anything which has an empirical content
for the individual and a meaning which may make it the object
of activity is a " social value ". Any datum—food, tools, money,
a piece of music, an institution, a scientific theory, a fashion,
physical or psychological traits, etc.—may become a " social
value " by being the object of an attitude. It is the contact with
an attitude which makes an object a " value " (either positive
or negative), and, inversely, it is the value which evokes attitudes.
This correlation of values and attitudes implies the correlation
of individual and culture, and it explains the mechanism by
which personality is the counter-part and subjective expression
of a general social situation.

Attention has been drawn to this close connection between
personality and culture by the many changes of personality
types which can be observed in our present culture as the result

[1] John Dewey : *Human Nature and Conduct* (Henry Holt, New York, 1922)
[2] Robert Park : *Human Nature, Attitudes and the Mores* (Henry Holt, New York, 1931).
[3] W. I. Thomas and Florian Znaniecki : *The Polish Peasant in Europe and America* (Knopf, New York, 1927).
[4] John Dewey has employed the term " habit ", and Znaniecki the term
" tendency " in the same sense.

of modern division of labour, of migration, of changes from country to town life, of the emancipation of subject races or classes. The great mobility of modern life brought about many conflict situations and necessitated many adjustments. Those groups which are in a state of transition afford the most obvious examples of the intimate relation between personality traits and culture. The most " natural " traits, habits, or beliefs reveal their connection with a cultural pattern if divorced from their normal setting, or become causes of conflict in a new situation. Just as a particular language is the normal expression of thought in one social environment but not in another, so are many " normal " habits and traits not transferable to another milieu or become reasons of acute self-consciousness. A person whose natural idiom is a country dialect will feel embarrassingly aware of it in the company of people who attach importance to correct and accent-free speech ; a small, dark and temperamental individual will become self-conscious of his physical characteristic in a community in which tall, fair persons of phlegmatic temperament are the norm or the ideal ; the family mores of the Polish peasant become causes of acute internal crises in the Polish immigrant in the United States ; a woman who walked about in trousers, a decade or two ago, was not only considered masculine, but was in fact a masculine type, while to-day, when it has become a generally accepted manner of dress, the costume is no longer associated with psychological characteristics. In this way, any habit, psychological trait or even physical characteristic is shown to be part of a social pattern when torn from its context.

A number of studies have been made, and more are being made, on the relation of personality traits to the social group, many of them with particular reference to ambivalent types characterized by membership of two different cultures. *The Polish Peasant in Europe and America* by W. I. Thomas and F. Znaniecky, *Colour, Class and Personality* by Robert Sutherland, *The Problem of the Marginal Man* by Everett V. Stonequist, *Human Migration and the Marginal Man* by R. E. Park are a few examples.

Sex and Society, a study on the personality traits of women in a transitional phase between subjection and emancipation, gives another particular aspect of the same problem and has to be viewed as a contribution to the discussion of the wider topic of *Personality and Culture*.

From the point of view of the sociology of knowledge it is one part (but a very representative part) of the new perspective which functionalizes fixed traits of human character and explains them by the social context in which they have been acquired. It represents the most radical change in our outlook and in our approach to the problems of Man and Society.   As this perspective is still in the making it is too soon to describe its limitations.

REFERENCES

W. I. THOMAS : *Sex and Society, Studies in the Social Psychology of Sex* (Chicago University Press, and T. Fisher Unwin, London, 1907).
" The Persistence of Primary Group Norms in Present-Day Society and Their Influence on Our Educational System " (in *Suggestions of Modern Science Concerning Education* (Macmillan, New York, 1918).
The Unadjusted Girl (Little, Brown & Co., Boston, 1931).
AND FLORIAN ZNANIECKY : *The Polish Peasant in Europe and America* (Knopf, New York, 1927).
E. T. HILLER : *Principles of Sociology* (Harper Bros., New York and London, 1933).
KIMBALL YOUNG : *Social Psychology* (2nd Edition, F. S. Crofts & Co., Inc., New York, 1945.)   To be published in the International Library of Sociology and Social Reconstruction.   (Kegan Paul, London).
JOHN DEWEY : *Human · Nature and Conduct* (Henry Holt & Co., New York, 1922).
ELLSWORTH FARIS : " Attitudes and Behaviour " (*Amer. Jour. of Sociol.* 1928, Vol. 34).
" The Concept of Social Attitudes " (*Jour. Appl. Sociol.*, Vol. 9, 1924–5).
R. E. PARK : *Human Nature, Attitudes and the Mores* (Henry Holt, New York, 1931.)
" Human Migration and the Marginal Man " in *Personality and the Social Group*, ed. Burgess, Chicago, 1929.
E. B. REUTER : " The Social Attitude " (*Jour. Appl. Sociol.*, 1922–3, Vol. 13).
E. T. KRUEGER AND W. C. RECKLESS : " The Nature of Personality " in *Social Psychology* (Longmans Green, New York and London, 1931).
EVERETT V. STONEQUIST : " The Problem of the Marginal Man " (*Amer. Jour. Sociol.*, 1935, Vol. 41).
ROBERT L. SUTHERLAND : *Colour, Class and Personality* (Amer. Council of Education, Washington, 1941).
JOHN LANGDON-DAVIES : *History of Woman* (Jonathan Cape, London, 1928).

CHAPTER XI

SUMMARY AND CONCLUSIONS

There is no doubt that it is generally assumed in our civilization that a great many psychological traits are linked to sex. By the most elementary classification human qualities are roughly divided into two classes corresponding to the division between male and female. This basic assumption is still maintained, although to-day the dividing line between the two sets of mental characteristics is no longer as clearly drawn as it used to be. The fact that it is increasingly realized that so-called " masculine " traits are, in varying degrees, found in women and " feminine " traits in men, does not, however, dispose of the original division, but makes it, on the contrary, more imperative to investigate what in fact are called feminine and what masculine characteristics.

There exists, to use Walter Lippmann's term, a " stereotype " of femininity in our society. It underlies practical activities in the most various departments of social life, ranging from simple questions of everyday conduct and etiquette to problems of education, of vocational choice, social work, employment policy, crime prevention and treatment of criminal offenders, press, film, literature, political campaigning and the advertising and selling of goods as well as ideas. What is more, this stereotype of femininity serves as a pattern of conduct to the growing girl, influences her life plan, and so contributes in shaping her character.

Although there can be no doubt as to the existence in our society of a Platonic idea of femininity, difficulties arise when we attempt to define it. For there are almost as many opinions as there are minds, and it is hard to find even two essential characteristics on which the common man or the majority of experts would agree. Some authors have tried to single out one fundamental trait as the general clue to the feminine character. G. Heymans,[1] for instance, thinks this basic quality to be emotionalism ; Gina Lombroso [2] explains it as altrocentrism ; for W. Liepmann [3] it is vulnerability ; and in S. Freud's view the essential of femininity is a " preference for passive aims ".

[1] *Die Psychologie der Frauen*, transl. from the Dutch (Winter, Heidelberg, 1924).
[2] *The Soul of Woman* (Jonathan Cape, London, 1924).
[3] *Die Psychologie der Frau* (Berlin and Vienna, 1920).

Even if we restrict ourselves to the relatively short list of authors treated in this study we find not only contradiction on particular points but a bewildering variety of traits considered characteristic of women by the various authorities. An attempt to draw up a table of feminine traits, and to list the respective authors' agreement or disagreement on each point must fail because there is hardly any common basis to the different views. The difficulty is not only that there is disagreement on specific characteristics and their origin, but that the emphasis is laid on absolutely different attributes.

The traits which do recur comparatively more often than others, although with various qualifications, in the different theories are : passivity, emotionality, lack of abstract interests, greater intensity of personal relationships, and an instinctive tenderness for babies.

This is, however, only a very short extract of the many traits considered typically feminine by the various authors, and agreement, even on these few points, is far from being complete, as a brief summary will show.

Havelock Ellis thinks the relatively more passive sexual rôle of the female has far-reaching psychological consequences, although this biological passivity has been greatly reinforced by social conventions and repressions. Whatever its origin, it has conditioned and increased such mental traits as receptivity and submissiveness. It is also connected with modesty which, though largely modifiable by fashion and custom, is more essentially a feminine trait. Among the other characteristics recorded by Havelock Ellis are : disvulnerability, i.e. greater power of resistance to major disturbances, notwithstanding a disposition to be more subject to minor oscillations ; affectability or suggestibility, i.e. quicker psychic and physical response to stimuli. Connected with this trait is the greater emotionality of women, their tact, their practical realism. There is generally found in women a lack of abstract interests, a dislike of rigid rules and principles, an aversion to analytical thinking and an inclination to act on impulse rather than upon deliberation. Women on the whole show less tendency to vary from type and thus produce less abnormalities, i.e. less genius and less idiocy. The feminine type is physically, and in a certain sense mentally, nearer to the infantile type than man, and, as according to Havelock Ellis's theory the child is not only father of the man but of Superman, woman thus represents a more advanced stage in the scale of phylogenetic evolution, and evolutionary progress therefore implies increasing feminization of the human race.

In *Otto Weininger's* view woman has one purpose in life and only one essential interest : sexuality. Both in the type of mother and in that of courtesan she is either indirectly or directly concerned with matters of sex. She has no moral standards of her own, and the constant compliance with extraneous standards has produced in her mendacity, hypocrisy, and the disposition to hysteria. She has no capacity for clear thought, no memory other than the ability to repeat memorized matter. Her judgment is uncertain and her sensibility poor except for tactile sensations. She is sentimental, but incapable of deep emotions. She has no desire for individual immortality, and no appreciation for permanent values ; she has no intellectual conscience, no relation to logic, and she lacks individuality and an independent will.

Although for *Sigmund Freud* femininity is essentially characterized by passivity and the lack of a male sex organ, he associates a number of psychological traits with woman's constitutional disposition. These are : modesty, vanity, inclination to envy and jealousy, lack of social conscience or social justice, a generally weaker moral sense (a weaker " super-ego " in Freud's term), inferior capacity and a limited urge for sublimation (i.e. for cultural interests), greater disposition to neuroses, particularly to hysteria, a weaker sex urge, masochistic tendencies, earlier arrest of psychological development (" rigidity "), and an antagonistic attitude towards civilization as the enemy of family and sexual life, woman's main concern.

According to *Alfred Adler*, the feminine character is circumscribed by woman's inferior social position and her resulting inferiority feelings. " Femininity ", to him, is a symbol for all those traits which in our culture obstruct social success : weakness, timidity, shyness, passivity, prudishness, submissiveness, hyper-sensitiveness, the sense of being pushed aside and of being at a disadvantage, and the realization of actual futility. These are the traits the individual—whether man or woman—tries to overcome by a " masculine protest ", the terms " masculine " and " feminine " being used here in a symbolic sense and in accordance with social conventions.

Helen B. Thompson has found women to possess better memories —both with regard to rapidity of memorizing and to duration— to have less social but more religious consciousness than men, to show better results in association tests, but to be of inferior ingenuity. Thompson's experiments did not disclose any marked differences in intellectual interests, methods of work, in type of mental activity or average capacity, in the intensity of emotions or in the degree of impulsiveness of action. She thinks, however, that women show a greater tendency to inhibit the expression of their emotions and that, owing to different social influences, their attention is distributed in a different way. She does not countenance Havelock Ellis's views about variability, but maintains that general statements about women should not transcend the limits of the normal. Within those limits no difference in variability between the sexes can be found.

In contrast to these findings, based on experiments with one specific class of women, namely students, *L. M. Terman* and *C. C. Miles* in their vast experimental study have established notable differences between the sexes both in their interests and their emotional disposition. Disclaiming the possibility of discovering an " eternal feminine " these two authors find femininity in our present-day Western civilization marked by interests in domestic affairs and aesthetic objects and occupations, by a preference for sedentary and indoor occupations and for " ministrative " jobs, and by a generally weaker intensity of interests. Women, in their opinion, are more compassionate and sympathetic than men, and that in a personal, concrete sense, not on humanitarian principles ; they are more emotional in general and more expressive of their emotions ; they are severer moralists, but more ready to admit weaknesses in themselves, and are less self-asserting.

Femininity, in *Mathias and Mathilde Vaerting's* view, does not exist as such. In a society with sex inequality there is a difference of characteristic traits and functions between the sexes according to their either subordinate or dominant social position. The subordinate sex, which in our society happens to be the feminine, is charged with housework and family cares and has developed traits of domesticity. It plays the passive part in courtship, is expected to be faithful and chaste, reserved and bashful. Its members are the younger partners in the marriage relationship. They are valued for their grace and beauty to the extent at times of being treated as mere dolls, thereby being conditioned to love bodily adornment and finery to excess. They are taken as the passive objects of erotic art. In all such spheres, in fact, they are regarded as things and used as instruments by the superior sex. The subordinate sex is therefore characterized by obedience and submission, by emotional dependence on the marriage partner, by fearfulness, and by prevailing through indirect means. It shows an inferior intelligence, restricted interests outside the home, inferior physical capacity, adiposity, and relatively more monogamous inclinations. But every one of these traits is not linked to sex but to the subordinate social position of women and can be found in members of the other sex in the history of other races.

Margaret Mead, too, believes the association of psychological traits with sex to be accidental rather than based on constitutional facts. She does not, however, endeavour to relate certain of these mental characteristics to the inferior social position of women. She considers it impossible to lay down any hard and fast rules as to the effect of a particular social rôle on the psychological traits of the persons occupying that rôle. As she points out, passivity, responsiveness, fondness for children, timidity, coquetry, playfulness, emotional dependence, are in some societies found in both men and women and are absent in both in other cultures ; in some societies they are characteristic of men, in others of women. The disposition to hysteria which, in our civilization, is largely found in women, is in Margaret Mead's view a characteristic condition of the cultural deviant, that is of the individual unable to adjust himself to the demands of his culture.

The traits which *W. I. Thomas* registers as characteristic of woman in our civilization and which have developed owing partly to organic conditions and partly to historical tradition are : a certain passivity, stability, endurance, greater disvulnerability and tenacity on life, a " quality of motherhood, capable of being transferred to any subject calling for sympathy, a doll, a man, or a cause " ; a certain reluctance to undertake changes, but greater adaptability to new conditions ; a peculiar code of morality concerned mainly with bodily habits, such as purity, chastity, modesty, and, as a consequence, a limitation of interests and attention to enhancing her person. Under male dominance women have developed trickery, hypocrisy, and a tendency to prevail by passive means. In view of their superior endurance and superior cunning their capacity for intellectual work may be assumed to be, under equal circumstances, at least as great as man's, but has been directed into unproductive channels and adopted the form of intrigue rather than invention.

This list of feminine traits could be extended almost indefinitely, in proportion to the number of authors considered. In addition to traits already mentioned it would include such others as an infantile type of sexuality and narcissism,[1] exhibitionism and a sensitive " herd instinct " which makes woman " follow fashion by force of a compelling instinct " and prompts her " to approve of orthodox and disapprove of unorthodox conduct ",[2] patience, discipline, orderliness, conscientiousness, linguistic abilities [3] and many others.

The impression one gains from this variety of descriptions is definite only on one point : namely, the existence of a concept of femininity as the embodiment of certain distinctive psychological traits. What, however, is considered essential to this concept depends to a large extent on personal bias and valuations, and on the social-historical vantage-point of the observer. There is a long line of development from the classical Aristotelian definition to modern ideas. Whereas the first said :

Woman is more compassionate than Man, more ready to weep, but at the same time more jealous, more querulous, more inclined to abuse. In addition she is an easy prey to despair and less sanguine than Man, more shameless and less jealous of honour, more untruthful, more easily disappointed and has a longer memory. She is likewise more cautious, more timid, more difficult to urge into action, and she requires a smaller quantity of food.[4]

A typical modern comment sounds as follows :

When physiological differences are left out of account there is little evidence to indicate any very striking differences between men and women except for a tendency for women to be more personal and emotional in their interests than are men. That this difference is innate, however, is extraordinarily doubtful. A much simpler and more plausible explanation may be seen in the culture of the group which places a premium upon each member conforming to the stereotyped responses of his sex. The regimen of training through which the little girl passes emphasizes the necessity of reacting to persons rather than to things. Sexual differences thus grow out of our double standards and may be expected largely to disappear as women participate in the activities of men.[5]

This line of development roughly passes through three stages. In the first, chiefly supported by metaphysical and religious argu-

[1] Paul Bousfield : *Sex and Civilization* (Kegan Paul, London, 1925).
[2] C. W. Cunnington : *Feminine Attitudes in the Nineteenth Century* (Heinemann, London, 1935).
[3] G. Heymans : *Die Psychologie der Frauen* (Winter, Heidelberg, 1924).
[4] *De animalis historia.*
[5] Ernest R. Mowrer : *The Family, its Organization and Disorganization* (Univ. of Chicago Press, 1932).

ments, woman is denied a soul. Femininity, at that point, is considered a "kind of natural defectiveness".[1] Woman is thought of as a sort of under-developed human being, with all the external attributes but without the essential qualities of humanity : without individuality, intellectual capacity, or character.

The second phase is marked by the discovery that, in Tennyson's words, "Woman is not an undeveloped man, but diverse", with the emphasis on "diverse". Woman is thought to be in every respect the reverse of man.

There are thus two human souls [says a French social philosopher of the nineteenth century],[2] that is a masculine soul and a feminine soul. Thus, woman not only has a soul, whatever impertinent misogynists may have thought, but she has a soul essentially different from ours, a soul which is the inverse of ours, inverse and complementary. *Different* in mind and heart, *different* in imagination and character, intimately and essentially *different* woman brings us a new spiritual world and not only a more or less watered down re-edition of the spiritual world of man. [And, as he was writing at the time when woman's emancipation was beginning, he adds] : And one can say that in future the sphere of the human mind will have its old and its new psychical world just as the terrestrial globe, since Columbus, has its old and new continent. Human genius and love will be doubled thereby . . .

This view, most popular at the end of the last and the beginning of this century and coinciding with the golden age of natural sciences, found its strongest support among biologists. But it was maintained by philosophers too, on the basis of dualism as a necessity of thinking. As Nietzsche said :

To be mistaken in the fundamental problem of Man and Woman is to deny the abysmal conflict and the necessity of an eternally hostile tension : perhaps even to dream of the same rights, the same occupations, the same demands, the same duties ; this is a typical sign of shallow-patedness, and a thinker who has shown himself shallow on this most dangerous point—shallow in his instincts !—must be put down as altogether suspicious, nay, more, as exposed and unmasked ; probably he will be found wanting in all the fundamental questions of life, including those of future life, and be incapable of reaching any profundity.

To mistake, however, categories of thought for norms governing reality means forcing life into a straight-jacket. It is as impossible to do justice to human existence by applying to it epistemological criteria as it is to judge organic life by the applica-

[1] Aristotle : *De generatione animalium.*
[2] Jean Izoulet : *La Cité Moderne, métaphysique de la sociologie.* Quoted from Cath. van Tussenbroek : "Over de Aequivalentie van Man en Vrouw" (Amsterdam), 1898.

tion of geometrical norms.   The rules governing the one system are not transferable to the other.   It does not impair their validity that they are not generally applicable.   Within the scope of epistemology dualism is an effective principle for reducing chaos to a system.   But on that account to deduce a psychological bi-polarity of human beings means to destroy not chaos but variety.

The growing recognition of this fact marks the third and latest stage in the development of society's attitude toward women.   Two factors, closely interrelated, characterize this phase.   The one is the growing conviction, based on sociological and psychological evidence, that personality traits are " by-products of immediate interests and incentives " [1] and develop in accordance with the individual's social rôle in a given culture. Among the circumstances determining this social rôle, and thus the shaping of personality traits, sex is only one.   Social class, religious background, age, race, vocation, family relationship, early training, opportunities for development, social tradition and conventions, individual physical and psychological dispositions, are others.   " Traits of personality, as expressed in a social rôle, are products of all the factors which affect the conception which others possess and which the person possesses both of the nature of the rôle itself and of the qualities which the person brings to the rôle." [2]

The logical inference of this train of thought is a view to which increasing individualism has led through other channels as well :   the view that individual differences prevail over differences between whole groups.

Moreover, it is, in our particular case, supported by the growing participation of women in all spheres of public life with the resultant doubts as to the validity of the traditional co-ordination of sex and psychological qualities.   Although the present time is a period of transition and the effects of tradition are still very strong, it is already becoming clear that the more of the formerly masculine functions women fulfil the more of those traits previously thought " masculine " they generally develop.   It therefore becomes more and more obvious that those traits are not the effect of innate sex characters but of the social rôle and are changing with it.

---

[1] Wilton P. Chase.
[2] E. T. Krueger and W. C. Reckless : *Social Psychology,* chapter " The Nature of Personality " (Longmans Green, New York and London, 1931).

The task of the sociologist at this particular juncture is not, as has been suggested by some, the creation of a " sociological woman, a sexless, bloodless creature ". Nor is it up to him to deny the influence of physiological facts upon psychological qualities. The contribution the sociologist has to offer to the discussion of this problem consists in an attempt to define more closely the concept of mental traits of sex by marking out its limits. His procedure is a conclusion from the negative. By eliminating those feminine traits which are due to other factors than sex he narrows down the definition of psychological sex character, making it at the same time more definite. His aim is not to prove that the organic constitution does not exert some influence, but rather to elucidate the nature of this influence by excluding those traits which can be shown to be due to such factors as a cultural pattern, including social functions, historic tradition, prevailing ideologies, etc. He therefore has to bring the problem into a wider context and to view it against different backgrounds.

The co-ordination and sociological examination of different formulations of the same problem as attempted in this study, is one of the various methods which can be adopted. Its chief aim is to outline the scope of the problem and, by indicating its different aspects, to make possible a closer understanding and higher degree of objectivity.

Another interesting and fruitful approach is a comparison between personality traits of women and other social groups in similar position, such as immigrants, Jews, converts, conquered people, American Negroes, Westernized natives, intellectuals who break away from the social groups and classes in which they originated without completely being free from their allegiance to them,[1] and the like. All these groups have certain personality traits and attitudes in common which have been made the subject of special sociological study. A considerable literature has been published, mainly in America,[2] on the personality type of the so-called " marginal man ", i.e. the person who lives in two

[1] viz : " The Sociological Problems of the ' Intelligentsia ' " in K. Mannheim's *Ideology and Utopia* (Kegan Paul, London, 1936, pp. 136–46).
[2] *R. E. Park* : " Human Migration and the Marginal Man " in *Personality and the Social Group* (ed. Burgess, Chicago, 1929). *Everett V. Stonequist* : " The Problem of the Marginal Man " (*Amer. Jour. of Sociol.*, Vol. 41, July, 1935). *Robert L. Sutherland* : *Colour, Class and Personality* (Amer. Council of Education, Washington, 1942). (Summary of an extensive study, comprising 6 volumes, by the Amer. Youth Commission on the effects upon personality development of Negro youth of their membership in a minority racial group.) And others.

different worlds simultaneously. He is a participant in two cultural systems, one of which is, by prevailing standards, regarded as superior to the other. This bi-cultural situation presents itself to the individual as a personal problem of adjustment to two different sets of values.

Ambitions run counter to feelings of self-respect. Recognition by the dominant group is wanted, but its arrogance at the same time resented. Pride and shame, love and hate, and other contradictory sentiments mingle uneasily in the nature of the marginal personality. The two cultures produce a dual pattern of identification and a divided loyalty, and the attempt to maintain self-respect transforms these feelings into an ambivalent attitude. The individual may pass in and out of each group situation several times a day ; thus his attention is repeatedly focussed upon each group attitude and his relationship to it.[1]

He feels he belongs with both groups to a greater, common unit —to a nation, to Western Civilization, to Humanity—but his contact with the dominant group constantly reminds him of his being " different ". Seeing himself both through the eyes of his own and the superior group—or, in C. H. Cooley's metaphor, seeing his self reflected from two different looking-glasses at the same time—sharpens his sense of being part of an " out-group ". The awareness of his relation to his group never leaves him completely and produces a sort of solidarity of fate. He knows that whatever he does, for good, and particularly for bad, will not be considered as an individual act but as " characteristic " of his group. And he reacts by feeling personally honoured by any honour conferred upon a member of his group, and by being filled with shame for the baseness of anyone of them. This peculiar relatedness to their group made Weininger state that women and Jews lacked " the sense of the value of their own personality ", and in the fact that Jews shared in this trait he saw a proof of their femininity. But it is in both—and in other marginal groups—a heightened sensitivity to the summary judgment of the dominant group. It is the natural correlative of the fact that the dominant group really is inclined to generalize about characteristics of the outsiders. The same qualities are valued differently according to whether they are manifested in members of the dominant group or in members of the subordinate group, and traits taken for granted in members of the " in-group " receive a peculiar emphasis if possessed by members of the " out-

[1] E. V. Stonequist : *The Problem of the Marginal Man*, op. cit.

group ". In Wilenski's *Introduction to Dutch Art*, for instance—
a book stressing the mutual interaction and influence of various
painters on each other and maintaining that every one of them
embodies the art of all his predecessors—a chapter on the woman-
painter Judith Leyster is introduced : " Women painters, as
everyone knows, always imitate the work of some man . . . But
women painters can occasionally contribute something pleasing
of their own in their pastiches . . .",[1] as if not all the other
artists had revealed both the influence of their masters as well as
their own style. " Woman is news ", says Margaret Cole,[2] in
the same way as " Man bites dog " would be news. But the
same applies to Jews, to Negroes, or to foreigners. Against this
feeling of being in the limelight the " marginal personality "
reacts by being acutely susceptible to criticism by others. His
self-respect is easily offended and every unfairness doubly resented
with the feeling of the socially weaker : " They think because
you are a foreigner (a Jew, a woman, etc.) they can treat you
like dirt." This touchiness may, at least in part, account for the
" irritability " regarded by various authors as a typically feminine
trait. Weininger's reproach : " They are more occupied with
what will be said of what they think than by the thoughts themselves," refers to an attitude which springs from the same origin.

While the marginal person resents criticism by others and is
extremely sensitive to the fact of being indiscriminately " put
all in one class " he, at the same time, unconsciously adopts the
majority standards. He is highly critical of the deficiencies of
his own group, an attitude which very often involves self-contempt
and self-hatred. Jewish self-hatred is almost proverbial ; most
studies of the Negro problem agree in reporting their extreme
race-consciousness and such facts as, for instance, that Negroes,
even within their own group, value their fellows with lighter
skin colour higher than the more negroid ones. The general
contempt of women shown by women—and particularly by the
more cultivated ones—is commonly known. The fact that so
many women intensely dislike women's organizations or clubs
or other purely feminine company cannot be accounted for solely
on the ground that women " instinctively " prefer the company
of the other sex. It is much more due to the fact that the accumulation of so many of their own despised kind is almost unbearable

[1] R. H. Wilenski : *An Introduction to Dutch Art* (Faber and Gwyer, Ltd., London,
1929).
[2] Margaret Cole : *Marriage, Past and Present* (J. M. Dent and Co., London, 1938).

to them.   It is as if they would see their own grimace reflected from a multiple distorting mirror.

The adoption of the majority standards has as another consequence the increased exertion on the part of the marginal person to be equal to or even better than the superior group in achievements highly valued by them.   Here again, one has only to quote the instances of Jewish ambition, or the bigotry of religious converts, as cases in point.   With regard to women, both what Freud calls the " masculinity complex " and Adler's " masculine protest " represent this kind of compensatory mechanism.

It is, moreover, characteristic of all the groups concerned to enter the labour market as outsiders and therefore to be willing to undercut prices.   Members of all these groups provide relatively cheap labour and are therefore resented as competitors unless their admission is restricted to second-rate occupations and as yet unestablished lines of trade.   " As the women thrust out the men, they thrust them upward ", says Elon Wikmark in *Die Frauenfrage des schwedischen Bürgertums*,[1] and this applies to outsiders of various other kinds, too.

All these groups have a vital interest in the promotion of a humanitarian, universalist outlook, in the abolition of discrimination against people on account of their race, creed, sex, or nationality, and in a legal order that puts right before might. If it be assumed that the general trend of social development goes in the direction of humanism, democracy and internationalism, it may therefore be said that these groups represent a progressive element.   (The issue is somewhat obscured, in the case of women, by the fact that in the course of centuries women have developed many substitute gratifications which they consider privileges and to which they cling emotionally more than to equal rights.)

This enumeration of " marginal " personality traits does not pretend to be exhaustive.   In a closer study it would, moreover, be necessary to distinguish between those people who differ from the majority group in physical as well as mental traits and those who differ in cultural tradition only and therefore have an easier chance of assimilation.   The intention here was not to give a detailed study, but to indicate a way of approach.   The comparison between the psychology of women and of other groups with which they have nothing in common except a similar social position helps to weed out those traits in their psychology which

[1] Halle, 1905.

are probably due to social conditioning, and thus furthers our understanding of the problem.

Another sociological approach to our problem which commends itself is a record of changes undergone by the feminine character during recent years in accordance with and as a result of woman's changing social rôle. Living, as we do, in a time of transition, we are in a particularly favourable position to observe the development of new traits and attitudes and the disappearance of traditional ones. A study, undertaken from this angle, of the film, the daily press and contemporary literature would yield rich material.

Changes noted would have to be classified according to their motivation into those due to (a) changed social functions, (b) a changed sexual morality, and (c) the changed status.

Even after a merely cursory survey it is possible to make the following observations. As seen in the first chapter, woman has during the last decades acquired a great number of new functions, but has lost hardly any of her old ones. Accordingly she has developed more new traits to be listed in group (a) of our classification than she has given up as a result of obsolescent functions. She has not only acquired a great many practical abilities (from writing business correspondence, keeping accounts, serving customers, or nursing sick and wounded, to driving cars or tractors, attending to telephone and telegraph communications, doing skilled and unskilled work at the most various machines in industry and apparatuses in research institutes, including both strenuous physical work and skilled techniques as well as responsible management) but has become more self-reliant and generally more efficient. The young girl of to-day travelling on her own all over the globe reads with a certain amused amazement the posters still decorating the walls of station waiting-rooms in which the Salvation Army and other charitable institutions offer their help to women stranded on arrival. Following the wider range of activities open to them women of to-day have more objective and impersonal interests than their mothers and grandmothers who never left the circle of their home and family. Girls, to-day, are interested in sport, in travel, in books, in politics—even if their political interest is said to be usually less keen than men's —in business organization and technical problems, and they have adopted a generally more inquisitive attitude as to how things work, which is the basis for scientific interest. In pursuance of their business obligations they have quite naturally assimilated a contractual morality, i.e. they have accepted the standards of conduct ruling public life, as contrasted to the behaviour patterns appropriate to the more intimate relationships within the family, or in courtship.   This makes many of them seem " businesslike " or " governing ", etc., compared to their previous sentimentality. Personal achievement has inspired them with self-confidence and they give proofs of a self-assertiveness which formerly was thought to be a masculine prerogative.   Accordingly they have more courage to trust their own judgment and are less dependent on other people's opinion.   No longer would they act on the advice given to a young lady of the last century : " It is not enough that she is pure and loyal—she must avoid everything that might induce the ill-natured to think disrespectfully of her ",[1] but would —particularly if they are of the urban type—rather adopt the " manly " device : " be just and fear not ".

Of the traditional feminine functions none has completely disappeared, but it may be said that, owing partly to improved technical methods and partly to a changed social organization domestic work no longer occupies a central position in the life of middle-class women.   As a consequence domesticity is no longer a chief virtue.   Not that a modern woman is not expected to run a house efficiently—the standards of cleanliness, hygiene and culture have, on the contrary, constantly gone up—but rather she is expected to be capable of doing housework with her left hand, so to speak, and must never be monopolized by it.   Of the qualities which a man looks for in a woman, domesticity is one of the least.   It has definitely lost its sex appeal. William Cobbett's story [2] of how he fell in love with his future wife sounds like a strange tale to many young people to-day. He was a young man, hardly over twenty then.

It was now dead of winter and, of course, the snow several feet on the ground and the weather piercing cold . . .   In about three mornings after I had first seen her our road lay by the house of her father.   It was hardly light, but she was out on the snow, scrubbing out a washing-tub.   " That's the girl for me," said I when we had gone out of hearing. . . .

She was, by the way, only thirteen at that time.   It would be worth investigating whether many of our young men, and from which groups, would react in a similar way.   And it would be

---

[1] " Advice to Young Ladies " (from the *London Journal* of 1855 and 1862), Methuen & Co., London, 1933.
[2] Told in *Advice to Young Men*, Routledge, London, first published in 1829.

equally interesting to learn whether many young men to-day would take, or agree with, Cobbett's advice, given in his chapter " To a Lover " : " The things you ought to desire in a wife are : (1) Chastity ; (2) sobriety ; (3) industry ; (4) frugality ; (5) cleanliness ; (6) knowledge of domestic affairs ; (7) good temper ; (8) beauty." To-day in ever widening circles it is becoming more important for a woman to be able to make her living than to be thrifty and sober, more important to possess *savoir faire* than knowledge of household affairs, more important to be attractive and a " good sport " than to be chaste.

A changed sexual morality seems to put less and less premium on modesty, " propriety ", passivity and virginity.

It is important in this connection to note in how many of the love stories shown on the screen—which, after all, are intended to appeal to the average taste and reflect bourgeois morality— the woman takes the active part ; and if this may not be a general practice, it at least does not shock the feelings of the average cinema-goer as " indecent " and " improper ", as it certainly would have shocked his elders.

It would lead too far to discuss here in detail the extent to which these trends in sexual morality have been caused by woman's changed social position, and what effect they have on it. The causal chain seems to be this : through the acceptance of a great variety of new functions, through socially valuable and remunerative work woman's status has been improved ; many of her inferiority feelings tend to disappear ; as a consequence she is more inclined to regard herself as an equal partner, and more resentful of the double standards of morality valid until recently. She has lost in the process a good deal of her timidity, her passivity, her " masochistic tendencies " and her traditional technique of prevailing by indirect means.

If we have kept in mind our first list of feminine traits we must recognize that by this method of examining the changes that have taken place a not inconsiderable number of characteristics originally listed as feminine can thereby be eliminated as being the result of social conditions and subject to alterations.

A sociological study of the problem of femininity does, however, not necessarily have to be comparative—comparing either feminine traits with those of other social groups or with characteristics of women at different times. Special studies of particular and restricted topics are also apt to reveal valuable material. It would, for instance, be of extreme interest to undertake research into the effect of discouragement on feminine creativeness, for modern psychology tends more and more to stress the importance of stimulation—by example, active encouragement or a cultural pattern which promotes individuality —on achievement. In a study on the *Psychology of Invention*,[1] made already in 1898, Josiah Royce wrote : " Inventions seem to be the results of the encouragement of individuality," and he maintained that, although genius was innate, " talent is somehow due to a social stimulation which sets their habits varying in different directions. And this stimulation is of the type which abounds in periods of individualism ". Psychology has since increasingly emphasized the need of encouragement in education ; so much so, that nowadays it seems almost self-evident that an atmosphere in which, for instance, a person has to protest that " any reputation for learning she might have won " was due to " inevitable accident " (" I have always carefully avoided it and ever thought it a misfortune "[2]) could do nothing but frustrate any interest and innate ability. The premium on conformity to given conventions, and the opprobrium attaching to all kinds of deviations from the norm in which feminine education mainly consisted, are bound to have inhibited the expression of so much talent as may have existed. The actual extent of this effect cannot, of course, be measured, since its very nature is to frustrate and to deprive of their means of expression those it has most strongly affected. Not many authentic reports have been recorded like that of Thomas More's daughter, Margaret, who

wanted to help in the great work of Erasmus, her father's friend. Erasmus was making a new Latin translation of the New Testament, and Margaret, who was, as Erasmus himself said, " an elegant Latinist ", decided she would make the concordance. One day her father found her in tears over the work. He took the manuscript from her and explained to her that such was not a woman's work. He was kind, and said he was proud of her desire to do the task, but to allow her to do it would be a mistake. It would consume her, he explained, and leave no residue either of emotion, or thought, and that would be very sad for her happiness as a woman. Women, he taught her, must save all their energies for the race. He turned her imagination gently away from scholarship and directed it upon one whom he called " yon tall stripling ", and Margaret, who adored her father, believed him to be right and obeyed him.[3]

[1] *Psychol. Review*, Vol. V, 1898.
[2] Lady Mary Wortley Montague, quoted from Irene Clephane : *Towards Sex Freedom* (The Bodley Head, London, 1935).
[3] Quoted from Margaret Lawrence's *We Write as Women* (Michael Joseph, London, 1937).

But apart from the anonymous legion of maybe mediocre talents who were doomed to remain dumb, an interesting undertaking would be to trace the influence of this discouragement in the works of women, who in spite of the hostile atmosphere surrounding their work succeeded in producing something. This would not be too difficult a task, for hardly any woman author fails to reflect in some way or other these difficulties. From the bitter lament of Lady Winchilsea (born 1661)—

> How are we fallen ! Fallen by mistaken rules,
> And Education's more than Nature's fools ;
> Debarred from all improvements of the mind,
> And to be dull, expected and designed ;
> And if someone would soar above the rest,
> With warmer fancy, and ambition pressed,
> So strong the opposing faction still appears,
> The hopes to thrive can ne'er outweigh the fears.
>
> .   .   .   .
>
> Alas ! A woman that attempts the pen,
> Such a presumptuous creature is esteemed,
> The fault can by no virtue be redeemed.
> They tell us we mistake our sex and way ;
> Good breeding, fashion, dancing, dressing, play,
> Are the accomplishments we should desire ;
> To write, to read, or think, or to enquire,
> Would cloud our beauty, and exhaust our prime,
> Whilst the dull manage of a servile house
> Is held by some our utmost art and use.[1]

—to the fresh cynicism of the contemporary poetess Stevie Smith—

> Girls ! although I am a woman
> I always try to appear human.

—there is an infinite variety of reactions against that experience of having to struggle against obstruction. In some form it can almost always be traced.

The discouragement does not so much consist in actual prohibition, but is rather exercised by subtler means : by ironic smiles, shrugs of the shoulder, ridicule of the " femmes savantes ", and contempt—whether expressed in an overtly misogynous attitude, in a matter of fact assumption of masculine superiority, in an overemphasis of the contrast between the character and abilities of the two sexes, or in condescending sympathy with the poor little girls who so hopelessly strive to compete with men.

---

[1] Quoted from Virginia Woolf's *A Room of One's Own* (Hogarth Press, London, 1929).

Listen to Beatrice Webb's report of her first meeting with Professor Marshall (when she was no longer an inexperienced young girl, but had a considerable record of social work behind her and went to him to discuss a new research which she proposed to undertake), and you will find all the paraphernalia of this technique in his argument :

He was

holding that woman was a subordinate being, and that, if she ceased to be subordinate, there would be no object for a man to marry. That marriage was a sacrifice of masculine freedom and would only be tolerated by male creatures so long as it meant the devotion, body and soul, of the female to the male. Hence the woman must not develop her faculties in a way unpleasant to the man : that strength, courage, independence were not attractive in women ; that rivalry in men's pursuits was positively unpleasant. Hence masculine strength and masculine ability in women must be freely trampled on and boycotted by men. Contrast was the essence of the matrimonial relation : feminine weakness contrasted with masculine strength ; masculine egotism with feminine self-devotion. " If you compete with us we shan't marry you," he summed up with a laugh.

Beatrice Webb goes on recording in her diary on March 8, 1889—

the little professor, with bright eyes, shrugged his shoulders and became satirical on the subject of a woman dealing with scientific generaliza-tions : not unkindly satirical, but chaffingly so. He stuck to his point and heaped on flattery to compensate for depreciation . . . I came away liking the man and with gratitude for the kindly way in which he had stated his view, refreshed by his appreciation, and inclined to agree with him as to the slightness of my strength and ability for the work I proposed to undertake. Still, with the disagreeable masculine characteristic of persistent and well-defined purpose I shall stick to my own way of climbing my own little tree . . . [1]

Not many women would have the energy and " well-defined purpose " to persist in their " masculine " endeavours against these odds.

The strength of the argument consists in the fact that it is backed by a solid body of public opinion. It only requires the gentle form of friendly flattery : " Oh, but as a woman you don't have to be logical ! " to eliminate a woman from a discussion and put her in her " proper place " outside the masculine world of intellect.

There are even some kinds of " encouragements " dealt out to women which had an almost irresistible negative effect. No

---

[1] Beatrice Webb : *My Apprenticeship,* op. cit.

better check could have been put on the intellectual work of
women than by the attitude represented in the following counsel [1] :

> Harriet asks in what way she can pass the dull evenings in the
> country ? She requires something to enliven her spirits. The society
> of a lover would be a radical remedy : but as she appears in that
> respect to be a neglected and destitute young lady we recommend some
> useful study. Drawing, music, books, unless the temperament is
> sanguine, soon pall upon the taste. Needlework is also monotonous,
> but these occupations might be combined with some novel pursuits.
> A game of chess with an old bachelor would be a relief, but if there
> is no one at hand, why something else must be recurred to. We can
> think of nothing at present but the study of some science. Within the
> past few years chemistry has been very popular with ladies who find
> time hanging heavily on their hands.

The attitude behind this advice is clearly that intellectual
work is, if at all, a suitable interest for unattractive spinsters.
Who would, under such circumstances, be eager to bear the
stigma ?

It is not suggested here that the relative paucity of feminine
achievement in the arts and sciences is merely or mainly the
result of discouragement. Domestic cares, for instance, have been
named as another cause, absorbing as they do, or did, a pre-
ponderating part of women's energy. Havelock Ellis has pointed
out in his *Study of British Genius* that the women who did get
on in the world were those who either did not marry at all or
late in life or else so young that they " escaped from, or found
a *modus vivendi* with, domestic and procreative claims ".

Domestic affairs, not on account of the time and energy
they demand, but for the state of mind they produce, have
often been mentioned as impediments to feminine creativeness. Helen Rosenau, for instance, gives the following explanation for it : " The processes of form require power of
concentration, an aptitude which is diametrically opposed to
the education of the average housewife, who has constantly to
diffuse her attention on various matters to keep her house in
order. Indeed, housekeeping is perhaps a real education in
the diffusion of thought . . ." [2]

By others (Karen Horney or Gina Lombroso for example)

---

[1] Again taken from *Advice to Young Ladies*, a compilation of extracts from
the correspondence column of the *London Journal* of 1855–62 (London, 1933). Note
the condescending and censorious tone of this advice to a worried questioner. The
change of tune which has taken place since, obviously under the influence of spreading
psychological knowledge, is remarkable.

[2] Helen Rosenau : " Creativeness in Women ", *Cont. Review*, August, 1941.

it has been maintained that the impulse to productivity is only one, in men and women, and while in men it produces creative achievement, in women it finds an outlet in procreation. Or, in other words, men create because they are unable to bear children.

If we selected discouragement as a topic for investigation it was not because we thought it the only clue to the complicated problem, but because it, no doubt, is an additional impediment, no matter how many other factors may obstruct feminine creativeness, and therefore deserves a closer study.

We do not believe that, when these and many other approaches to the problem of the " feminine character " have been exhausted, femininity will, like a phantom, dissolve into nothing. On the contrary, the residue of typically feminine traits, connected with woman's specific constitution, which is likely to remain after all is said and done about social conditioning, will have more substance and a greater scientific validity.

BIBLIOGRAPHY

ABENSOUR, LÉON: *Histoire Générale du Féminisme des Origines à Nos Jours*, Paris, 1921.
—— "Advice to Young Ladies" from the *London Journal*, 1855–62, Methuen, London, 1933.
ABRAHAM, K.: "Manifestations of the Female Castration Complex", *Internat. Jour. of Ps.-An.*, 1922, *3*.
ACHESON, E. M.: "A Study of Graduate Women's Reactions and Opinions on Some Modern Social Attitudes and Practices", *Jour. Abn. and Soc. Psych.*, 1933, *28*.
ADLER, ALFRED: *The Practice and Theory of Individual Psychology*, Kegan Paul, London, 1924.
—— *The Case of Miss R.; The Interpretation of a Life Story*, New York, 1929.
AIKINS, H. A.: "Man, Woman and Habit", *Western Reserve Univ. Bull.*, 13, No. 3. 1910.
ALLEN, C. N.: "Studies in Sex Differences", *Psychol. Bull.*, 1927, *24*.
—— "Recent Studies in Sex Differences", *Psychol. Bull.*, 1930, *27*.
ALLPORT, G. W.: "Attitudes", in *A Handbook of Social Psychology*, ed. C. Murchison, Clark Univ. Press, Worcester, Mass., 1935.
AMFITEATROV, A.: *Women in the Social Movement in Russia*, Geneva, 1905.
ANASTASI, ANNE: *Differential Psychology*, Macmillan, New York, 1937.
ANGELL, J. R. AND THOMPSON, H. B.: "A Study of the Relation between Certain Organic Processes and Consciousness", *Psychol. Rev.*, 1899, *6*.
ANGUS, S. Y.: "The Higher Education of Girls and the Employment of Women", M.A. Thesis, London University, 1931.
ARGELANDER, A.: "Geschlechtsunterschiede in Leistung und Persönlichkeit des Schulkindes", *Ztschft. f. päd. Psychol.*, 1931, *32*.
ARMSTRONG, C. P.: "Sex Differences in the Mental Functioning of School Children", *Jour. Appl. Psychol.*, 1932, *16*.
ATKINSON, C.: "Sex Differences in the Study of General Science", *Jour. Educ. Res.*, 1931, *24*.
BACHOFEN, J. J.: *Mutterrecht und Urreligion*, first published in Stuttgart, 1861.
BAILYN, LOTTE: "Notes on the Role of Choice in the Psychology of Professional Women", *Daedalus*, 1964, Vol. 93, No. 2, pp. 700–710.
BAKER, E. F.: "Women in the Modern World", *Annals of the Amer. Acad. Pol. and Soc. Sci.*, 1929, *232*.
BANISTER, H.: "Sentiment and Social Organization", *Brit. Jour. Soc. Psychol.*, 1932, *22*.
BARKLEY, K. L.: "A Consideration of the Differences in Readiness of Recall of the same Advertisements by Men and Women", *Jour. Appl. Psychol.*, 1932, *16*.
BATESON, G.: "Cultural Determinants of Personality", in J. V. McHunt, ed.: *Personality and the Behaviour Disorders*, New York, 1944.
BÄUMER, GERTRUDE: *Die Frau in Gesellschaft und Staatsleben der Gegenwart*, Stuttgart, 1914.
BEACH, FRANK, ed.: *Sex and Behaviour*, Wiley, New York, London, 1965.
BEARD, MARY RITTER: *On Understanding Women*, Longmans Green, New York and London, 1931.
—— "The Nazis Harness Women Power", *To-day*, Vol. 1, 1934.
BEAUCHAMP, JOAN: *Women who Work*, Lawrence & Wishart, London, 1937.
BEAUVOIR, SIMONE DE: *The Second Sex*, transl. and ed. H. M. Parshley, Cape, London, 1953.

BEBEL, AUGUST: *Woman in the Past, Present and Future*, Modern Press, London 1885.
—— *Die Frau und der Sozialismus*, Stuttgart, 1891.
BELFORT BAX, E.: *The Fraud of Feminism*, Grant Richards, London, 1913.
BÉLOT, GUSTAVE: *Les Problèmes de la Famille et le Feminisme*, Paris, 1930.
BENEDICT, RUTH: *Patterns of Culture*, Houghton Mifflin, Boston, and Routledge, London, 1934.
BERNARD, JESSIE: *American Family Behaviour*, Harper Bros., New York and London, 1942.
—— *Academic Women*, Pennsylvania State University Press, 1964.
BERNARD, L. L.: *An Introduction to Social Psychology*, Holt, New York, 1926.
BESANT, ANNIE: *An Autobiography*, Fisher Unwin, 1893.
BLANCHARD, PHYLLIS: " The Sex Problem in the Light of Modern Psychology ", in *Taboo and Genetics*, Kegan Paul, London, 1931.
BLEASE, W. LYON: *The Emancipation of English Women*, Constable & Co., London, 1910.
BLOCH, IWAN: *The Sexual Life of Our Time in its Relation to Modern Civilization*, transl. Eden and Cedar Paul, London, 1908.
BONAPARTE, K.: " Passivity, Masochism and Femininity ", *Internat. Jour. of Ps.-An.*, 1936, *21*.
BOOK, H. M.: " A Psycho-physiological Analysis of Sex Differences ", *Jour. Soc. Psychol.*, Nov. 1932.
BOOK, W. F. AND MEADOWS, J. L.: " Sex Differences in 5929 High School Seniors in Ten Psychological Tests ", *Jour. Appl. Psychol.*, 1928, *12*.
BOOTH, MEYRICK: *Woman and Society*, G. Allen & Unwin, London, 1929.
BOSANQUET, HELEN: *The Family*, New York, 1923.
BOTT, ELIZABETH: *Family and Social Network*, Tavistock, London, 1957.
BOUSFIELD, PAUL: *Sex and Civilization*, Kegan Paul, London, 1925.
BRAUN, LILY: " Die Anfänge des Frauenbewegung ", *Archiv f. Soz. Gesetzgebung und Statistik*, 1899, *13*.
—— *Die Frauenfrage*, Leipzig, 1901.
BRECKINRIDGE, S. P.: *Women in the Twentieth Century*, McGraw-Hill Book Co., New York, 1933.
—— *Marriage and the Civil Rights of Women*, Univ. of Chicago So. Sci. Monogr., Chicago, 1931.
BRIFFAULT, R.: *The Mothers. A Study of Origins of Sentiments and Institutions*, Macmillan, New York, 1927.
BRITT, S. H.: *Social Psychology of Modern Life*, Farrar and Rinehart, New York, 1940.
BRITTAIN, VERA: *Lady into Woman: A History of Women from Victoria to Elizabeth II*, Dakers, London, 1953.
BROOKS, W. K.: " Woman from the Standpoint of a Naturalist ", *Forum*, 1896, *22*.
BROOM, M. E.: " Sex Differences in Mental Ability Among Junior High School Pupils ", *Jour. Appl. Psychol.*, 1930, *14*.
BROWN, D. S.: " Sex-role Development in a Changing Culture ", *Psychol. Bull.*, 1958, *55*.
BROWN, J. F.: *Psychology and the Social Order*, McGraw-Hill, New York, 1936.
—— " The Origins of the Antisemitic Attitude ", in: I. Graeber and S. H. Britt: *Jews in a Gentile World: The Problem of Antisemitism*, Macmillan, New York, 1942.
BÜCHER, KARL: *Die Frauenfrage in Mittelalter*, Tübingen, 1910.
BUCURA, C. J.: *Die Eigenart des Weibes*, Vienna, 1918.
BÜHLER, C.: " Das Problem der Differenz der Geschlechter ", *Deutsche Mädchenbildung*, Vol. 3, Teubner, Leipzig, 1927.

BURGESS, E. W.: " The Family and the Person ", *Publ. Amer. Sociol. Soc.*, XXII.
—— " Family Tradition and Personality ", in *Social Attitudes*, ed. Kimball Young, Holt, New York, 1931.
BURNHAM, W. H.: " Sex Differences in Mental Ability ", *Educ. Rev.*, 1921, *62*.
BURT, C. AND MOORE, R. C.: " The Mental Differences Between the Sexes ", *Jour. Experi. Ped.*, 1912, *1*.
BUTLER, JOSEPHINE: *The Education and Employment of Women*, Macmillan & Co., London, 1868.
—— Ed., *Woman's Work and Woman's Culture*, Macmillan & Co., London, 1869.
BUTLER, R. M.: *A History of England 1815–1918*, Home Univ. Library, London, 1928.
CALVERTON, V. F. AND SCHMALHAUSEN, S. D.: *Sex in Civilization*, Macauley, New York, 1929.
—— *Woman's Coming of Age*, Liveright, New York, 1931.
CARPENTER, J. AND EISENBERG, P.: " Some Relations between Family Background and Personality ", *Jour. Psychol.*, 1938, *6*.
CARROLL, W. A.: " Influence of the Sex Factor upon Appreciation of Literature ", *School and Society*, 1933, *3*.
CARTER, H. D. AND STRONG, E. K.: " Sex Differences in Occupational Interests of High School Students ", *Person. Jour.*, 1933–4, *12*.
CASTLE, C. S.: " A Statistical Study of Eminent Women ", *Arch. Psychol.*, 1913, *27*.
CHOMBART DE LAUWE, PAUL HENRI, ed.: *Images de la femme dans la société*, Les Editions Ouvrières, Paris, 1964.
CLARK, F. I.: *The Position of Women in Contemporary France*, P. S. King & Son, London, 1937.
CLEPHANE, IRENE: *Towards Sex Freedom*, The Bodley Head, London, 1935.
COBBE, FRANCES POWER: *Woman's Work and Woman's Culture*, ed. Josephine Butler, Macmillan & Co., London, 1869.
—— *The Life of Frances Power Cobbe as Told by Herself*, London, 1904.
COBBETT, WILLIAM: *Advice to Young Men*, Routledge, London, 1887, first published in 1829.
COLE, MARGARET: *Marriage Past and Present*, J. M. Dent & Sons, London, 1938.
COLLET, CLARA E.: *Educated Working Women*, King & Son, London, 1902.
COLLIER, V. M.: *Marriage and Careers*, Channel Bookshop, New York, 1926.
COMMINS, W. D.: " More About Sex Differences ", *School and Soc.*, 1928, *28*.
—— " Community of Ideas of Men and Women ", *Psychol. Rev.*, 1896, *3*. Essays by M. W. Colkins, Jos. Jastrow, Cordelia Nevers, Anny Tanner.
CONRAD, H. S. AND JONES, H. E.: " Psychological Studies of Motion Pictures: Adolescent and Adult Sex Differences in Immediate and Delayed Recall ", *Jour. Soc. Psychol.*, 1931, *2*.
—— " Sex Differences in Mental Growth and Decline ", *Jour. Educ. Psychol.*, 1933, *24*.
COOK, EDW. T.: *The Life of Florence Nightingale*, Macmillan, London, 1925.
COOLEY, C. H.: *Social Organization*, Scribner, New York, 1909.
COURTNEY, JANET E.: *The Adventurous Thirties*, Oxford Univ. Press, London, 1933.
—— *The Women of My Time*, London, 1934.
CRUX, J. AND HAEGER, F.: " Männlich-Weibliche Differenzierung ", *Ztschft. f. Sex.-Wiss.*, 1930, *17*.
CUNNINGTON, C. W.: *Feminine Attitudes in the 19th Century*, W. Heinemann, London, 1935.
CUNOW, HEINR.: " Die ökonomischen Grundlagen der Mutterherrschaft ", *Die Neue Zeit*, 6, Jahrg., Ed. 1.
DAHLSTRÖM, EDMUND, ed.: *The Changing Roles of Men and Women*, Duckworth, London, 1967.

DALY, C. D.: "The Psychology of Man's Attitude Towards Woman", *Brit. Jour. Med. Psychol.*, 1930, *10*.

DANA, R. T.: *Relative Efficiency of Men and Women Workers*, London, 1927.

DAVENPORT, ISABEL: *Salvaging American Girlhood: A Substitution of Normal Psychology for Superstition and Mysticism in the Education of Girls*, Dutton, New York, 1924.

DAVIES, H. B.: *Factors in the Sex Life of 2,200 Women*, Harper, New York, 1929.

DAWSON, C. A. AND GETTYS, W. E.: *An Introduction to Sociology*, New York, 1939.

DEGLER, C. N.: "Revolution without Ideology: the Changing Place of Women in America", *Daedalus*, 1964, Vol. 93, No. 2, pp. 653-70.

DELL, FLOYD: *Love in the Machine Age*, Farrar & Rinehart, New York, Routledge, London, 1930.

DEUTSCH, HELENE: "The Psychology of Women in Relation to the Function of Reproduction", *Internat. Jour. of Ps.-An.*, 1925, *6*.

—— "Psychoanalysis of the Neuroses", *Internat. Jour. of Ps.-An. Library*, 1932.

—— *Psychology of Women*, Grune & Stratton, New York, 1944.

DEWEY, JOHN: *Human Nature and Conduct*, Holt, New York, 1922.

DICKINSON, R. L. AND REAM, L.: *A Thousand Marriages*, Williams and Wilkins, Baltimore, Md., 1931.

—— *The Single Woman*, Williams and Wilkins, Baltimore, 1934.

DOLLARD, JOHN: "Culture, Society, Impulse and Socialization", *Amer. Jour. of Soc.*, V. 45, 1939.

—— *Caste and Class in a Southern Town*, Yale Univ. Press, Oxford, 1937.

EELS, W. C. AND FOX, C. S.: "Sex Differences in Mathematical Achievement of Junior College Students", *Jour. Educ. Psychol.*, 1932, *23*.

ELLIS, HAVELOCK: *Man and Woman. A Study in the Secondary and Tertiary Sexual Characters*, 8th rev. ed., Heinemann, 1934, first published in 1894.

—— *Studies in the Psychology of Sex*, F. A. Davis Co., Philadelphia, 1898-1902.

—— *A Study of British Genius*, Hurst & Blackett, London, 1904.

—— *Sex in Relation to Society*, 1910.

—— *The Task of Social Hygiene*, Constable & Co., London, 1912.

—— *Marriage To-day and To-morrow*, 1929.

ENGELS, FRIEDR.: *The Origin of the Family, Private Property and the State*, Chicago, 1902, first published, Zurich, 1884.

FARIS, ELLSWORTH: "The Concept of Social Attitudes", *Jour. Appl. Sociol.*, 1924-5, *9*.

—— "The Attitudes and Behaviour", *Amer. Jour. Sociol.*, 1928, *34*.

FAWCETT, MILLICENT GARRETT: *Women's Suffrage*, The People's Books, London, 1912.

—— *What I Remember*, Fisher Unwin, London, 1924.

FENICHEL, O.: "Psychoanalysis of Antisemitism", *Amer. Imago*, 1940, Vol. I.

FERENCZI, SANDOR: *Versuch einer Genitaltheorie*, 1924.

FERRERO, G.: "Woman's Sphere in Art", *New Review*, Nov. 1893.

—— *The Problem of Woman from a Bio-Sociological Point of View*, Turin, 1894.

—— "The Problems of Women from a Bio-Sociological Point of View", *The Monist*, Vol. 4, No. 2, first published in Turin, 1894.

FIELD, ALICE W.: *Protection of Women and Children in Soviet Russia*, New York, 1932.

FIGNER, VERA: *Memoirs of a Revolutionist*, transl. Martin Lawrence, London, 1929.

FINOT, JEAN: *The Problems of the Sexes*, Putnam, New York, 1913.

FIVE WOMEN: *Our Freedom and Its Results*, Hogarth Press, 1936.

FLEMMING, E. G.: "Sex Differences in Emotional Responses", *Jour. Gen. Psychol.*, 1933, *8*.

FLUGEL, J. C.: *The Psychoanalytic Study of the Family*, Hogarth Press, London, 1931.

FOLSOM, JOS. KIRK: *The Family and Democratic Society*, Wiley, New York, and Chapman & Hall, London, 1943.

FORSTER, R. C. AND WILSON, PAULINE PARK: *Women after College. A Study of the Effectiveness of their Education*, New York, 1924.

FREEMAN, F. S.: *Individual Differences; The Nature and Causes of Variations in Intelligence and Special Abilities*, 1936.

FREUD, SIGM.: *Three Contributions to the Theory of Sex*, Coll. Papers, first published in 1904–5.

—— *Civilized Sexual Morality and Modern Nervousness*, Coll. Papers, first published in 1908.

—— *Totem and Taboo*, Kegan Paul, London, 1919.

—— *The Psychogenesis of a Case of Homosexuality in a Woman*, 1920, Coll. Papers.

—— " The Psychology of Women ", Chap. 1, 33, *New Introductory Lectures on Ps.-An.* Hogarth Press, London, 1933.

—— " Some Psychological Consequences of the Anatomical Distinction between the Sexes ", *Internat. Jour. of Ps.-An.*, 1927.

—— *Civilization and its Discontents*, Hogarth Press, London, 1934, first published in 1930.

—— *Analysis Terminable and Unterminable*, 1937.

FRIEDAN, BETTY: *The Feminine Mystique*, Gollancz, London, 1963.

FRIEDENTHAL, A.: *Das Weib im Leben der Völker*, Berlin, 1910.

FROMM, ERICH: " Die gesellschaftliche Bedingtheit der Psychoanalytischen Therapie ", *Ztschft. f. Sozialforschung.*, 1935.

—— *The Fear of Freedom*, Internat. Lib. of Sociol., Kegan Paul, London, 1942.

FURNESS, C. F.: *The Genteel Female. An Anthology*, Knopf, New York, 1931.

GEORGE, W. L.: *The Story of Women*, Chapman & Hall, London, 1925.

GOLDENWEISER, ALEXANDER: " The Cultural Approach to Problems of Social Development ", in *Contemporary Social Theory*, ed. H. E. Barnes, Howard Becker and F. B. Becker, Appleton, New York and London, 1940.

GOODE, W. J.: *World Revolution and Family Patterns*, The Free Press, New York and Collier-Macmillan, London, 1963.

GOODENOUGH, F. L.: " The Consistency of Sex Differences in Mental Traits at Various Ages ", *Psychol. Rev.*, 1927, *34*.

GOODSELL, WILLYSTINE: *The Education of Women*, Macmillan, New York, 1923.

—— *A History of the Family as a Social and Educational Institution*, Macmillan, New York, 1927.

—— " Families of College and Non-College Women ", *Amer. Jour. of Sociol.*, March, 1936.

—— *The Problems of the Family*, Appleton, New York, 1928.

GORE, M. S.: *Urbanization and Family Change*, Bombay, Popular Prakashan, 1968.

GRAVES, A. J.: *Woman in America*, Harper Bros., New York, 1838.

GROSSE, ERNST: *Die Formen der Wirtschaft und die Formen der Familie*, Freiburg i.B., 1896.

GROVES, E. R.: *Marriage*, Holt, New York, 1933.

—— *The American Family*, Lippincott, New York, 1934.

HALLE, FANNINA: *Woman in Soviet Russia*, Routledge, London, 1933.

HAMILTON, G. V.: *A Research in Marriage*, Boni, New York, 1929.

HARDING, ESTHER: *The Way of All Women*, London, 1933.

HARNIK, J.: " The Various Developments Undergone by Narcissism in Men and Women ", *Internat. Jour. of Ps.-An.*, 1924, *5*.

HARPER, E. B.: " Personality Types: A Note on Sociological Classification ", *Soc. Sci.*, Vol. I.

HARTLEY, RUTH E.: " Children's Concepts of Male and Female Roles ", *Merrill-Palmer Quart.*, 1960, *6*.

HARTLEY, RUTH E.: " A Developmental View of Female Sex-Role Definition and Identification ", *Merrill-Palmer Quart.*, 1964, *10*, also in Biddle, B. J. and Thomas, E. J., eds., *Role Theory*, John Wiley, 1966.

HARTMANN, H.: " Psychoanalysis and Sociology ", in A. S. Lorand, ed.: *Psychoanalysis To-day*, Intern. Univ. Press, New York, 1944.

HAYS, H. R.: *The Dangerous Sex: the Myth of Feminine Evil*, Putnam, New York, 1964.

HEIDBREDER, E.: " Introversion and Extroversion in Men and Women ", *Jour. Abn. and Soc. Psychol.*, 1927, *22*.

HEILMANN, J. D.: " Sex Differences in Intellectual Abilities ", *Jour. Educ. Psychol.*, 1933, *24*.

HEYMANS, G.: *Die Psychologie der Frauen*, Winter, Heidelberg, 1924.

HILL, GEORGIANA: *Women in English Life from Medieval to Modern Times*, 2 vols., R. Bentley & Sons, London, 1806.

HILLER, E. T.: *Principles of Sociology*, Harper, New York and London, 1933.

HINKLE, BEATRICE: " On the Arbitrary Use of the Terms 'Masculine' and 'Feminine' ", *Psycho-An. Review*, 1920, 7.

—— " Masculine and Feminine Psychology ", in *The Recreating of the Individual: a Study of Psychological Types and their Relation to Psychoanalysis*, pp. 284–335, 1921.

HIPPEL, TH. G. V.: *Ueber die bürgerliche Verbesserung der Weiber*, Berlin, 1792.

History of Woman Suffrage, 6 vols., ed. Elizabeth Cady Stanton, Susan B. Anthony, and Mathilda J. Gage, New York, 1881–1922.

HOBHOUSE, L. T.: *Morals in Evolution*, Chapman & Hall, London, 1906.

HOLLINGWORTH, L. S. AND MONTAGUE, H.: " The Comparative Variability of the Sexes at Birth ", *Amer. Jour. Sociol.*, 1914–15, *20*.

—— " Sex Differences in Mental Traits ", *Psychol. Bull.*, 1916, *13*.

—— " Comparison of the Sexes in Mental Traits ", *Psychol. Bull.*, 1918, *15*.

—— " Differential Action upon the Sexes of Forces which Tend to Segregate the Feebleminded ", *Jour. Abn. Psych.*, 1922, *17*.

HOLST, AMALIE: *Ueber die Bestimmung des Weibes zur höheren Geistesbildung*, Berlin, 1802.

HOLTBY, W.: *Women and a Changing Civilization*, John Lane, London, 1934.

HORNEY, KAREN: " On the Genesis of the Castration Complex in Women ", *Internat. Jour. of Ps.-An.*, 1924, *5*.

—— " The Flight from Womanhood: The Masculinity Complex in Women as Viewed by Men and by Women ", *Internat. Jour. of Ps.-An.*, 1926, 7.

—— " The Problem of the Monogamous Ideal ", *Internat. Jour. of Ps.-An.*, 1928, *9*.

—— *The Neurotic Personality of Our Time*, Kegan Paul, London, 1937.

—— *New Ways in Psychoanalysis*, Kegan Paul, London, 1939.

HUGHES, E. C.: " Personality Types and Division of Labour ", *Amer. Jour. Sociol.*, Vol. 33, No. 5.

HUGHES, M. V.: *A London Girl of the Eighties*, University Press, London, 1937.

HURD, A. W.: " Sex Differences in Achievement in Physical Sciences", *Jour. Educ. Psychol.*, 1934, *25*.

HUSBAND, R. W. AND LUDDEN, M. J.: " Sex Differences in Motor Skills ", *Jour. Exper. Psychol.*, 1931, *14*.

HUTCHINS, GRACE: *Women Who Work*, Martin Lawrence, London, 1934.

HUTCHINSON, E. J.: *Women and the Ph.D.*, Greensboro, N. Car. Coll. for Women, 1929.

HUXLEY, JULIAN: *Sex Biology and Sex Psychology*, Lecture given to the Brit. Soc. f. Sex. Psychol., Oct. 1922, publ. Pelican Books, London, 1939.

INTERNATIONAL LABOUR OFFICE: *The Law and Women's Work. A Contribution to the Study of the Status of Women*, Geneva, 1939.

JEPHCOTT, A. P.: *Girls Growing Up*, Faber, London, 1942.

Johnson, W. B. and Terman, L. M.: " Some Highlights on the Literature of Psychological Sex Differences Published since 1920 ", *Jour. Psychol.*, 1940, 9.

Jones, Ernest: " Early Development of Female Sexuality ", *Internat. Jour. of Ps.-An.*, 1927.

—— " Phallic Phase ", *Internat. Jour. of Ps.-An.*, 1933.

Josey, C. C. and Miller, C. H.: " Race, Sex and Class Differences in Ability to Endure Pains ", *Jour. Soc. Psychol.*, 1932, 3.

Jung, C. G.: *Psychological Types*, Kegan Paul, London, 1933.

Kingsbury, Susan M.: *The Economic Status of University Women in the U.S.A.*, U.S. Govt. Printing Office, Washington, 1939.

Kinsey, Alfred C., and others: *Sexual Behaviour of the Human Female*, W. B. Saunders, Philadelphia and London, 1953.

Kirkpatrick, Clifford: " Measuring Attitudes Towards Feminism ", *Sociol. and Soc. Res.*, 1936, 20.

—— " Inconsistency in Attitudinal Behaviour with Special Reference to Attitudes Towards Feminism ", *Jour. Appl. Psychol.*, 1936, 20.

—— " A Comparison of Generations in Regard to Attitudes Towards Feminism ", *Jour. Genet. Psy.*, 1936, 39.

—— " Recent Changes in the Status of Women in Germany ", *Amer. Sociol. Rev.*, Vol. 2, No. 5, 1937.

—— *Nazi Germany; Its Women and Family Life*, Bobbs Merrill & Co., New York, 1938, London, 1939.

Knight, M. M.: " The New Biology and the Sex Problem in Society ", in *Taboo and Genetics*, Kegan Paul, London, 1931.

Komacrovsky, Mirra: " Cultural Contradictions and Sex Roles ", *Amer. Jour. of Sociol.*, Nov. 1946.

—— " Functional Analysis of Sex Roles ", *Amer. Sociol. Review*, Aug. 1950.

—— *Women in the Modern World, Their Education and Their Dilemmas*, Little, Brown & Camp, Boston, 1953.

—— *Blue-Collar Marriage*, Random House, New York, 1964.

Krueger, E. T. and Reckless, W. C.: " The Nature of Personality ", in *Social Psychology*, Longmans Green, New York, 1931.

Ladies' Pocket Book of Etiquette, 7th ed., George Bell, London, 1840.

Laird, D. A. and McClumpha, T.: " Sex Differences in Emotional Outlets ", *Science*, 1925, 62.

Lang, E. M.: *British Women in the 20th Century*, T. Werner Laurie, London, 1929.

Langdon-Davies, J.: *A Short History of Woman*, Jonathan Cape, London, 1928.

Lange, Helene und Bäumer, Gertrude: *Geschichte der Frauenbewegung in den Kulturländern*, Berlin, 1901.

—— Eds., *Handbuch der Frauenbewegung*, Berlin, 1901–6.

Lasswell, H. D.: " The Contribution of Freud's Insight Interview to the Social Sciences ", *Amer. Jour. of Sociol.* XLV, 1939.

—— " Person, Personality, Group Culture ", *Psychiatry*, Vol. 2, 1939.

Lawrence, Margaret: *We Write as Women*, Michael Joseph, London, 1937.

Lee, P. R.: " Changes in Social Thought and Standards which Affect the Family ", *Family*, July, 1923.

Lehmann, H. C. and Witty, P. A.: " Sex Differences: Some Sources of Confusion and Error ", *Amer. Jour. Psychol.*, 1930, 42.

Leigh-Smith, Barbara: *A Brief Summary in Plain Language of the Most Important Laws Concerning Women*, London, 1854.

Leland, C. G.: *The Alternate Sex*, New York and London, 1904.

Liepmann, Wilh.: *Psychologie der Frau*, Berlin and Vienna, 1920.

Lilar, Susanne: *Le Malentendu du Deuxième Sexe*, Presses Universitaires de France, Paris, 1970.

LINCOLN, E. A.: *Sex Differences in School Children*, Warwick & York, Baltimore, 1927.

LINDSAY, BEN AND EVANS, W.: *The Companionate Marriage*, Boni, Liveright, New York, 1925.

LINTON, RALPH: " The Effects of Culture on Mental and Emotional Processes ", *Research Publications of the Assoc. for Nervous and Mental Diseases*, Vol. 19, 1939.

—— " Age and Sex Categories ", *Amer. Sociol. Rev.*, 1942, 7.

—— *The Cultural Background of Personality*, Appleton-Century-Crofts, New York, 1945.

LIPMANN, O.: " Psychische Geschlechtsunterschiede ", *Beihfte z. Ztschft. f. angew. Psychol.*, 1914, 5.

LOMBROSO, CESARE: *Sensibility of Women*, Read at the Internat. Congr. of Exp. Psych., London, 1892. Report in " Mind ", N.S., Vol. I, 1892.

—— AND FERRERO, G.: *La Donna Delinquente, la Prostituta, e la Donna Normale*, Turin, 1893.

LOMBROSO, GINA: *The Soul of Woman*, Jonathan Cape, London, 1924.

LOURBET, JACQUES: *La femme devant la science contemporaine*, Paris, 1896.

LOUTITT, C. M.: " A Bibliography of Sex Differences in Mental Traits ", *Tr. Sch. Bull.*, 1925–6, 22.

LOWIE, R. H. AND HOLLINGWORTH, L. S.: " Science and Feminism ", *Sci. Mthly.*, Sept., 1916.

LUDOVICI, A. M.: *Woman, A Vindication*, Constable, London, 1923.

LUND, F. H.: " Sex Differences in Type of Educational Mastery ", *Jour. Educ. Psychol.*, 1933, 23.

LUNDBERG, G. A.: " Sex Differences on Social Questions ", *Sch. and Soc.*, 1926, 23.

MACCOBY, ELEANOR E., ed.: *The Development of Sex Differences*, Stanford Studies in Psychol., California, 1966, Tavistock, London, 1967.

McDERMATT, J. F. AND TAFT, N. B., ed.: *Sex in Art. A Symposium*, Harper, New York, 1932.

MACLENNAN, S. F.: *Primitive Marriages*, Edinburgh, 1865.

—— *The Patriarchal Theory*, London, 1885.

MALINOWSKY, B.: *Sex and Repression in Savage Society*, Kegan Paul, London, 1927.

—— *The Sexual Life of Savages*, Kegan Paul, London, 1929.

MANNHEIM, K.: *Ideology and Utopia*, Kegan Paul, London, 1936.

—— *Man and Society in an Age of Reconstruction*, Kegan Paul, London, 1939.

MARTINDALE, HILDA: *Women Servants of the State, 1870–1938*, Allen & Unwin, London, 1938.

MARTINEAU, HARRIET: *Household Education*, London, 1849.

MASLOW, A. H.: " Dominance Feeling, Behaviour and Status ", *Psychol. Rev.*, 1937, 44.

—— " Dominance, Personality and Social Behaviour in Women ", *Jour. Soc. Psychol.*, 1939, 10.

MASON, OTIS T.: *Women's Share in Primitive Culture*, Appleton, New York, 1924.

MAURER, ROSE: " Recent Trends in the Soviet Family ", *Amer. Sociol. Rev.*, June, 1944.

MAY, GEOFFREY: *Social Control of Sex Expression*, Allen & Unwin, London, 1930.

MAYREDER, ROSA: " A Survey of the Woman Problem ", transl., Heinemann, London, 1913, from *Zur Kritik der Weiblichkeit*, 1905.

MEAD, MARGARET: *Coming of Age in Samoa. A Psychological Study of Primitive Youth for Western Civilization*, New York, and Jonathan Cape, London, 1928.

MEAD, MARGARET: *Growing Up in New Guinea*, New York and G. Routledge & Sons, London, 1930.
—— *Sex and Temperament in Three Primitive Societies*, Routledge, London, 1935.
—— *The American Character*, Penguin Books, 1944.
—— " The Cultural Approach to Personality ", *Trans. of N.Y. Ac. of Sc.*, Vol. 2, Jan., 1944.
—— *Male and Female*, Morrow, New York, and Gollancz, London, 1949.
MEAKIN, A. M. B.: *Woman in Transition*, Methuen, London, 1907.
MEINERS, CHRISTOPH: *History of the Female Sex*, transl. London, 1908, 4 vols., first published in German, 1788–1800.
MELTZER, H.: " Sex Differences in Forgetting Pleasant and Unpleasant Experiences ", *Jour. Abn. and Soc. Psychol.*, 1931, *25*.
MENCKEN, H. L.: *In Defence of Women*, Knopf, New York, 1926.
MESSERSCHMIDT, R.: " The Suggestibility of Boys and Girls between the Ages of Six and Sixteen ", *Jour. Genet. Psychol.*, 1933, *43*.
MEWS, HAZEL: *Frail Vessels: Woman's Role in Women's Novels from Fanny Burney to George Eliot...*, Athlone Press, London, 1969.
MICHELET, J.: *Les femmes de la Revolution*, Paris, 1885.
MILES, C. C.: " Sex in Social Psychology ", Chapter 16, in *Handbook of Social Psychology*, ed. C. Murchison, Clark Univ. Press, Worcester, Mass., 1935.
MILL, JOHN STUART: *The Subjection of Women*, Longmans & Co., London, 1906, 1st publ., 1869.
MÖBIUS, P. J.: *Beitrage zur Lehre von den Geschlechtsunterschieden*, Halle a. d. S., 1903.
MOORE, T. H.: " Further Data Concerning Sex Differences ", *Jour. Abn. and Soc. Psychol.*, 1922, *17*.
MORE, HANNAH: *Structures*, London, 1799.
MORGAN, C. LLOYD: " Individual and Person ", *Amer. Jour. Sociol.*, Vol. 34, No. 4.
MORGAN, L. H.: *Ancient Society, Researches in the Lines of Human Progress from Savagery through Barbarism to Civilization*, New York and London, 1877.
MORRISON, A. H.: *Women and Their Careers*, Nat. Fed. of Business and Professional Women's Clubs, New York, 1934.
MOSCHER, C. D.: " Woman's Physical Freedom ", *Woman's Press*, New York, 1923.
MOSHINSKY, PEARL: " The Relation between the Distribution of Intelligence and the Social Environment ", Ph.D. Thesis, London Univ., 1937.
MOWRER, E. R.: *The Family, its Organization and Disorganization*, Univ. of Chicago Press, Chicago, 1932.
MUDROW, L.: " Die Stellung ehemaliger Abitutientinnen zu Studium, Beruf und Ehe ", *Archiv. f. Rassen u. Geschlechtsbiologie*, 1936, *30*.
MYRDAL, ALVA: *Nation and Family*, International Library of Sociology and Social Reconstruction, Kegan Paul, London, 1945.
—— AND KLEIN, VIOLA: *Women's Two Roles: Home and Work*, Routledge & Kegan Paul, London, 1956, and Humanities Press, New York, 2nd revised ed. 1968.
Myself When Young, by Famous Women of To-day, ed. Margot Oxford, London, 1938.
NEFF, W. F.: *Victorian Working Women, 1832–1850*, Allen & Unwin, London, 1929.
NEVINSON, MARY: *Ancient Suffragettes*, London, 1911.
NEWITT, HILARY: *Women Must Choose*, V. Gollancz, London, 1932.
NIGHTINGALE, FLORENCE: *Suggestions for Thought*, London, 1853.
NORTHROP, A. C.: " The Successful Women of America ", *Po. Sci. Mo.*, 1903–04, *64*.

NYE, F. I. AND HOFFMAN, LOIS W., eds.:   *The Employed Mother in America*, Rand
    McNally, Chicago, 1963.
NYEMILOV, A. V.:   *The Biological Tragedy of Woman*, transl., Allen & Unwin,
    1932.
OGBURN, WILLIAM F.:   *Social Change*, Huebach, New York, 1923.
OGLESBY, C.:   *Business Opportunities for Women*, Harper, New York, 1932.
OPHUISEN, J. H. W. VAN: " Contributions to the Masculinity Complex in
    Women ", *Internat. Jour. Ps.-An.*, 1924, *5*.
OTTOLENGHI, S.:   *La Sensibilité de la femme*, Revue scient. Series 4, Vols. 5–6.
Our Towns, A Close Up, Report by the Hygiene Committee of the Women's
    Group on Public Welfare, Oxford Univ. Press, London, 1943.
PANKHURST, EMMELINE GOULDEN: *Suffrage Speeches from the Dock*, Woman's
    Press, London, 1913.
—— *My Own Story*, Eveleigh Nash, London, 1914.
PANKHURST, E. SYLVIA: *The Suffragette*, Sturges & Walton Co., New York,
    1911.
—— *The Suffragette Movement. An Intimate Account of Persons and Ideals*, Longmans
    Green, New York and London, 1931.
—— *The Home Front. A Mirror to Life in England during the World War*, Hutchin-
    son, London, 1932.
PARK, R. A.:   " Human Migration and the Marginal Man ", in *Personality
    and the Social Group*, ed. E. W. Burgess, Chicago, 1929.
—— " Personality and Cultural Conflict ", *Publ. Amer. Sociol. Soc.*, Vol. 25.
—— *Human Nature, Attitudes and the Mores*, Henry Holt, New York, 1931.
PARK, R. A. AND BURGESS, E. W.:   *Introduction to the Science of Sociology*, Univ.
    of Chicago Press, Chicago, 1924.
PATERSON, D. G. AND LANGLIE, T. A.:   " The Influence of Sex on Scholar-
    ship Ratings ", *Educ. Admin. and Super.*, 1926, *12*.
PATRICK, G. T.W.:   " The Psychology of Woman ", *Pop. Sci. Mthly.*, 1895, *47*.
PEARSON, K.:   " The Chances of Death and Other Studies in Evolution ",
    Chap. 8, *Variation in Man and Woman*, Arnold, London, 1897.
PEIRCE, A.:   *Vocations for Women*, Macmillan, New York, 1933.
PERCIVAL, A. C.:   *The English Miss To-day and Yesterday*, Harrap & Co.,
    London, 1939.
PETERS, J. L.:   " The Institutionalized Sex Taboo ", in *Taboo and Genetics*,
    Kegan Paul, London, 1931.
PFEIFFER, EMILY: *Women and Work*, Trubner, London, 1888.
PINCHBECK, IVY: *Women Workers and the Industrial Revolution*, Routledge,
    London, 1930.
PLETSCH, E. M.:   " A Study of Certain Characteristics of Women in 'Who is
    Who in America' ", *Who is Who in America*, Vol. 17, 1932–3.
PLOSS, H. H. AND BARTELS, P.:   *Woman, A Compendium*, 1st ed., 1885, latest ed.,
    1935.
POPP, ADELHEIDE: *The Autobiography of a Working Woman*, transl., Fisher
    Unwin, London, 1912.
PRATT, E. A.:   *Pioneer Women in Victoria's Reign*, George Newnes, London,
    1897.
PRESSEY, L. W.:   " Sex Differences Shown by 2,544 School Children on a
    Group Scale of Intelligence with Special Reference to Variability ",
    Jour. Appl. Psychol., 1918, *2*.
PRUETTE, L.:   *Women and Leisure. A Study of Waste*, Dutton, New York, 1924.
PUCKETT, H. W.:   *Germany's Women Go Forward*, Univ. Press, Columbia, New
    York, 1930.
PUTNAM, EMILY J.:   *The Lady*, Putnam, London, 1910.

PYLE, W. H.: " Sex Differences and Sex Variability in Learning Capacity ", *School and Soc.*, 1924, *19.*

RADO, SANDOR: " The Fear of Castration in Women ", *Ps.-An. Quarterly*, 1933.

REID, MRS. HUGO: *A Plea for Women*, W. Tait, Edinburgh, 1843.

REUTER, E. B.: " The Social Attitude ", *Jour. Appl. Sociol.*, 1922–3, *13.*

REUTER, E. B. AND RUNNER, J.: *The Family*, McGraw-Hill, New York, 1931.

RIESMAN, DAVID: *The Lonely Crowd*, Yale University Press, New York, 1950.

—— " Two Generations ", *Daedalus*, 1964, Vol. 93, No. 2.

RIVENBURG, N. E.: *Harriet Martineau, An Example of Victorian Conflict*, Philadelphia, 1932.

RIVIÈRE, JOAN: " Womanhood as Masquerade ", *Internat. Jour. Ps.-An.*, 1939, *10.*

ROBERTSON, J. M.: *A History of Freethought in the Nineteenth Century*, Watts & Co., London, 1929.

ROGERS, ANNIE M. A. H.: *Degrees by Degrees*, Oxford Univ. Press, London, 1938.

ROMANES, G. J.: *Mental Differences between Men and Women*, Nineteenth Century, May 1887.

ROSSI, ALICE S.: " Equality Between the Sexes: an Immodest Proposal" , *Daedalus*, 1964, Vol. 93, No. 2.

RÜHLE-GERSTEL, ALICE: *Freud und Adler*, Dresden, 1924.

—— *Das Frauenproblem der Gegenwart*, Hirzel, Leipzig, 1932.

RUSSELL, BERTRAND: *Marriage and Morals*, New York and Allen & Unwin, London, 1929.

RUSSELL, DORA: *Hypatia, or Woman and Knowledge*, Kegan Paul, London, 1925.

SACHS, HANNS: " The Wish to be a Man ", *Internat. Jour. of Ps.-An.*, 1920, I.

SCHARLIEB, MARY, M. D.: *The Bachelor Woman and Her Problems*, Williams & Norgate, London, 1929.

SCHIRMACHER, KÄTHE: *Die Moderne Frauenbewegung*, Leipzig, 1909, transl., Macmillan, New York, 1912.

SCHMIDBERGER, G.: " Ueber Schulfleiss und Schulaufmerksamkeit bei Knaben und Mädchen ", *Ztschft. f. pad. Psychol.*, 1931, *32.*

—— " Ueber Geschlechtsunterschiede in der Rechenbegabung ", *Ztschft. f. pad. Psychol.*, 1932, *33.*

SCHREINER, OLIVE: *Woman and Labour*, Fisher Unwin, London, 1911.

SELIGMAN, C. G.: " Anthropology and Psychology ", *Jour. of the Royal Anthr. Institute*, LIV, 13, 1924.

SIMMEL, E.: " Zur Psychologie der Geschlechter ", *Psychoanalyt. Bewegung*, 1933, *5.*

SIMMEL, GEORG: " Das Relative und das Absolute im Geschlechterproblem ", in *Philosophische Kultur*, Leipzig, 1911.

SIX POINT GROUP: *Status of Women in Great Britain and Principal Differences of Law in the Dominions*, London, 1937.

SKAGGS, E. B.: " Sex Differences in Moral Attitudes ", *Jour. Soc. Psychol.*, 1940, *2.*

SMITH, JESSICA: *Women in Soviet Russia*, Vanguard Press, New York, 1928.

SMITHIES, E. M.: *Case Studies in Normal Adolescent Girls*, Appleton, New York, 1933.

SNYDER, A. AND DUNLAP, K.: " A Study of Moral Valuation by Male and Female Students", *Jour. Comp. Psychol.*, 1924, *4.*

SPENCER, A. G.: *Woman's Share in Social Culture*, Philadelphia, 1913.

SPIEGELBERG, W.: *Der Papyrus Libbey; ein ägyptischer Heiratsvertrag*, Strassburg, 1907.

SPRING-RICE, M.: *Working Class Wives*, Pelican Books, London, 1939.

STAGNER, R.: "Differential Factors in the Testing of Personality: I. Sex Differences ", *Jour. Soc. Psychol.*, 1932, *3*.

STERN, BERNH. J.: *The Family, Past and Present*, Commission on Human Relations, Appleton-Century Co., New York and London, 1938.

STOKE, S. M. AND WEST, E. D.: "Sex Differences in Conversational Interests ", *Jour. Soc. Psychol.*, 1932, *2*.

STONEQUIST, E. V.: "The Marginal Man ", *Amer. Jour. Sociol.*, 1935, *41*.

STRACHEY, RACHEL C.: *The Cause; A Short History of the Women's Movement in Great Britain*, G. Bell & Sons, London, 1928.

—— *Careers and Openings for Women*, Faber & Faber, London, 1935.

STRASSER, NADYA: *Die Russin*, S Fischer, Berlin, 1917.

STRONG, EDW. K., Jr.: *Vocational Interests of Men and Women*, Stanford University Press, 1943.

SUTHERLAND, R. L.: *Colour, Class and Personality*, Amer. Council of Education, Washington, 1941.

SUTTIE, J. I.: "Mental Stresses of Adjustment in Women ", *Brit. Med. Jour.*, September, 1922.

SVEISTRUP, HANS AND ZAHN-HARNACK, AGNES VON: *Die Frauenfrage in Deutschland. Strömungen und Gegenströmungen 1790-1930*, Hopfer, Burg, 1934.

TANDLER AND GROSZ: *Die biologischen Grundlagen der sekundaren Geschlechtsmerkmale*, Berlin, 1913.

TAYLOR, W. S.: "A Critique of Sublimation in Males: A Study of Forty Superior Men ", *Genet. Psych. Monogr.*, 1933, *13*.

TENENBAUM, JOSEPH: *The Riddle of Woman*, The Bodley Head, London, 1939, first published in U.S.A., 1936.

TERMAN, L. M. AND MILES, C. C.: *Sex and Personality; Studies in Masculinity and Femininity*, McGraw-Hill, New York, 1936.

TERMAN, L. M. AND TYLER, L. E.: "Psychological Sex Differences ", N. L. Carmichael, ed.: *Manual of Child Psychology*, 2nd ed., Wiley, New York, 1954.

THOMAS, CATHERINE: *Women in Nazi Germany*, Gollancz, London, 1943.

THOMAS, W. I.: *Sex and Society, Studies in the Social Psychology of Sex*, Fisher Unwin, London, 1097.

—— "The Persistence of Primary-Group Norms in Present-day Society and their Influence in our Educational System ", in *Suggestions of Modern Science Concerning Education*, Macmillan, New York, 1918.

—— *The Unadjusted Girl*, Little, Brown & Co., Boston, 1931.

THOMAS, W. I. AND ZNANIECKY, FLORIAN: *The Polish Peasant in Europe and America*, A. Knopf, New York, 1927.

THOMPSON, CLARA: "The Role of Women in this Culture ", *Psychiatry*, Vol. 4, 1941.

—— "Cultural Pressures in the Psychology of Women ", *Psychiatry*, Vol. 5, 1942.

—— "'Penis Envy' in Women ", *Psychiatry*, Vol. 6, 1943.

THOMPSON, H. B.: *The Mental Traits of Sex*, Chicago University Press, Chicago, 1903.

THOMPSON, WILLIAM: *Appeal of One Half of the Human Race, Women, against the Pretensions of the other Half, Men*, London, 1825.

THORNDIKE, E. L.: "Sex Differences in Status and Gain in Intelligence Scores from Thirteen to Eighteen ", *Ped. Sem.*, 1926, *33*.

—— "On the Variability of Boys and Girls from Thirteen to Eighteen ", *Ped. Sem.*, 1926, *33*.

TICKNER, F. W.: *Women in English Economic History*, J. M. Dent & Sons, London, 1923.

TUSSENBROEK, CATHERINE VAN: *Over de aequivalentie van Man en Vrouw*, Amsterdam, 1898.
VAERTING, MATHILDE AND MATHIAS: "Die Monogame Veranlagung des Mannes ", *Ztschft. f. Sex. Wiss.*, 1917.
—— *The Dominant Sex. A Study in the Sociology of Sex Differentiation*, transl., Allen & Unwin, London, 1923 of *Die weibliche Eigenart im Männerstaat und die männliche Eigenart im Frauenstaat*, Karlsruhe, 1923.
VALENTINE, C. W.: "The Reliability of Men and Women in Intuitive Judgments of Character ", *Brit. Jour. Psychol.*, 1929, *19.*
WALLER, W.: *The Family*, Dryden Press, New York, 1938.
WEBB, BEATRICE: *My Apprenticeship*, Longmans, London, 1926.
WEBB, SIDNEY: "Alleged Differences in the Wages paid to Men and Women for Similar Work ", *Econ. Jour.*, 1891.
WEBER, MARIANNE: *Ehefrau und Mutter in der Rechtsentwicklung*, Tübingen, 1907.
WEININGER, OTTO: *Sex and Character*, transl., Heinemann, London, 1906, first published in Vienna, 1903.
WELLMANN, B. L.: "Sex Differences ", Chap. 15 in *Handbook of Child Psychology*, ed. C. Murchison, Clark Univ. Press, Worcester, Mass., 1933.
WESTERMARCK, E. A.: *History of Human Marriage*, Macmillan & Co. London, 1891.
WEXBERG, ERWIN: *Individual Psychology and Sex*, Jonathan Cape, London, 1931.
WHIPPLE, G. M.: "Sex Differences in Intelligence Test Scores in the Elementary School ", *Jour. Educ. Res.*, 1927, *15.*
WHITE, E. M.: *Woman in World History: Her Place in the Great Religions*, London, 1924.
WHITING, O. W. M.: "Socialisation Process and Personality ", in *F.K. Hsu*, ed., *Psychological Anthropology*, Dorsey Press, Homewood, Ill., 1962.
WIESE, L. A.: *Ueber die Stellung der Frauen im Altertum und in der christlichen Zeit*, Berlin, 1854.
WIETH-KNUDSEN, K. A.: *Feminism, A Sociological Study of the Woman Question from Ancient Times to the Present Day*, transl. from the Danish, Constable, London, 1928.
WINGFIELD-STRATFORD, ESME: *Victorian Trilogy*, Routledge, London, 1930–3.
—— *Women in Professions*, Internat. Congress of Women 1899, Fisher Unwin, London, 1900.
WINSLOW, M. N.: *Married Women in Industry*, U.S. Govt. Print. Off., Washington, 1924.
WINSOR, A. L.: "The Relative Variability of Boys and Girls ", *Jour. Educ. Psychol.*, 1927, *18.*
WOOD, ETHEL M.: *Mainly for Men*, V. Gollancz, London, 1943.
WOOLLEY, H. T.: "Psychology of Sex ", *Psychol. Bull.*, 1910, *7.*
—— "Psychology of Sex ", *Psychol. Bull.*, 1914, *11.*
WRESCHNER, A.: "Vergleichende Psychologie der Geschlechter ", *Wissen und Leben*, 1911, *4.*
YOUNG, F. F.: "Balance and Imbalance in Personality ", in *Social Attitudes*, ed. Kimball Young, New York, 1931.
YOUNG, KIMBALL: *Social Psychology*, 2nd ed., Crofts, New York, 1945 and International Library of Sociology and Social Reconstruction, Kegan Paul, London, 1946.
ZACHRY, C. B.: "Social Adjustment and Sex Education ", *Jour. Nat. Educ. Assn.*, 1932, *21.*
ZILBOORG, GREGORY: "Masculine and Feminine. Some Biological and Cultural Aspects ", *Psychiatry*, Vol. 7, 1944.

INDEX OF NAMES

SUBJECT INDEX

Ability, differences in, 99, 106
Active-passive contrast, 81
Affectability, 46, 164
Age, effects of, 110
—, relative, 119
Ambivalence of feeling, 68
Amorality, 58, 61, 62
Anabolic constitution of woman, 146
Animus and *anima*, 63
Anthropological approach, 125–42
Anthropology, 94–5
Anti-semitism, *see* Jews
Anti-slavery, 17
Apes and man, 48–9
Arapesh, 129–32, 134
Art, 68
Association, 99
Attention, 99, 156
Attitudes and values, 127, 160

Beauty, 120–1
Bible, and male superiority, 91
Biological approach, 37–52
Birth-control, 95
Bi-sexuality, 57, 68, 80–1
Brain formation, 42

Capitalism, expansion of, effects, 92
Castration complex, 75
Causation, error of exclusive, 141
Changes, recent, in feminine character, 175
Characteristics, congenital and acquired, 146
Charity Organization Society, 18
Chartists, 38
Chicago, University of, 98
" Clinging vine " type, 11
Communism, 26
Complementariness of Sexes, 45
Conditioning, social, 132 ff.
Conflicts, in " emancipated " women, 157
Conservatism, organic, 47
Constitutional differences, 42, 146
Contagious Diseases Acts, 18

Co-ordination of science, need of, 144
Courtesan, as type, 61
Courtship, 118
Couvade, 118
Cultural change, effects of, 32–3
— —, rate of, 31
— pattern, and study of individuals, 89
— patterns, contrasting, study of, 94–5
Culture, integration and, 126
—, personification of, 139
—, variations in, 128
—, women and, 78, 79

" Decline," 12–13
Definition of the situation, 149
Democracy, and feminism, 23
Differences, individual and group, 170
Discouragement, effects of, 178 ff.
Discrimination against women, present-day, 28
Displacement of men by women, 30
Disvulnerability, 46, 164
Domesticity, reduced appeal of, 176
Dominance feelings, 108
Double standard, 118
Doubt, 93
Dress, 120

Economic crisis, effects of, 101
Education, nineteenth-century, 14–15
—, women's, 18, 29, 158
Egypt, Ancient, 118, 119
Élite groups, 114
Emotion, inhibition of expression of, 99
Emotional aspects of equality, 26
— differences, 107
Employed women, proportion of, 30
Enfranchisement, 25
—, first attempts at, 38
—, municipal, 38
Environment, and constitution, 113–14
—, and M–F score, 110